PROFIT FROM TIME

Profit from Time

Speed up business improvement by implementing Time Compression

Ian C. Gregory and Simon B. Rawling

Programme Contributors
Adrian Beesley
Gordon Brace
Paul Chapman
Mike Cox
Jud Gretton
Matthew Holmes
Mike James-Moore
Jay Jina
Stan Manton
Stuart Passey
Tom Ridgman
Dev Sharma
Sylvan Sitkey
Gary Smith
Baback Yazdani

Programme Director
Professor S. K. Bhattacharyya

First published 1997 by
MACMILLAN PRESS LTD
Houndmills, Basingstoke, Hampshire RG21 6XS
and London
Companies and representatives
throughout the world

ISBN 0–333–712 05–6

A catalogue record for this book is available
from the British Library

This book is printed on paper suitable for recycling and
made from fully managed and sustained forest sources.

10 9 8 7 6 5 4 3 2 1
06 05 04 03 02 01 00 99 98 97

Typeset in Great Britain by
Aarontype Limited, Bristol

Printed and bound in Great Britain by
Creative Print & Design (Wales), Ebbw Vale

This book is dedicated to the memory of the late **Mike Cox**, a valued and respected member of our team for his honesty, candidness and humour – whose presence is sorely missed at the conclusion of our research

Contents

List of Figures

List of Tables

List of Abbreviations

BIW	Body in White
BOM	Bill of Materials
BOR	Bill of Routings
BPR	Business Process Re-engineering
CAA	Civil Aviation Authority
CAD	Computer Aided Design
CAM	Computer Aided Manufacture
CBU	Cable Business Unit
CNC	Computer Numerical Controlled
DFMA	Design for Manufacture and Assembly
DNA	Decision Node Analysis
EDI	Electronic Data Interchange
FMEA	Failure Mode and Effect Analysis
JIT	Just in Time
MLT	Manufacturing Lead Time
MOQ	Minimum Order Quantity
MRP	Material Requirements Planning
MRPII	Manufacturing Resource Planning
NVA	Non-Value-Adding
OPT	Optimized Production Technology
QFD	Quality Function Deployment
SBU	Strategic Business Unit
SKU	Stock Keeping Unit
SPC	Statistical Process Control
SSADM	Structured Systems Analysis and Design Methodology
TBPM	Time-Based Process Mapping
TCP	Time Compression Programme
TLA	Three Letter Acronym
TQM	Total Quality Management
VA	Value-Adding
WIP	Work in Progress
WMG	Warwick Manufacturing Group

Preface and Acknowledgements

Since its origins in 1992, the Time Compression Programme at the Warwick Manufacturing Group, University of Warwick, has worked alongside managers in our partner companies to help them to gain benefits from a time-based approach to business. In order to do so we found that it was vitally important for us to be able to transfer our expertise to the managers who owned the processes we were working on, thereby ensuring that appropriate improvements were made to these processes. Whilst working directly with managers has proved to be an effective way of transferring our expertise, the objectives of the Time Compression Programme included its dissemination to industry at large. We felt that one of the best means of doing so was through writing this book.

The companies we worked with were typical of what we see in industry. Few were the superstars often featured in management books, although all had the objective of reaching the standards set by such companies. Through working with the management of these companies we have identified the type of things that they need to see in a book to allow them to time-compress business processes. This book is aimed principally at the needs of these managers. The work presented has been carried out within the academic tradition of 'action research'. We do however believe that a test of good research is its usefulness and so the demonstration of academic rigour has been sacrificed to keep this book concise and readable.

We have taken an approach that provides a combination of theory, published practice, examples from our own experience and practical techniques we have developed to get time-based improvements under way. We have applied the principles of Time Compression not only to business processes but also to the techniques for improving business processes. Thus this book contains the following elements:

- Theory to explain why Time Compression is effective as a business improvement approach
- Theory to explain our approach to implementing these changes

- An overview of the Time Compression techniques that have been published to show managers what they can do. These have been grouped into a set of 'generic solutions'. We have included suggested reading to allow managers to find out more
- A description of the process we used in the implementation of improvements and how Time Compression techniques can be used within this process itself
- Case studies to allow managers to see how we used the techniques to improve business performance and to show what is possible
- A detailed description of how to use Time-Based Process Mapping, a tool which we have developed and found to be extremely useful for promoting a time-based approach to business improvement
- A description of the other tools and techniques we have used

We hope that these elements will provide all of the information needed to allow a manager to begin to make improvements to their company's business processes.

The Time Compression Programme has benefited from the work of many people. In the first instance recognition must go to the contributors of this text, namely Adrian Beesley, Gordon Brace, Paul Chapman, Mike Cox, Jud Gretton, Matthew Holmes, Mike James-Moore, Jay Jina, Stan Manton, Stuart Passey, Tom Ridgman, Dev Sharma, Sylvan Sitkey, Gary Smith and Baback Yazdani. In addition, many members of the Warwick Manufacturing Group have made substantial contributions to the research programme, especially Arindum Bhattacharya, Julian Coleman, Andrew Klapatyj, Mike Newton, Dan Park, Rajat Roy, Mark Smalley, Andrew Walton, Richard Wilding and many others who provided their expertise to our partner companies. Finally we are indebted to Professor S. K. Bhattacharyya for providing us with a vision of the future and the environment in which our ideas could flourish. We sincerely appreciate the support and dedication of all the people involved; this book has been created from their work.

We are also grateful to all of the employees of the partner companies of the Time Compression Programme for their enduring support and enthusiasm. The companies are: Airbus Industries, Avro International Aerospace, BAe Aerostructures, BICC Cables, Brita-Finish, British Aerospace, British Airport Authorities, British Airways, British Steel, Building Research Establishment, Charles Letts, Clearplass, Coats Viyella, Counterpart, Crosby Doors, Fairey Hydraulics, G&A Manufacturing, GEC, GKN Hardy Spicer, GPT,

H&R Johnson Tiles Limited, Hartwells, Hi-Shear Fasteners, IMI, Jetstream Aircraft, Kesslers International, LandRover, LTI Carbodies, LucasVarity, Lucas Wiring Systems, Maganese Bronze Components, Marvic Empe, Massey Ferguson, Premier Sheet Metal, President Office Furniture, Racal, Renold Chain, Rolls-Royce, Rover Body and Pressings, Rover Group, Short Brothers, Smiths Industries, Textured Jersey, Tuftane Limited and Ward Engineering.

In addition, a special thank you to the Engineering and Physical Sciences Research Council (EPSRC) for its support to all Research Engineers enrolled on the Engineering Doctorate Programme.

Acknowledgement is gratefully made to Simon & Schuster for permission to reprint Figures 2.2, 2.4 and 11.8 from M. E. Porter, *Competitive Advantage: Creating and Sustaining Superior Performance* © 1985 Michael E. Porter; and to MCB University Press for permission to reprint Figure 4.1, from J. B. Houlihan, 'International Supply Chain Management', *International Journal of Physical Distribution and Materials Management*, 17(2) (1987). Every effort has been made to trace all copyright-holders, but if any have been inadvertently omitted the publishers will be pleased to make the necessary arrangement at the earliest opportunity.

Finally, our thanks go also to the Department of Trade and Industry for initiating this research into improving the effectiveness, efficiency and competitiveness of UK manufacturing industry. Its commitment and encouragement throughout the programmes were greatly appreciated.

IAN C. GREGORY
SIMON B. RAWLING

Introduction

This book is designed to provide managers with all of the information required to begin to use Time Compression as the basis for business improvement or strategic advantage. In the first two chapters we provide an overview of the subject and show how a time-based approach can be used to gain competitive advantage. These provide the context for the more detailed techniques covered in the remainder of the book. Chapters 3 and 6 introduce the two major sections of the book, techniques for Time Compression and implementing Time Compression. In Chapters 3, 4 and 5 we describe the techniques available for Time Compression of business processes. We have covered the full range of techniques and included suggested reading to allow managers to find out more about them. In Chapters 6, 7, 8 and 9 we describe how to go about implementing business improvements based upon Time Compression and explain how the techniques of Time Compression can be used to speed up the change process. Finally in Chapters 10 and 11 we describe the tools we have used and provide a detailed self-help guide for our most valuable tool, Time-Based Process Mapping.

Throughout the book we have included case studies from our work to show the reader how we used the techniques of Time Compression to improve business performance. We have used a system of symbols to cross-reference these case studies with the approaches to Time Compression covered and the tools and techniques used. This will help the reader to understand our approach to real problems. There are two sets of symbols:

- In Chapter 3 we describe the fundamental concepts behind Time Compression. Our research has shown us that many of these techniques follow similar underlying principles, leading us to create a set of 'generic solutions' for Time Compression. The 'generic solutions' provide a checklist of possible ways to time-compress a given process. The 'generic solutions' and their symbols are summarized on p. 38ff. The 'generic solutions' used by the different techniques described and those used in case studies are indicated by a symbol in the margin.

- In Chapter 11 we describe the different tools and techniques that we have found useful. These and their symbols are summarized on p. 234ff. Where a tool or technique has been used in a case study this is indicated by the use of its symbol in the margin.

1 Why Time Compression?

INTRODUCTION

Business is in disarray. The world is getting a smaller place. Countries that a few years ago were sleepy backwaters are now thrusting forth into global markets with a low cost base and a management cadre educated in the best western universities. Their companies have learnt all that we have to teach them and built upon that to gain advantage in the market-place. We react to stay in the game. We try to change the culture of our businesses to take on the challenge, yet the harder we try the more our corporate dinosaurs seem to stand still. Programmes such as MRPII, Total Quality Management and Business Process Re-engineering have promised much but the results show success rates of at best 20 to 30 per cent. Even so, the desire to find the Holy Grail of competitiveness burns ever more fiercely. In the early 1990s the idea of time-based competition became popular in the United States as the next source of competitive advantage. The case studies presented showed enormous benefits, particularly in becoming more responsive to customers through shorter lead-times. In 1992 the Time Compression Programme was set up in the UK. Our mission was to investigate this phenomenon to see if it could be used to aid the competitiveness of UK manufacturing industry. Just as it has helped the competitiveness of companies elsewhere in the world, we found that not only did Time Compression deliver the benefits it promised, but that our approach was able to fill the crucial gap between a company's processes and its people to accelerate the change process, in effect to time-compress it.

The existence of this gap has caused companies enormous problems in adapting to the world around them. How many companies have installed a sophisticated computer system only to find that its employees would not use it the way it was meant to be used? How many companies have spent thousands on training courses, yet have never seen business benefits from them? The need for a means to tie together all of the strands of business change has never been greater.

1

You may well ask how Time Compression achieves this. Time is a fundamental measure of business performance. Lead-time, delivery time, cycle time, process time, business is full of time. Despite the old adage 'Time is Money', most of it is wasted. Typically 95 per cent of the lead-time of a product is spent idly. Surely no business in its right mind can afford to see such waste in its operations, yet time after time we have discovered the same thing. Why is such waste so prevalent? It is because we are not looking for it. The essence of Time Compression is to seek this wasted time and eliminate it. It is not the Holy Grail of management, yet it sheds a bright new light on a familiar situation, bringing to life new opportunities for both strategic advantage and business improvement. We invite you to read on to discover for yourself the new opportunities Time Compression can bring to your world.

WHAT IS 'TIME COMPRESSION'?

We define Time Compression as:

the reduction of wasted time throughout a business

Perhaps you are thinking that your employees are working hard already and there is little scope for reducing the time they waste. If so you are probably right. Looking at your business through spectacles of a Time Compression hue will allow you to see the opportunities for reducing the wasted time of your product, not that of your people. The lead-time of your product is the time it takes to turn raw materials from the ground into an item in the hands of your customer. It is by taking the perspective of the product that opportunities are to be seen and their enormous benefit felt. Table 1.1 gives some examples of improvements we have seen.

As you can see, Time Compression is not just confined to manufacturing things. We have found it equally valid in the product development areas of a business, in their administration and in the supply chain. You can also see that Time Compression is equally applicable to all sectors of industry. Since time is a fundamental of business thinking this is hardly a surprise.

The use of time as a tool for developing and measuring competitiveness is not new. However, what is new is that even in the best examples, the underlying time-based strategy has not always been explicitly articulated. Even where the notion of time has been articulated, there

Table 1.1 *Time Compression performance improvements*

Rolls-Royce (*Aero engines*) Time to prototype	Component development lead-time reduced from 3.5 years to 1 year Greater flexibility for change during evolution of the design
H&R Johnson (*Cramic tiles*) Time to supply	Lead-time reduced from 10 days to 2 days Pipeline inventory reduced by 3 weeks Product range increased by 400 lines Service levels up to 96%
Coats Viyella (*Knitwear*) Time to market	Design lead-time reduced by 75% Improved quality of information Reductions in process inventory
Short Brothers (*Aerospace*) Time to receive	Supplier lead-time reduction from 16 weeks to 2 days Removal of £3.5m of current stock 400 part numbers removed
Massey Ferguson (*Tractors*) Time to manufacture	Reduced cell lead-time by 70 days for 29 items Increase in stock turn ratio of 24% 10% reduction in inventory

has been the drawback that the tools, techniques and processes have remained largely hidden. The practising manager is thus left with a feeling that although the cases discussed seem interesting and show how Time Compression or for that matter Total Quality Management or Business Process Re-engineering or some other business improvement philosophy might work, it fails to give sufficient insight into *how to do the same in the specific context of a given business.*

The research carried out by the Time Compression Programme at the Warwick Manufacturing Group, an industrially based research project which has been under way since November 1992, has led us to reach three important conclusions:

- **Time is an exceptional way to think about business performance**
- **Time is a major source of competitive advantage**
- **Time is an extremely effective enabler in implementing strategic change**

Throughout this book we will show you how we reached these conclusions and give practical examples of how your organization can use time to enhance its performance.

The most important of these conclusions is the last. Knowledge of an innovative and beneficial strategy can only be turned into results through effective change management. Effective change management requires many things. One is a balance between the 'hard' task-based elements of a system, for example new technology or business process re-engineering, and the often neglected 'soft' human and behavioural elements. It also requires consistency of approach, careful resourcing, clear ownership and focus. During the course of the Time Compression Programme we realized that the principles of Time Compression were not only applicable to business processes in a company, they were also applicable to the process of changing a company. In the latter half of the book we will show you how we have used the principles of Time Compression to accelerate the change process.

WHAT TIME COMPRESSION IS NOT

There have been many managerial references to the reduction of time which are not Time Compression, for example time and motion studies or time management techniques. These techniques are about making **people** work faster. This book is not about making people work faster, it is about making a **product move faster** through a factory or office, or making a new design move faster through the new product process. Our approach looks at the flow of the product and reduces the period of time during which it is **not** worked on, a period which is significantly longer than the amount of time people spend working on the product.

THE HISTORY OF TIME COMPRESSION

The current interest in time as a business focus was brought to prominence by George Stalk and Thomas Hout, two US consultants, in their 1990 book *Competing Against Time*. They explicitly identified that a focus on time can result in significant competitive advantage, showing that time-based companies grew at three times industry norms and were twice as profitable as their main competitors.

Time has also been a major strand of thought for the management pioneers of the early twentieth century. Whilst Henry Ford is best known for the mass production system, there is unmistakable evidence that time was a key element in his understanding of manufacture.

'Time waste differs from material waste in that there can be no salvage. The easiest of all wastes, and the hardest to correct, is the waste of time, because time does not litter the floor like wasted material. In our industries we think of time as human energy.'[1]

Ford had a particularly strong notion of the importance of time in a supply chain context as he explained in his book *Today and Tomorrow*. 'The time element in manufacturing stretches from the moment the raw material is separated from the earth to the moment when the finished product is delivered to the ultimate consumer.' 'Our production cycle is about eighty hours from the mine to the finished machine in the freight car, or three days and nine hours instead of the fourteen days which we used to think was record breaking.'[2]

The next revolution in production system design was the advent of the Toyota Production System with its focus on Just-in-Time manufacture. The purpose of the Toyota Production System is to increase profits through completely eliminating waste and producing the necessary items in the necessary quantities at the necessary time. Again there is a strong implicit understanding of the importance of time. The *kanban* system adopted to pass demand information through the system requires smooth production which in turn requires short lead-times. This is so that required parts can be produced promptly each day in line with demand. Toyota achieved short lead-times through small batch sizes. These were achieved mainly through short set-up times and multi-skilled workers. Toyota benefited considerably through flexibility in its production process and showed the world that product variety, low cost and good quality are not mutually exclusive.

Finally in 1990 the importance of time as a way of thinking about business performance was explicitly stated and brought to prominence in the management literature. We have shown that the importance of time underlies the thinking of many well-known innovators in management techniques, particularly within manufacturing. The history of thinking about business in terms of time provided a basis for our research and some established techniques and principles to help us along our way.

THE TIME COMPRESSION PROGRAMME

The question being asked by industry in the early 1990s was how the ideas behind Time Compression could be turned into practical

changes and real performance improvements. The research carried
out by the Time Compression Programme since 1992 was initiated to
help show UK companies how to use the philosophy of a time-based
approach to improve their competitiveness in the rapidly changing
world of the 1990s. Our objectives were to provide practical methods
and demonstrators of performance improvement through Time
Compression.

The programme was initially funded jointly by the Department
of Trade and Industry (DTI) and by industry itself. At a value of
£3 million it was the largest research contract ever awarded by the
DTI. Its base in the Warwick Manufacturing Group at the University
of Warwick enabled us to do pragmatic research based upon the real
needs of industry. The Warwick Manufacturing Group is recognized
as the leading European institution in bridging the gap between
industry and academia. Our approach to the research was to build a
Time Compression Club of companies whose employees worked with
our researchers to develop and implement time-based business
improvements. Our methodology was based on the traditions of
'Action Research'. Our philosophy was to transfer our skills and a
method of thinking about Time Compression and business improvement to company employees so that they could continue to improve
without external help.

The programme started with a number of base assumptions:

- **There are no shortages of methodologies for Time Compression.**
  The work of Stalk and Hout[3] and other authors provided a body
  of theory and language which we used as a base for our work.
  We also assumed that Time Compression was based on the
  application of common-sense principles to complex situations.
  The assumption proved to be only partially true as it was
  necessary to develop a number of unique tools to provide focus
  for our analyses.
- **There is a cultural block to adoption and management of change**.
  The literature on the subject of change management indicates
  that the most likely barrier to the successful implementation of
  Time Compression is the 'soft' area of company culture and
  the behaviour of the individuals within the organization. Our
  research has confirmed the importance of this.
- **Time Compression as part of a strategy**. The literature on Time
  Compression suggested that initiatives which focus on a narrow
  part of a business process or are aimed at low-level objectives

tend to redistribute the wasted time/effort into other parts of the process. Although these initiatives can achieve up to 50 per cent improvement in the process measures, they do not lead to bottom-line benefits. Accepting this as an assumption we therefore ensured that Time Compression work was carried out as part of an overall strategy, thus resulting in overall business benefits. An analogy of this can be clearly seen in project management exercises where shortening non-critical activities can have no benefit to the total programme and shortening critical activities is only of value until the critical status is transferred to another activity. Instead a holistic approach has to be taken to the plan.

Since the beginning of the programme we have worked with over forty companies on over fifty projects. Our work has encompassed industrial sectors including the following:

- Aerospace
- Automotive
- Ceramics
- Electricals
- Furniture
- Jewellery
- Steel
- Textiles

We have found that the principles of Time Compression are equally applicable to each of these disparate industrial sectors. The research contained in this book has been compiled from the experience we have gained through working with numerous companies within each of these sectors.

BUSINESS PERFORMANCE AND TIME

Businesses discover the need for Time Compression in a number of different ways – as a differentiation strategy for customer service, as part of a cost reduction/waste elimination programme, through problems arising in day-to-day operations and as a requirement for enabling other initiatives. These drivers can be divided into two groups:

- Time as a strategy
- Time as a management tool

Both can be used for increasing competitive advantage.

Time as a Strategy

Beginning with strategy, it is first necessary to look at the nature of competitive advantage, the traditional objective of a business being to deliver value to a customer at a lower cost than the competition. The philosophy behind a time-based strategy demands that businesses deliver the most value for the least cost as rapidly as possible. So, the focus of management attention must shift from cost to time.

All previous attempts at business improvement have focused on cost reduction and quality improvement. Whilst a great deal of progress has been achieved through these focuses, our experience suggests that the obvious opportunities for improvement have now been taken by most companies. Time is the other fundamental element of competitive advantage. Traditional thinking suggested that you could not have low cost and high quality or low cost and fast delivery or fast delivery and high quality. The quality movement of the 1980s proved that good quality actually reduced costs. Similarly, thinking in terms of time allows different opportunities for business improvement to be seen. In effect it follows the old adage of allowing you to 'see the wood for the trees'. A focus on time does not necessarily mean that costs will go up or quality come down. Benefits to all three can be achieved by taking a holistic view. Time, quality and cost are closely interlinked through factors such as inventory and system turbulence, and so have to be addressed together for lasting business benefits to be gained.

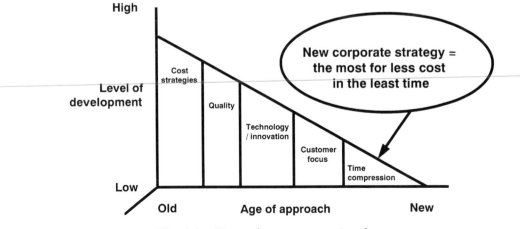

Fig. 1.1   *Time: the next strategic advantage*

So, to date business strategy has evolved to become:

- **Cost-focused**, using the power of mass production to bring products to a large-scale consumer base, driving down cost
- **Quality-focused**, the customer being no longer satisfied with just owning a product but expecting higher and higher quality standards
- **Technology/innovation-focused**, to achieve strategies of differentiation
- **Customer-focused**, identifying specific end user needs and tailoring products to secure customers
- the newest strategy, **Time Compression** – providing the most value for the least cost in the least time

Time as a Management Tool

Time as a management tool has been embedded in the manufacturing industry since the advent of Taylor's Scientific Management Principles. Lead-time, standard hours, clocking time, throughput, velocity ratios and so on, are just some of the measures utilized in manufacturing. The vocabulary of time is in common usage, is well-understood and so provides a firm foundation for Time Compression activities. The development of some of these metrics and concepts of personal time management in process management, particularly paperwork and supply chain processes, gives an immediate focus for efficiency improvements. Thus one of the major advantages of a time-based approach is the universal nature of time as a measure. The commonly used measurement systems of cost and quality are both complex and easily misinterpreted.

- Cost can be interpreted in a wide variety of ways. Indeed cost is really an abstract, arithmetical measure that is frequently misunderstood by those without finance-based training and access to accounting standards. Cost is also a lagging indicator. By the time it is known it is often already too late to use the figures to identify problems as they happen.
- There are many ways to quantify quality. Most rely on statistics or attributed values and again can be easily misunderstood by those who have not been explicitly trained in their use.

- Time is a measure that all people understand. Every person
instinctively knows how long a second, minute or hour is. Every
clock in the world uses the same units of time. Time is therefore a
measure that all people, from directors to operators, can relate to.
A focus on compressing time is equally easily understood. Time is
a common measure of performance, but also it is a real measure
that can be recorded objectively and in real time. Indeed time is
such a fundamental measure that it provides the basis for many
accounting measures, for example, costs are often based on
'standard times'. The ease with which time can be recorded
objectively and as events unfold means that it tends to force
analysis of events to a physical level. It is easy to see where an
item clocks up valuable lead-time as it can be seen doing so,
sitting in a warehouse or an in-tray or being reworked.

The commonality of time as a measure allows it to cross boundaries
of communication, be they between countries or between departments
within a company. It offers equal opportunities to compete on a global
basis, contrary to wage rates, trade barriers, market size and currency
rates. Perhaps the best illustration of the universal nature of time as a
measure is the example of Asea Brown Boveri (ABB), a global
company of over 200 000 employees. It challenged each of its seventy
operating units to cut their lead-times by 50 per cent in a time-based
improvement programme labelled 'T50'. Impact on corporate performance has been excellent with a strong impact on profit, a
reduction in lead-time in the range of 30 to 75 per cent, a 10 per cent
improvement in already high levels of delivery performance and a
20 per cent reduction in work in progress.[4]

Table 1.2   *Summary of TCP results*

	Average improvements
Manufacturing	65%
Product development (complex)	34%
Administration	47%
Product development (simple)	74%

Table 1.3 Time Compression and international performance

Company and product	Objectives	Nature of Time Compression	Results
Atlas Doors (USA) (Industrial doors)	Enter established market by offering fast and effective customer service	Order entry Reduced manufacturing set-up times Reorganization on product basis Logistics tracking system	15% growth v. 5% industry average 10% return on sales v. 2% industry average 20% price premium Delivery time one-third industry average
Black & Decker (Handtools and appliances)	Regain market share against new competition	Compression of new product development lead-time Closer links between marketing and design	18% growth v. 9% industry average 60 new products in 18 months Return on sales doubled in two years
Wal-Mart with Procter & Gamble (Consumer goods to retail outlets)	Increase the level of customer service with reduced inventories and cost savings	Improvement in information flows through supply chain Replenishment of stock every two days v. two weeks industry average	Investment in inventory one-quarter that of competition 37% growth v. 8% industry average 51% return on inventory v. 28% industry average
Ralph Wilson Plastics (USA) (Decorative laminates (as Formica))	Market share in specifically targeted areas	Deliver out of stocks in ten days v. 30-day average Compressed order processing and manufacturing processes	Growth 3× industry average Profitability 4× industry average

CREATING ADVANTAGE THROUGH
TIME COMPRESSION

The benefits of Time Compression are not limited to time savings. Almost any symptom of an inefficient system can be traced down by time mapping techniques and the clear focus on time improvements can stimulate innovative efforts that enhance both the function and performance of processes. However, as shown in Table 1.2, the most clearly identifiable performance improvements are in lead-time reduction.

Whilst our research has focused on the use of Time Compression within UK industry there are many examples of its use in other parts of the world. The examples in Table 1.3 taken from Stalk and Hout's book illustrate the universal applicability of the approach.

All these above examples demonstrate that thinking about business performance in terms of time has immense potential for improving business performance. What Time Compression provides is a mechanism to achieve similar advantages in the specific context of your business. The remainder of this book is dedicated to showing you how to do this.

We believe that time is a fundamental of business and that Time Compression is a valuable way of gaining both operational improvements and strategic advantage. Please read on and make up your own mind.

2 Time Compression and Business Strategy

In the introductory chapter we outlined the key principles of Time Compression and its history, showing that many companies all over the world have obtained remarkable results through the application of Time Compression. In this chapter we will enter a wider-ranging discussion on how Time Compression fits into existing ideas of strategy and how it can be used to gain real competitive advantage for your business.

In the modern business world it is evident that everything is changing at an increasingly fast pace. Developing nations are providing new markets and new competition, technology is advancing and opening up new ways of doing business, and legislation is changing due to pressures such as those on the environment. The challenge for companies is to react to these changes to maintain competitive advantage in their existing markets, whilst further developing these changes into new opportunities. By doing so companies will be able to increase their revenues and the profit that gives them their freedom.

Reacting to changes and creating new opportunities rely on different abilities. Reacting to changes requires that new competencies must be developed to form new or better forms of competitive advantage in that company's market. Creating new opportunities to exploit the markets of the future requires the building up of entirely new competencies, for example in new technologies. Time-based strategies provide a technique that can be used to help develop these new competencies. Time Compression provides the means to optimize the use of time in a business and can motivate an organization towards competing in a changing environment.

WHAT IS STRATEGY?

Business strategy is a broad subject which has inspired an enormous number of books and articles. Our intention is to provide a simple introduction to the idea of developing a strategy and an explanation of how a focus on time can be used to deliver competitive advantage.

The first step in developing a strategy is to ask yourself the following questions:

- What is your company good at?
- Why do your customers buy your products and not those of your competitors?
- Who are your competitors, both in the UK and world-wide?
- Why do people buy your competitor's products?

Having asked yourself these questions for the present, ask yourself how these will change in the future. How does your company need to change so as to take account of these changes and thrive in the future?

There are many books on the subject of strategy which describe the dynamics of industries and competitive advantage, many using the framework provided by Michael Porter in his 1985 book *Competitive Advantage*.[1] He suggests that in determining a strategy it is vital that you have an understanding of:

- Your competitors and their relative sources of competitive advantage
- Potential new entrants to your industry and their likely competitive advantage
- Potential products that may substitute those that you offer
- The likely response and receptiveness of customers to your new source of advantage
- Constraints to delivering your new advantage provided by powerful suppliers or legislation

More recently the emphasis has changed to looking at the idea of 'core competencies', a concept suggested by Hamel and Prahalad in their book *Competing for the Future*.[2] Quite simply these are the things that you do well that your competitors cannot match. If these competencies are well-chosen and developed then they will provide the source of your competitive advantage into the future.

Through understanding your core competencies, your customers, your competitors and your own ambition, you should be able to develop a vision of where your company is trying to go. The vision, combined with tangible objectives, should describe how you intend to turn your company's core competencies into profitable sales, both now and in the future. It will thus be possible to identify which activities will need to be improved and the priorities in doing so. It is unwise to change everything at the same time. If the vision and objectives are chosen well it will also be possible to use them to direct change throughout the company and motivate employees into achieving the desired outcome. We discuss the importance of the choice of vision and objectives in the context of change in Chapter 7.

SOURCES OF COMPETITIVE ADVANTAGE

Competitive advantage is gained from offering customers a set of benefits which are not easily available from your competitors. The value which these benefits provide to a customer relative to the price and benefits offered by competitors determines the ability of a company to sell its products.

Over time these sources of competitive advantage will change. To take an example of this, in the 1980s quality was seen as a factor that would win orders in many industries. The efforts of companies to deliver quality has resulted in some industries where every competitor now has first-rate quality. This means that quality is no longer an attribute that will encourage a customer to buy one particular product, yet any product without quality will be at a disadvantage in the market-place. Thus quality has changed from an attribute that differentiated a product from its competitors to an attribute that is required to qualify a product to be considered at all

Today, in the 1990s customers are also beginning to take low cost for granted whilst moving their attention to the availability of the product as soon as the need arises. This shift forces companies to seek alternative mechanisms by which competitive advantage can be gained. The effectiveness of each of these, that is, whether they are qualifiers or differentiators, is determined by the structure of the industry they compete in.

In order to compete, your product will require a number of attributes in order for it to provide value for money to a particular market. Some of these attributes will be those which any product in that market must possess, others will differentiate your product from those of your competitors. There are many attributes which may differentiate your product. Some of the most common are:

- **Short delivery times** – being able to meet customer needs more quickly than competitors
- **Delivery reliability** – delivering goods to customers exactly when they are required when competitors cannot
- **Functional performance** – providing products that perform their benefits better than those of competitors
- **Product quality** – providing products which are better made and more reliable than those of competitors
- **Strong branding** – providing a particular image that competitors cannot replicate
- **Customer support** – providing after-sales support and service to customers better than competitors
- **Sales techniques** – providing a customer service through sales techniques, for example catalogue retailing or technical sales
- **Customized products** – providing exactly the product a customer requires where competitors have only limited offerings
- **Financial engineering** – providing financial incentives for purchase, for example interest-free credit

Companies that build their strategies on providing these type of advantages become much more powerful competitors than traditional companies who base their strategies on cost alone. These cost-based strategies typically require businesses to drive down costs regardless of the effects on customer response times. Hence, sourcing from low-wage countries, divesting business units and consolidating plants become the norm.

Once you have understood the competitive environment in which your business lives and have developed a vision to direct your company into the future it is time to look at turning this vision into action. The sources of competitive advantage you have identified as being critical to your business's future will almost certainly rely on you becoming better at some activities. Everything you offer to customers will be dependent upon a series of activities.[3] Some of these activities will add both cost and value to a product, others will add only cost. All will add time. Michael Porter described this series of value-adding activities as the 'value chain'.[4] More recently it has evolved into the idea of the 'business process'. In order to gain competitive advantage through any differentiating attribute, the business process which performs that function must be both effective and responsive.

TIME-BASED STRATEGY

Some of the common sources of competitive advantage identified rely upon carrying out activities faster than competitors. If the vision of your company's future relies upon doing things faster, then Time Compression will be of value to you. Time Compression allows your company to provide the most for the least cost in the least time.

Reducing the time taken to do a series of activities makes it possible to be more responsive to the needs of customers. This may take the form of:

- Reducing the time between taking an order and delivery to customers
- Reducing the time to respond to a customer's query, problem or complaint
- Reducing the time taken to service a product
- Reducing the time taken to produce a quotation or tender
- Reducing the time taken to produce a customized or out-of-stock product
- Reducing the time taken to undergo credit checks
- Reducing the time taken to produce a new product in response to market changes or a competitor's new products

Adoption of a strategy which sees time as the fundamental element will help to promote a perspective which identifies opportunities to become more responsive. Focusing on time reduces the wastage of time in every aspect of the business. It cuts across the boundaries of functional departments, different factories and different companies. In doing so it unites all activities around a common theme, the reduction of time to become more responsive to customers. Time also provides a universal performance measure for the objectives set for each activity. Everyone understands the units of time. Time-based performance measures exist in real time. It is possible to see time being used up during a process as the seconds tick by.

This ease of understanding of time and the fact that time is something that we are all conscious of means that it is extremely powerful in facilitating change. It provides a clear link between strategy and operational issues including business improvement. It helps to identify opportunities for business improvement. It provides a clear and understandable set of performance measures. We discuss the benefits of time as an approach to change in more detail in Chapter 6.

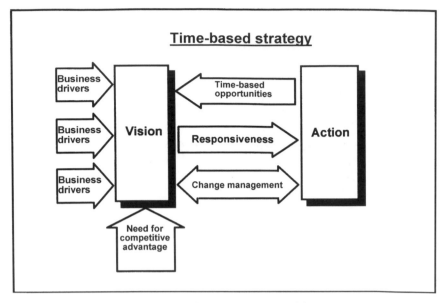

Fig. 2.1   *Time-based strategy and business*

The Time Compression Programme focused upon improving the business processes of the supply chain and the new product process. We will now discuss the strategic benefits which a time-based strategy brings to these major business processes. Whilst we do not specifically cover the strategic advantage available from the Time Compression of other business processes, close analogies of those discussed are usually valid. To give an idea of the activities which constitute the two business processes we focus on within this book we have developed a model for each based upon the generic activities suggested by Porter in his concept of the 'value chain'.[5] We have found these to be valuable tools to help identify strategically relevant activities within the business processes.

The Supply Chain

Effective management of the supply chain is an increasingly popular way to gain advantage through increased responsiveness and, more commonly, reduced costs. We have found that most past effort has been spent looking at the manufacturing process, shown here as internal logistics. As you can see this is a tiny element of the overall supply chain and in most of the companies we have seen it is the most

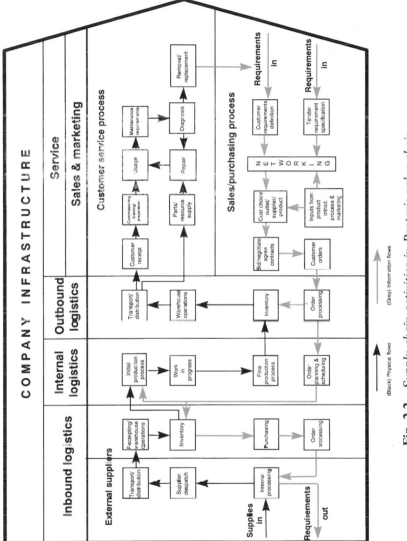

Fig. 2.2 *Supply chain activities in Porter's value chain*

effective element. In general there is far more scope for reduction of
the overall lead-time between taking an order and delivering it by
looking at the other activities.

There are five common objectives for the improvement of the
supply chain through Time Compression:

- To reduce lead-times between taking orders and delivery of
  product
- To improve delivery reliability
- To provide extra product variety in acceptable lead-times
- To provide customized products in acceptable lead-times
- To reduce cost

Reducing delivery lead-time
The shorter the delivery time, the quicker a company can satisfy a
change in demand from their customers. This type of responsiveness
to their changing needs can endear a supplier to its customers. More-
over, a consumer or company that is in a hurry and desperately needs a
component will often pay more to get it. Short lead-times also mean
that customers do not need to hold as much raw materials stock, which
results in a cost saving. It may be possible to persuade them to pay a
premium price for this convenience. High levels of responsiveness will
result in greater loyalty from customers and therefore more business.
They are also addictive. Once a company gets used to short component
lead-times it finds it hard to accept longer times again. This sort of
responsiveness has an additional benefit in that it tends to result in more
stable demand. This stability allows the lead-time to be shortened
further still. The mechanism which creates this is discussed in more
detail in Chapter 4 on 'Time Compression and the Supply Chain'.

Improving delivery reliability
In some industries Just-in-Time production is becoming increasingly
common. One of the key requirements is that deliveries are accurate
and on time. The penalties for failure can be immense. In other
industries delivery reliability may be a factor which differentiates
your company from its competitors. Poor delivery performance is
usually a factor of inability to cope with changes in demand, excessive
reliance on finished goods stock, quality problems or poor communication. Time Compression can help companies to react quickly to
changes in demand, reduce the magnitude of those changes and
reduce reliance on stock.

Another effect of shortening lead-times is the reduction in the forecasting horizon required. There is a saying in industry that there are only two types of forecast, a wrong one and a lucky one. It is certainly true that the further ahead a company tries to forecast, the more likely the forecast is to be wrong. It is usually necessary in industry to forecast only as far ahead as the lead-time for a particular product. Orders within the lead-time period are usually met from stock. If the lead-time is reduced then the forecast period can be shorter. This results in a more reliable forecast and therefore in less risk of stock-outs or obsolete stock. This will result in improved delivery reliability.

Providing variety
Shortened lead-times in manufacturing, the supply chain and product development help factories to deliver a variety of products without the traditional cost penalty of doing so. By reducing the overall lead-time, complexity of a product and set-up times, and by using smaller production batches, the production of a particular product can be scheduled more frequently. This improves the variety of products available to a customer at any given time. Reducing lead-times for products allows more variants to be held for the same stock level or allows out-of-stock products to be made within acceptable lead-times with a lower level of stock. The provision of variety means that customers' requirements are more closely met, resulting in more sales.

Providing customized products
Time Compression can be used to provide products which are tailored to the exact requirements of customers in acceptable lead-times. This can be done by reducing the time taken to design the changes, to procure components and to manufacture the product. Provision of customized products may result in more sales and perhaps a premium price.

Reducing cost
Using time as a focus for improvement within the supply chain also increases profit through reducing cost. Since it is possible to both increase responsiveness and reduce cost we believe that it is better to focus on gaining extra sales through responsiveness rather than through cost reduction. Costs decrease for a number of reasons:

- **Reduced quality costs** – one of the key elements in improving quality is to reduce the time between an error being made and it being detected. The sooner the error is detected the smaller the amount of product affected by it. Reducing lead-times has a positive effect on the speed of feedback and hence quality costs are reduced.

- **Increased productivity** – one key element of Time Compression is the elimination of non-value-adding time. This means that tasks that are not actually adding any value in the customer's eyes can be identified and eliminated, resulting in increased productivity. Stalk and Hout stated that the reduction in costs through increased productivity could be as much as 20 per cent.[6]

- **Reduced working capital** – in most cases manufacturing lead-time is proportional to work-in-progress levels. Shorter lead-times mean less work in progress. In addition we have already mentioned the potential for decreased raw material and finished goods stock. Less inventory results in reduced working capital, reduced floor area and reduced cost of managing and protecting stock

- **Risk reduction** – the reduction in the forecasting horizon results in less risk from the forecasting process. This translates into smaller finished goods stocks and less possibility of obsolete stock, thereby reducing costs. If lead-time can be compressed to less than that required by customers it may be possible to eliminate the cost of the forecasting function entirely.

These links between Time Compression and profit are summarized in the causal loop diagram in Figure 2.3. If you are unfamiliar with causal loop diagrams an explanation can be found in Chapter 11 on diagnostic tools.

New Product Development

In our experience the new product process is less effectively managed than many other processes. There are three main reasons for this: the traditional, functional nature of most product development activities, the focus on utilization of people and the inherent difficulty in determining how long the process will take due to the need to learn and improve designs. This provides enormous opportunity for gaining competitive advantage through time-compressing the new product process. The benefits of this are also enormous. Smith and

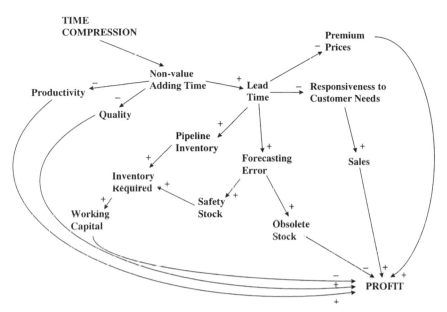

Fig. 2.3 *The relationship between time and profit in the supply chain*

Reinertsen pointed out that in some markets, a six-month delay in product introduction can reduce a product's life-cycle profits by 33 per cent.[7]

There are five common objectives for gaining competitive advantage through Time Compression of the new product process.

- To provide innovation in new products to make them the best and most up to date
- To imitate the new products of competitors
- To be more responsive to opportunities which arise for new products
- To reduce the risk of new products failing
- To reduce development costs

Providing innovation
The shortening of product development lead-time means that innovations can be exploited to maximum effect. If a company is innovating to improve its product faster than its competitors it will become increasingly competitive through speedy product design, development and introduction. This can give the innovation an effective monopoly for the early part of its life cycle, allowing the possibility of premium

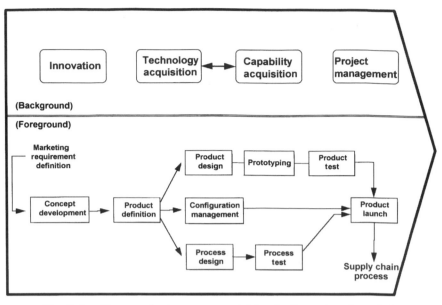

Fig. 2.4 *New product process activities in Porter's value chain*

pricing. Frequent innovations can result in slower competitors' products becoming less and less comparable. There are two additional benefits of Time Compression which improve the effectiveness of innovation as a strategy.

- **Increased product life cycle** – an advantage of shorter product development lead-times is that the innovation will get to market earlier, thereby increasing the length of time before competitors react and increasing the length of the overall product life cycle. Introducing a product earlier does not affect its withdrawal date.
- **Reduction of risk** – one approach to Time Compression involves the use of incremental innovation strategies. Having smaller development projects results in lower-cost projects which reduces the consequences of their failure and improves learning opportunities. Thus the cost–benefit equation of taking risks on innovations becomes more favourable.

Imitating competitors
If it is a company's competitors who are innovating, then reducing the time to develop imitations, perhaps better than the original, can help it to remain competitive.

Maximizing opportunities
In many businesses unexpected opportunities for a new product may arise occasionally. This may be as a result of, for example, competitors' new products or potential new customers. If product development lead-times are short then it is more likely that the market window of the opportunity can be achieved, resulting in a greater likelihood of product success.

Reducing risk of product failure
Shorter development lead-times mean that the specification for a product can be fixed later and with more certainty, thus improving the chances of the product's success. In contrast long lead-times allow markets to shift, competitors to introduce products that invalidate assumptions and developers to lose touch with the market. This tends to result in changes being required to the product specification which further increases the development lead-time and increases the likelihood of product failure.

Reduced development cost
The Time Compression of the new product process results in reduced development costs so long as it is achieved through the elimination of waste. Beyond this point it is necessary to invest money to reduce lead-time, thereby increasing costs. As we have already suggested, in industries which are sensitive to lead-time this type of cost overrun is small compared to the cost in lost sales of being late to market.

Development costs are reduced as a result of the following:

- **Productivity increase** –Time Compression results in non-value-adding activities being removed, for example, administrative tasks and the management of surplus, dormant projects. This increases the productivity of engineers.
- **Reduced rework** – the techniques involved in Time Compression improve cross-functional communication and speed up the learning process. This reduces the amount of rework which must be done, particularly at the later stages of the process where it costs most. The shortening of development lead-times also reduces the need for specification changes, reducing the rework which they entail.
- **Reuse of design** – some approaches to Time Compression of the new product process facilitate the reuse of design, for example,

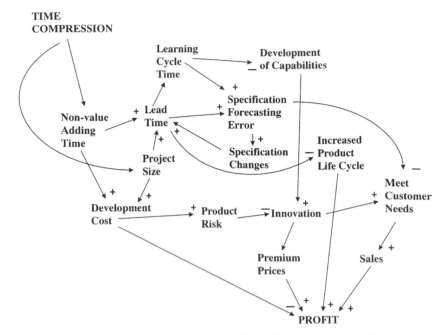

Fig. 2.5 *Relationship between time and profit in the new product process*

through modular architecture and incremental innovation. This can reduce overall design costs.

- **Reduced risk** – the reduction in the likelihood of product failure reduces the write-off costs of products failing.

These links between Time Compression of the new product process and profit are summarized in the causal loop diagram in Figure 2.5.

DEVELOPING NEW COMPETENCIES FOR THE FUTURE

In recent years management thinkers such as Hamel and Prahalad have asked whether exploiting existing markets is sufficient to ensure survival into the future.[8] They point out that many of the markets of the future have yet to come to maturity and are therefore still open to new entrants. The capability that the successful companies in these new markets will require is the ability to learn. This may be learning in pursuit of a new technology or learning in pursuit of a new managerial competence. Either way, time-compressing successive learning cycles can speed up the learning process.

In his book *The Fifth Discipline*, Peter Senge describes how many organizations have difficulties learning.[9] The most effective learning occurs when someone takes an action and experiences the results. However in many organizations the person who takes an action does not experience all of the effects of that action. Some of the effects of the action are displaced from the instigator by distance. They are experienced by someone else, somewhere else in the organization. They are also displaced in time. They happen so long after the action is taken that the causal link with the action is not understood. Using Time Compression techniques can reduce the delay between the action being taken and its results becoming apparent, thereby increasing the speed and effectiveness of learning. Time Compression also tends to encourage cross-functional working which makes the effects of distance less destructive to the learning process.

In the development of new products and technologies, speed of learning is increased by utilizing more opportunities to try out what has been developed. This may take the form of prototyping cycles[10] where the process of physically building and integrating the product highlights where problems still remain and where they have been overcome. It may also take the form of market launches of products. Where the exact markets for a completely new product are uncertain, the best way to find out what works is to launch a product and see what happens. In this situation traditional market research would be ineffective as customers do not realize the exact nature of their need. This learning can then be used to refine the product concept until it meets the needs of the market. The use of Time Compression in the new product process facilitates such an approach by allowing a product concept to be adapted to the new market quickly and at less cost than traditional techniques.

Increasing the frequency of product development projects also allows the knowledge built up within them to be transferred to other projects. As projects finish, their personnel can be moved on to start up projects without causing disruption. As the projects are relatively short in duration it is possible to maintain a stable project team for the duration of the project, facilitating learning within the project.

This approach can also be used to transfer the capability for change required in companies that are developing. Using a series of short, focused yet coordinated projects, the benefits of change can be realized quickly. The learning of employees involved in the projects occurs quickly as the time between action and experiencing its results is reduced. These experienced employees can be used to lead further projects, resulting in an exponential growth in change capability. Ultimately this will lead to a situation where all in the company are experienced in initiating and managing change, a condition often described in the management literature as being the ideal.

This chapter has developed the idea that using Time Compression can bring strategic benefits both in current markets and in developing those of the future. Its use in the supply chain can provide competitive advantage gained by having the shortest delivery times or by the provision of variety or customized products in reasonable time and at reasonable cost. In product development Time Compression can help your company to keep its products at the leading edge of its market and to capitalize on opportunities without incurring excessive risk or cost. In both cases we have shown that a time-based strategy usually reduces cost. It also provides the possibility to increase revenues by maximizing product life, providing better value which may attract a premium price, and most importantly by providing the right product for the changing needs of customers. It is this responsiveness to changing customer needs which makes time-based strategies so effective as a means of gaining competitive advantage, in short providing the most value for the least cost in the least time.

Having discussed the benefits of a time-based strategy it is time to explain how to obtain these massive improvements in performance. The next chapter reviews the fundamental principles of Time Compression. We will investigate the concept of value-added time and look at its application to different business processes, specifically supply chains, manufacturing and new product development. We will also discuss some of the common problems experienced within these business processes and how a focus on time can be used to help solve them.

Suggested Reading

G. Hamel and C. K. Prahalad, *Competing for the Future* (Boston, Mass., Harvard Business School Press, 1994).

M. E. Porter, *Competitive Advantage* (New York, The Free Press, 1985).

P. M. Senge, *The Fifth Discipline* (New York, Doubleday, 1990).

G. Stalk Jr. and T. M. Hout, *Competing Against Time: How Time Based Competition is Reshaping Global Markets* (New York, The Free Press, 1990).

3 The Fundamentals of Time Compression

There are two fundamental precepts behind Time Compression which are essential in understanding how to obtain performance improvements. These are:

- **Thinking in terms of business processes**
- **Value-adding time and non-value-adding time**

THINKING IN TERMS OF BUSINESS PROCESSES

The idea of business processes has been popular of late due to the high profile of Business Process Re-engineering (BPR), a concept brought to prominence by Hammer and Champy in their book *Re-engineering the Corporation*.[1] BPR has come in for a great deal of criticism based on the relatively large number of failures that have resulted. Both we and Hammer and Champy would argue that this is a result of poor implementation. The concept of 'business processes' is an extremely valuable tool for improvement.

Traditionally organizations have developed into business functions, for example, sales, marketing, manufacturing and finance. Even within these functions there were more functional departments, for example, manufacturing might have different groups of machines, a planning department and a separate maintenance department. Each of these functions was set up to excel at its particular task. A job passing through the factory would be passed from one department to another, receiving the benefits of excellence in each function it reached. Overall coordination between functions was limited as each was managed as an independent unit with coordination only taking place at board level. Thus it was commonplace for functions to be working against each other's interests, inadvertently reducing the effectiveness of the company as a whole. An example of this is where the purchasing function obtains the cheapest components it can, only

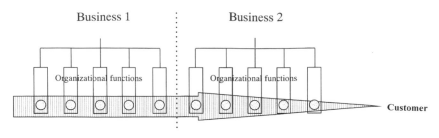

Business process

Fig. 3.1 *Introduction to business processes*

to find that the quality levels are so poor that rework on the shop floor increases, increasing overall cost to the company. The purchasing function is remote from the shop floor and so does not realize the effect that its policy is having.

Thinking in terms of business processes eliminates this problem. A business process is a sequence of activities that must be undertaken in order to produce a product, design or other end result, as exhibited in Figure 3.1. By thinking in terms of the business process, ignoring all of the functional boundaries that must be crossed, including those between the company, its suppliers and customers, it is possible to see opportunities to improve the performance of the company. Business processes may not be simple chains but may have parallel and intersecting processes covering elements like information generation and transfer. Whilst business processes provide a useful way of thinking about what happens in a company, it is important to remember that, due to the complexity of any company, there will always be knock-on effects to actions taken to improve a business process. Hence, it is important to stand back and take a view of the entire company when trying to change any element of it.

VALUE-ADDING TIME AND NON-VALUE-ADDING TIME

The lead-time of an item being designed or produced can be described as the sum of the time it takes to complete each activity required to design/produce it and the delays, waits and transfer activities between these operations. In our experience many of these activities are unnecessary and the handling and storage activities take up large proportions of the time. It is therefore useful to classify process time in terms of the value that it adds to the final design or product.

Value-adding time can be defined simply as:

Time when something is being done to the product that the customer cares about and would be willing to pay for

Value-Adding Time

Examples of value-adding time include anything where an item is processed for the first time and the customer requires that processing to be done.

Often we find that discussions over what is and is not value-adding get quite heated. This usually resolves around the question of who is 'the customer'. In the ideal world 'the customer' is the end consumer who goes into an outlet and buys a product. In some industries the end consumer might be government. In most companies, particularly suppliers near to the beginning of the supply chain, there is little or no visibility of the end consumer. We also find that in large companies customer-facing staff may be completely separate to those in operating divisions which can result in their staff not even understanding the needs of the company's immediate customer, let alone the end consumer. In cases such as these it is sensible to define 'the customer' as the consumer who is furthest away yet whose needs can be easily ascertained. This way there will be some value-adding time in the business process. It is, however, worth remembering that the wider the view of the business process taken, and the nearer to the end consumer 'the customer' is, the greater are the opportunities for improvement.

The definition of 'the customer' need not be constrained to the person buying your product. In the financial areas of the business 'the customer' may be the authorities which regulate companies. 'The customer' may also be the shareholder or any other group of people with whom a company works. The choice of the definition of 'the customer' should be based upon the objective of the process.

Another common area of debate around value-adding time surrounds the issues of shifts. If a factory has a single shift from 9 a.m. until 5 p.m., is the time between 5 p.m. and 9 a.m. value-adding or not? It can be argued that using two additional shifts would effectively reduce lead-time by two-thirds, so this time must be non-value-adding. We tend to solve this question by asking what the possibility of running additional shifts is and looking at the economics of the situation. If the answer is 'no way' then we will treat time as just that during the working day.

A similar problem is that of transportation. If a factory is making components in the UK to be assembled in Japan, is the transportation time value-adding or not? It can be argued that the building of a components factory next to the assembly plant would eliminate this time. Again we would ask the question as to whether this was feasible and look at the economics of the situation. If the answer was 'no way' then we would treat this time as though it were value-adding.

We are often asked if certification procedures are value-adding, be they based on quality standards such as ISO9000, or for other regulatory bodies such as the US Food and Drug Administration or the bodies setting standards for the design of aircraft, automobiles or ships. The answer is that if the customer would be unable or unwilling to buy these products without these levels of certification then the process as a whole must be value-adding. There may however, be opportunities within that process to remove non-value-adding activities based on the certification authority as the customer.

In some companies a product may be produced to a standard which is far higher than the customer needs. In this case it can be argued that the value-adding time is only that time which is spent on bringing the product up to the standard that the customer actually requires. Any additional work is non-value-adding.

Non-Value-Adding Time

The remaining time is classed as non-value-adding. There are many reasons why time might not add value. There are four major groupings of non-value-adding time:[2]

- Queueing time
- Rework time
- Decision-making time
- Waiting time

Queuing time
This is the time when an object is waiting to be worked upon by a value-adding process. The following are common causes of queuing time:

- **Batch size**. For example, if a batch of one hundred widgets is being processed by a machine that can handle one at a time, then 99 of the widgets are queuing at any time. Some will be queuing in front of the machine, others will be waiting for the remainder of the widgets to be processed. For the sake of simplicity it is best to assume that the processed widgets are also consuming queuing time, thereby making the queuing time equal to 99 multiplied by the value-adding time of the process. The same rules would apply to paperwork done in batches.
- **Work in progress**. If an activity is a bottleneck there may be several batches of work queuing to be worked upon. These would be consuming queuing time. Examples are items in in-trays, parts in buffer stores, projects on 'to-do lists'.
- **Inventory**. Items in a store are awaiting processing of some kind and so are, in effect, queuing.

Waiting time
This is time when items are waiting to be processed but not because other items are being processed ahead of them. Examples of waiting time are:

- **Breakdown** – waiting for machines that have broken down to be repaired
- **Sickness/holiday** – waiting for people who are sick or on holiday to return so that an item of work can be processed
- **Set-up time** – waiting for the set-up on a machine to be changed for a new product line
- **Material shortages** – waiting for necessary materials to be available to make an item

Decision-making time
This is a special case of waiting time and is often very well hidden. Work can be delayed because a decision is being made on what to do. Typical decisions include:

- **Capital approval** – waiting for approval to be made on expenditure
- **Scheduling** – waiting for a decision to be made on which order items are to be made in

Rework time

It is true to say that something is not adding value the second time it is done. This is rework. Examples of rework time are:

- **Quality defects** – rework to overcome errors in manufacture, design or processing of paperwork
- **Double handling** – this includes moving items from one type of storage medium to another
- **Redundant operations** – this involves collecting the same information twice when once would be sufficient, for example, typing items into a computer twice

TIME COMPRESSION IN BUSINESS PROCESSES

The majority of the opportunity for Time Compression is available as a result of the mismatches and poor communication between different departments and functions within an organization, and between different organizations within a supply chain. Our work showed that on average within a company the following overall process time was value-adding:

Manufacturing 5.9 per cent
Administration 2.6 per cent
Product development (complex) 46.5 per cent
Product development (simple) 13.4 per cent

In a supply chain less than 0.1 per cent of the total process time was value-adding. Other authors have described similar figures.[3] The scope for improvement is enormous. Typical opportunities include:

- **Stocking points** – many companies have stores of components, finished goods and semi-finished goods. Items in a store are waiting to be processed and therefore contribute to the lead-time of an item. Whilst some stock may be desirable to act as a buffer, many stocks at different points are likely to result in too much buffer stock and excessive lead-times. This was the case at H&R Johnson, a manufacturer of ceramic tiles, where large stocks were present throughout the supply chain. The removal of stock reduced the lead-time to the customer by seven days.

- **Batch size** – the larger the batch size of a product, the greater the number of items which are queuing at an activity at any given time. Therefore reducing the batch size reduces the queuing time for the items. This was illustrated in the machine shop at Massey Ferguson, a tractor manufacturer, where reducing transfer batch sizes from 180 to 30 resulted in lead-time reductions of 45 per cent.
- **Capital expenditure decision-making** – the decision-making process can slow down a business process. Senior management are busy and can take a long time to make decisions. One example of this was a company which took twelve weeks to sign off a capital expenditure decision on tooling. The tooling was always approved as the project had board approval anyway, and so the decision was not adding any value to the process.
- **Double handling** – this is typically caused through short-termism where management consider the efficiency of their own process whilst ignoring the effects throughout the business. This results in the rework of the product/information into a form which is meaningful and effective to each individual business function. A good illustration of this came from the Rover Group where the removal of double handling throughout a vehicle programming cycle delivered a significant reduction in lead-time, whilst improving the accuracy of supplier schedules through error elimination.
- **Stock types** – it is typical to find suppliers holding finished goods stock to buffer against customer schedule fluctuations and customers holding component stock to buffer against supply. From a supply chain context these are one and the same. Each business individually calculates and maintains stocks levels without consideration for the system in its totality. Within Lucas wiring companies, Lucas Rists and Lucas SEI, the identification of this factor enabled a substantial reduction in stock throughout the entire business. It will further reduce total supply chain stocks when Lucas attack the inventories between their business and their customers/suppliers.
- **Sequential tasks** – lead-time can be reduced by running tasks in parallel rather than in sequence. For example, staged information release in the manufacture of automotive press tooling allows the base casting to be procured at the same time that the detailed design work is done. This parallel working reduces the lead-time of the process by around 40 per cent.

- **Project overload** – this problem is caused by an imbalance between the number of projects in a system and the resources available to do them. This results in delays due to lack of focus and constantly changing priorities as urgent projects are expedited. It is extremely common in product development, for example at Jetstream Aircraft where improving project filtering and prioritization combined with purging the least important projects resulted in significant improvements in lead-time, delivery performance and productivity.

These opportunities seem clear and many of the solutions are commonly known. You may be asking yourself why such obvious inefficiencies have been built into a system for producing/designing things. We have mentioned the importance of taking a holistic view, looking at the organization as a whole and not just individual components of it. Inefficiencies like excess inventory, batch transfer and schedule manipulations were built into the system to protect it from the sudden changes in demand, priority and operating constraints that are placed upon it. Finished goods inventory exists so as to protect companies from stock-outs, because demand is unpredictable and lead-times to manufacture are longer than the customer's required lead-time. Raw materials inventory exists to protect companies from their suppliers' stock-outs and their long lead-times. Sometimes the combined amount of inventory is considerably more than that required to stabilize demand and supply. Some stock may therefore be removed through better co-ordination of stocking levels. It is only necessary to hold enough stock to cover the actual lead-time for the manufacture of the item required. Further improvements in stocking levels beyond this point are more difficult to achieve.

Similarly, in product development drawing sign-offs are a result of functional divides between different branches of engineering. Product changes protect the sales and marketing departments from long lead-times in the development function.

In every business process the causes of the opportunities for Time Compression have been very similar. Typically they are the organization of a business based on functional demarcations, build-ups of work to maximize utilization of employees regardless of fluctuations in demand, and the use of one set of inflexible resources to meet the requirements of a diverse set of customers. The similarity between these problems has led us to generate a range of generic solutions for improving a business process. Some of these solutions originate from manufacturing, some from product development, some from supply chain management. We believe that consideration of these solutions will generate ideas as to different options for improving a particular business process. Depending upon the particular circumstances of your business some of the options will prove useful, others less so. Our intention is to increase the number of options you consider. Table 3.1 summarizes these generic solutions. They are then explained in more detail in the text that follows.

The approaches of control, simplify and compress are related to the removal of non-value-adding time from the business process.

Table 3.1 *Generic solutions for Time Compression of a business process*

Group	Generic solution	Examples
Control	Control demand	Forecast, filter projects
	Control resources	Subcontract, flexible hours, excess resource
	Optimize throughput	MRPII, OPT, Finite Capacity Scheduling
	Increase process capability	Quality approaches, prototyping, clear specification
Simplify	Untangle flows	Cellular manufacture, modular design, distribution channel
	Reduce product complexity	Group technology
Compress	Straighten flow	JIT, cellular manufacturing
	Reduce work unit size	Reduce batch sizes, incremental innovation
	Eliminate echelons	Remove activities, remove supply chain tiers
	Waste elimination	Non-value-adding removal
Integrate	Improve communication	EDI, supplier scheduling
	Integrate entities	Partnerships, teamwork
Co-ordinate	Parallel working	Concurrent engineering, modular design
	Reorder activities	Late configuration
Automate	Automate value-adding	CAD/CAM, Robotics, IT systems
	Automate transfer	Conveyors, AGVs

As such they are relatively inexpensive, and often result in large benefits without affecting the value-adding activities. It is best to approach these in the order shown. It is difficult to simplify a process that is not in control, and difficult to compress a process which is complex. Integrate and coordinate are approaches based around doing the value-adding activities in a more effective manner. Integration may also help to reduce non-value-adding time through better information flows. As these approaches focus on the small, 5 per cent value-adding time they are generally less effective in compressing time than the approaches which focus on the 95 per cent non-value-adding time. The solutions which should be considered last are those which automate a process. These tend to be expensive. It is impossible to automate a process which is out of control as computers cannot cope with uncertainty or poor information. It is expensive to automate a process which has not been simplified, compressed and integrated as it is necessary to automate activities which are not required. Some solutions may incorporate a number of the generic approaches simultaneously, although care needs to be taken that the fundamental problems of controlling and simplifying a business process have been successfully tackled.

Control

In any business process, demand, resource capacity and lead-time are closely related. If demand rises above capacity, lead-times will increase unless resources are increased in line with demand. In order to maintain or reduce lead-time it is necessary to balance this equation effectively. Failure to do so leads to fluctuating demand in the supply chain or a state of 'project overload' in the new product process.

Control demand
The traditional approach to balancing the equation in a supply chain context is the use of forecasting and stock-holding. However, as we discuss in the next chapter, this approach usually leads to an unstable supply chain as it is impossible to get forecasts correct all of the time. Forecasting is a means of controlling demand. There are other ways of controlling demand, for example, booking new orders directly into a slot in the factory schedule.

Control resources

Alternatively the resource variable can be altered. This can be done through the use of subcontractors, through the use of temporary labour or, on a larger scale, building new factories. In these cases there will most likely be a lag between a requirement being identified and being resolved, leading to a mismatch between demand and capacity. Another alternative is the use of excess resource. This approach has advantages in that there is no lag or cost in changing resource levels within the available capacity, albeit there is pressure to keep the demand high.

Optimize throughput

Within any given business process there will be one activity which is a bottleneck and constrains the process as a whole. Bottlenecks are usually identified by the queues of product waiting to be processed by them. One approach to reducing lead-time is to ensure that the bottleneck is fully utilized by optimizing the flow of product through the business process. In the manufacturing process this tends to be done through the use of sophisticated computer systems such as optimized production technology (OPT) and finite capacity scheduling packages. The main problem with this method of lead-time reduction is that the bottleneck moves around depending upon product mix, absent employees and broken machines.

Increase process capability

One source of non-value-adding time is rework. In a production process this may be due to poor quality. In the new product process it may be due to mistakes in design, or more commonly it is inherent in the design process as the development staff learn how to make a product. Either way this rework delays the product and reduces overall capacity as it uses resources. It is possible to reduce this delay through improving quality. In the new product process it is possible to minimize the delays by using extra prototyping or modelling stages to highlight problems earlier in the project where they can be solved more easily.

Simplify

These generic solutions are concerned with improving the lead-times of business processes by removing sources of complexity. This complexity makes the processes more difficult to control, leads to confusion and possible errors and makes it difficult to meet the exact needs of different customers, particularly with respect to lead-time.

Untangle flows

In many organizations one business process is expected to cope with the differing requirements of a large number of different customers. In manufacturing this may be different requirements for quality, delivery time, or product design. In the new product process the same effect occurs due to the presence of different-sized development projects, engineering changes, queries from manufacturing and tenders in the same process. Using the same process for all of these differing requirements tends to lead to confusion and mediocrity of performance in all aspects including lead-time. One approach to reducing lead-time is to untangle these different requirements into a set of sub-processes which focus on the different requirements of different customers. In manufacturing this approach is often known as cellular manufacturing, in distribution it is known as distribution channels.

Reduce product complexity

Coping with different products or highly complex products tends to slow down a process because of the logistics of getting all of the different component parts to the right place at the right time and because of the variation in processing times that tend to occur between different activities. Simplifying the product can result in these tasks being simplified, reducing the lead-time of the product. There are two ways to simplify the product. One is to integrate components, thereby reducing overall component count for a given product. This makes purchasing and scheduling simpler, and can also make the product easier to assemble. The other approach is to standardize components across different products. This reduces the overall number of components which must be controlled. This makes it easier to purchase components and reduces the likelihood of mistakes being made.

 Compress

These generic solutions are concerned with the removal of non-value-adding time between different value-adding activities.

Straighten flow
This approach reduces non-value-adding time in a business process by bringing activities together and laying them out in the order in which they occur. If activities are close together it is possible to control flow through them much more effectively, reducing delays. In manufacturing it is seen in flow-line type production arrangements. This may be part of a Just-in-Time (JIT) system with *kanbans* to reduce the delays between stages.

Reduce work unit size
The most common cause of non-value-adding time is queuing time. One element of this is queuing time within a batch of product. If a batch size of ten products is used, then at any given activity nine of these are not being worked on, be they already processed or waiting for processing. If the processing time per product was one minute there would be nine minutes of non-value-adding queuing time for each product. By reducing the size of the batch to five products and having two batches, only four products are waiting. Thus the non-value adding time for each product in the batch would be reduced to four minutes. The same principle applies in the new product process and administration where work tends to be batched together and moved on.

Eliminate echelons
Sometimes non-value-adding time occurs as a result of activities which need not be done. These activities may be a result of using middlemen, for example wholesalers, or may be activities which have outgrown their usefulness and can now be removed. Removing these unnecessary activities increases control and reduces lead-times. It may also improve communication within the process. Good examples of opportunities are paperwork or buffer stores.

Removal of waste
In some cases there may be difficulties in compressing processes through echelon removal or straightening out the flow. It may still be possible to reduce lead-time through the removal of excessive stocks and other causes of non-value-adding time. Opportunities may be reducing decision-making time or changing methods for transferring product between activities.

Integrate

These generic solutions are concerned with reducing lead-times by integrating different value-adding activities so that they work more closely together and therefore more effectively. There are two different approaches to dealing with the information transfer which this entails. The first is to become better at transferring the information. The second is to integrate the two entities which need to work more closely.

Improved communication

One common cause of non-value-adding time is waiting for information to arrive. This may result in delays to initiating activities or in decision-making. In some cases the problem may be people not receiving information which could remove uncertainty or allow them to start early on a process. This may lead to rework when the information finally becomes known and is a factor in the system dynamics explained in the next chapter. Effective information transfer can overcome these problems and reduce lead-time. It can be enhanced through IT systems such as electronic data interchange (EDI) or Computer Aided Design/Computer Aided Manufacture (CAD/CAM).

Integrating entities

A second approach to resolving the problems of late or non-existent information transfer is to forge relationships between the departments or companies which need to communicate. By building up closer relationships the activities carried out by the different entities become integrated and act as one. This type of approach is seen in teamworking and partnership sourcing.

Coordinate

These generic solutions reduce lead-time by reorganizing value-adding activities so that they are done in the optimal order or in parallel.

Parallel working

One approach is to run value-adding activities in parallel where previously they were in sequence. This approach is popular in the concurrent engineering approach within the new product process.

Reordering activities
Sometimes it is possible to reduce lead-times by doing value-adding activities in a different order. This may make it possible to combine two activities, reduce transport between different activities or allow late configuration of products to a customer's exact requirements.

Automate

This generic solution is concerned with reducing time usage through using machines to speed up an activity.

Automating value-adding activities
This is the use of automation to speed up value-adding activities. An example of this is the use of IT systems to do computer-based activities faster or robots on a production line.

Automating transfer activities
This is the idea of using automated means to transfer products from one value-adding activity to another, thereby reducing non-value-adding time. For example it may include the use of conveyors or automated guided vehicles (AGVs).

SUMMARY OF BUSINESS PROCESSES

We must end this chapter with two caveats. The first of these is that the suitability of solutions to problems is incredibly context-specific. In the next two chapters we present a range of the most effective solutions and a framework for identifying and understanding the contexts in which they work best. We have also provided references so that you can find out more about them. It is vital that you assess these solutions and apply them to the context of your organization. Will they fit in with the systems you already have? How acceptable will they be to management and other employees? Are they the most cost-effective solutions in your organization? What needs to exist before they can be successfully implemented? We would also warn you against attempting to change too much at once. Change can get bogged down in 'project overload' just as easily as the new product process does.

Second, all of the solutions to problems offered in this chapter are dependent upon the people within the processes explored for their successful implementation. It would be unwise to implement multi-skilling or teamworking without consideration of job classifications and reward structures. It would be foolish to try to develop your company's supply chain without building internal capabilities to manage it effectively.

We have devoted four chapters of this book to choosing a suitable approach to change and to balancing the improvements of the business processes you are trying to time-compress with the ability of your employees to implement them successfully.

Suggested Reading

M. Hammer and J. Champy, *Reengineering the Corporation: a Manifesto for Business Revolution* (London, Brealy, 1994).

G. H. Stalk and T. M. Hout, *Competing Against Time: How Time Based Competition is Reshaping Global Markets* (New York, The Free Press, 1990).

CASE STUDY – COATS VIYELLA KNITWEAR

The Company

Coats Viyella Knitwear (CVK) is part of the global company with the same name. The business develops, designs and manufactures knitwear for a single customer, the retailer Marks & Spencer. When the project to transform the business was launched, CVK consisted of eight manufacturing plants spread over the north of England and Scotland. It had a turnover of about £90 million and employed over 4000 employees.

Strategic Drivers

The garment industry is one of the most traditional industries in the UK and over the last five years has begun to experience some major changes to its competitive environment. New names are emerging that have established strong positions in the market by creating highly responsive organizations that supply the high street buyer with a wide range of rapidly changing styles. These new organizations also make significant use of overseas manufacturers to supply garments at lower unit cost.

These shifts in the market have forced the larger retailers to take note of the changes and respond to the changing demands of the high street customer. Marks & Spencer will remain competitive in this market and is looking for increased innovation and flexibility in its supply chain. The effects of this are already being felt at Coats Viyella Knitwear. As the product life cycle is decreasing and both order quantitites and mixes become more variable, so design lead time must be reduced.

Traditionally Marks & Spencer have required predominantly classic designs of knitwear, requiring few design changes from year to year and with established sales figures for styles, size and colour ratios. This market has changed recently and is now weighted more in favour of fashion garments. These styles have more changes from year to year and have no previous sales record on which to base forecasts.

The trend for increased levels of change has led Marks & Spencer to begin to behave differently in their approach to placing orders for each season. The point at which they identify the styles that they have in mind is getting later in the year. The final selection of designs is also being left later. At the point where in the past they confirmed quantities, size and colour ratios, they are now providing only guidelines and are expecting Coats Viyella Knitwear to be able to react to the market throughout the season, both in design and quicker response manufacturing.

Although it will be several years before Marks & Spencer expect Coats Viyella Knitwear to take full responsibility for a build-to-order relationship, the business must begin to gear itself to such conditions in preparation. Such an exercise must consider not only the initial design process but also the manufacturing process including raw material supply and the means by which demand is identified and stock movement controlled.

The issues faced by the business – increasing levels of innovation, bringing new products to market faster – manufacturing greater levels of variety and responding rapidly to changes in demand, are all relevant to the principles of a Time Compression approach. It was recognized early on that whilst the overall principles were common the approach and tools used for development of the elements of the business were likely to be different across the new product introduction process, the manufacturing process and the supply chain so the development programme was split into these three areas.

The Programme of Change

Phase 1 – Defining the scope of the project
The initial period of investigation allowed the Time Compression project team to meet with key people from the organization to develop an understanding of the history of the business and the issues it now faced. This was supported by a sector review to determine the direction of the industry as a whole and to place Coats Viyella in the context of their competition.

This investigation phase culminated in a workshop attended by the directors of the business in which the Time Compression team presented the results of their work and proposed the three project streams. Having agreed the nature and scope of the project streams the workshop team identified the project structure for each one, who would champion the project from within Coats Viyella Knitwear, who would facilitate and co-ordinate it and what resources would be provided by the Warwick Manufacturing Group.

Given that the development of the business was likely to require significant changes in the roles and responsibilities of those working in the organization it was recognized at this stage that success would depend on a high level of involvement of people throughout the company.

New product introduction process
The development of this process was carried out over a 12-month period by a multi-functional and multi-level team (directors to clerical staff and technicians) from within Coats Viyella Knitwear. The project was led from within and championed by the Managing Director with WMG support in the form of two facilitators. The role of these facilitators was to design and run a series of workshops for the project team and to support investigation and development work throughout the programme.

The workshops were aimed at building a creative environment in which the project team could explore the issues faced by the business relate them to a time-based approach and to begin to develop an understanding of the possible solutions. These workshops were also used as a means of introducing a number of business development tools and process models.

The team selected a gateway model (shown in Figure 3.2), enabling them to build a new process from the ground up, focusing on specific, identified requirements. Having identified the key decision points in the process of bringing new ideas through design and into

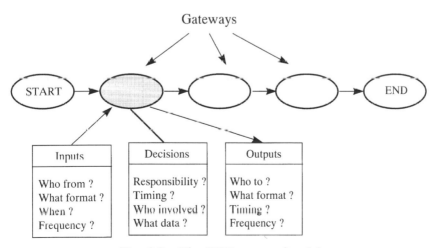

Fig. 3.2 *The CVK gateway model*

production the team was able to define the decision that needed to be made at each stage, the information required, who it would come from, who would make the decision and who would receive the results of the decision.

In order to involve as many people as possible in the process to gain ownership, the workshop team opened up the project to a large number of other people in the business at this stage. Each of the gateways in the process now had clear inputs and outputs so it was possible to pick small teams for each step whose task it was to design the detailed process. These teams were given four weeks to complete the definition of the processes, with support from WMG and the internal facilitator. Following this phase the original workshop team regrouped to fit the various elements of the process together eliminating duplicated and unnecessary tasks.

The final process was tested as a pilot scheme with a number of styles for a particular range being put through the new process alongside the traditional approach. This exercise highlighted the remain-ing implementation issues and the workshop team was able to plan the final stage of the project. The overall approach of involvement, support and communication ensured that everybody was aware of the issues, the likely benefits and the programme of changes, with the intention that change came through commitment and understanding rather than being forced through authority.

Manufacturing process

This project stream was run over a longer period of time – close to two years. Whilst the development of the new product introduction process focused on the creation of new ways of passing information, new decision points and new roles and responsibilites, the manufacturing stream was focused on the introduction of new machinery and the adoption of new working practices in the factory units. The business invested £17m in the latest technology knitting machines, radically reducing set-up and run times and ensuring consistent levels of quality that the older machinry could not provide.

Simulation tools were used to define optimum plant layouts and batch sizes, challenging many traditional beliefs about the most effective way to manufacture garments. As a result a number of pilot manufacturing cells were set up in both the knitting and make-up facilities. The aim of these pilot cells was to test the effects of changing working patterns on the information systems, roles and responsibility of employees, the management structure and the traditional piece-rate payment systems. The business had manufacturing facilities in a number of locations and pilots were run at each facility. It was recognized that each plant differed in its history and organization and therefore it was possible that the issues relevant to each factory would be very different.

The simulation work coupled with the results from the pilot studies resulted in a clear view of how the factory units could be best organized to ensure maximum levels of effectiveness. The lessons learnt were applied to the entire business and implementation across the business was planned by a team supported by the managing director and facilitators from both within Coats Viyella Knitwear and the WMG. This process has continued further with the work of full-time multifunctional project teams within several of the business units.

Supply chain project

Due to the substantial developments across the new product introduction and manufacturing processes, new arrangements with suppliers had to be established to cover the changed requirements for responsiveness and flexibility. In effect, the providers of raw materials were now on the critical path and the manufacturer's compressed lead-times were being restricted by yarn availability. Hence this project focused on developing faster information flows from end customer order through to raw material supplier, and compressed material lead-times from yarn supply through to despatch of the finished garments.

Time-Based Process Mapping the total supply chain identified supplier lead-times were far in excess of those anticipated. Consequently, a project was initiated in partnership with a number of key suppliers to identify the causes of waste and delays. Some suppliers represented 'flow' type products, those which were produced all year round at stable volumes. Others involved 'pathfinder' (high fashion) items which might only be required for one particular season. The diversity of these supply chains identified discrete characteristics requiring different solutions.

The analysis identified that inefficiency in the chain was caused by both customer and suppliers. Much of the waste was induced through customer puchasing policy, deficient scheduling, excessive inventory and ineffective channels of communication. The exchange of the diagnostic findings between customer and suppliers stimulated the generation of co-operative solutions, developing supply chains which worked effectively for all players within the chain. The learning from this process of working with a few suppliers will then be applied across the entire supply base. Due to the complexity and traditional nature of the supply chain, this work will continue over the next two years to achieve the final objectives.

Key Outcomes

The project required a significant degree of market and sales analysis giving Coats Viyella Knitwear an excellent view of the key strategic directions in which they must develop to become increasingly competitive in the future. The business has developed new processes, a new organization structure, new goals and measures and a clearer understanding of where its key strengths lie for serving the market.

A key development of the project is that Coats Viyella Knitwear have been able to develop a very good understanding of the uses and benefits of teamworking in manufacturing. They are now undertaking a major project to develop fully integrated 'Knit-to-Box' factories and hence benefit fully from their significant investments in new technology.

The organization has been changed to one that focuses fully on the process of delivering products to the customer rather than that of meeting individual functional goals. The decision-making process has been clarified with obvious milestones in the design process and clear responsibility at every stage and the use of an approach akin to simultaneous engineering.

Through this clarificaton of the route to the customer and the introduction of an approach that ensures development work is done as early as possible in the process, the company has reduced the lead-time for new product introduction by at least 50 per cent. The quality of information in the process has improved dramatically and more time is available to concentrate on the development of new techniques, processes and materials, allowing greater levels of innovation.

The introduction of new technology and new working practices in manufacturing has contributed to the reduction of manufacturing lead-times of up to 90 per cent with associated reductions in work in process inventory as the company's approach becomes 'build to order', not 'build to stock'.

Learning Points

- Ensure that as much of the development work is completed as early as possible in the new product process in order to reduce lead-times.
- Providing the customer with clear and concise information on which they can base their buying decision ensures that the best decision is made for both customer and supplier.
- The early involvement of manufacturing in the development process delivers reduced production lead-times.
- Support from the top must be present and seen in terms of both words and action.

The people who are actually involved in the process itself are the best source for generating a feasible, optimal solution.

4 Time Compression and the Supply Chain

The largest recognizable business process is that of the supply chain. This is the business process that converts raw material (from the ground, sea or air) into a consumable product. Even simple products such as nails have a complicated supply chain. For example, the iron must be extracted from the ground, turned into steel ingots, turned into wire, formed into individual nails, then packaged, sent to a warehouse and then a retailer before a customer can purchase. Within each of these stages there are many sub-stages; for example, the wire may need to be drawn into ever decreasing diameters by a series of machines, or the protective treatment may involve several coatings. In a similar manner, the blast furnace will need fuel and the steel-making process will need chemical additives. So, even for a simple product like a nail there are many links to other chains of supply.

In most industries there is more than one product available to the end consumer, arriving from a number of competing supply chains. For a commodity like a nail there will be little to choose between two competing products in terms of their functional performance. Thus the products will be differentiated by price, or by the service received by the retailer or end consumer. In more complex products the goods may be differentiated by their overall performance, functionality and design, a vast majority of which will be a consequence of the supplied components. For example, in the personal computer market of the mid-1990s, many customers already demand Intel components inside their computers before considering other features. High street fashion shoppers want DuPont's Lycra in many of their garments. Hence the supply of components becomes a critical determinant on the customer's ability to compete in the market-place. Parameters such as these form a function of supply chain effectiveness.

Thus the effectiveness or efficiency of any supply chain relies upon a number of interrelated issues:

- The end consumer pays for every activity undertaken within the supply chain and for the profit of each supply chain echelon.

If one part of the supply chain is inefficient, the supply chain as a whole loses sales due to the higher price of the goods relative to more efficient competitors.

- If one part of the supply chain is unresponsive to customer needs, the supply chain will be unresponsive to the end consumer's needs. This is overcome by using stock to protect demand to individual echelons of the supply chain. The holding of stock adds to the cost of the product.
- If any tier of the supply chain fails to share information regarding orders, sales volumes or capacities, the remaining supply chain players are left to rely on inaccurate forecasts, typically resulting in lost sales or increased inventories.
- If one supplier's technology or design is inferior, the functional performance of the end product as a whole will suffer, most likely resulting in lost sales.

In most industries the different parts of the supply chain will have different owners. Each of these owners typically tries to maximize its own returns independently of the other owners within the supply chain. The individual companies have focused on increasing their profit at the expense of their suppliers and customers. This serves to redistribute the profits of the supply chain amongst its members. It also generates ill will and lack of trust which damages the ability of the supply chain to increase the profit available and therefore limits the amount of profit to be shared out.

This somewhat blinkered approach to managing the supply chain has resulted in the structuring of supply chains that are far from perfect, indeed in some instances highly unstable. Component suppliers have, in the past, shown little regard for the satisfaction or the attraction of the ultimate customer, the task nearly always being left to the last link in the chain. Similarly, large customers have shown little regard for small suppliers with their use of cost-cutting policies and multiple sourcing.

This 'traditional' model of the manipulations of the supplier/ customer relationship has in fact worsened to what Lamming calls the 'stress' model.[1] This typically maintains 'big stick' purchasing, the exploitation of suppliers, the unacceptable order fluctuations and continual price pressures, but now the buyer insists on an 'open book' relationship where supplier costing policies can be scrutinized for 'savings'. Of course, since the supplier needs to maintain some degree of profitability they are forced to claw back costs on quality, service, or both. Along with the general state of the relationship between the buyer and supplier, this advocates supply chains which are associated with:

- poor product quality, high scrap rates and reduced inspection from supply;
- late or unreliable deliveries due to suppliers concentrating only on the high margin customers; and
- reduced communication, secrecy and deception. Information is typically inaccurate, late and mis-communicated.

Of course, these factors do not apparently present a problem where stock is tolerated. In theory, inventory and work in progress smooth any fluctuations from irresponsible customers, provide a buffer for all eventualities, allow the running of inefficient plants and procedures, and permit management to tolerate any functional or organizational mistrust. However, these luxuries just add to the cost of the product through the burdens of carrying inventory and reworking products. They also promote a phenomenon known as the 'Forrester Effect'.

CHARACTERISTICS OF THE SUPPLY CHAIN

Research initiated by Jay Forrester of MIT, in the 1950s, identified that if end user demand for a product increases, then the increase is rapidly transmitted along the supply chain, causing capacities and inventories to be proportionally increased to respond to the demand.[2] The time lags and uncertainties that exist within the supply chain cause these capacities and inventories to respond in a way that exceeds the original required demand increase. Consequently, the demand becomes amplified as it progresses down the supply chain, and as a result causes waste and confusion within the chain. The longer the delay in information getting from the market-place to the factory, the more distorted is the company's view of demand.

This phenomenon, commonly referred to as supply chain dynamics, is best described through Figure 4.1. Here it is implied that a retailer near to the final market will see relatively small and accurate changes in customer demand. However, the supplier of that company will have the view distorted by the retailer's policy on stocking and ordering. As the retailer frequently holds stock, it will probably wait until a proportion of the stock has been sold before

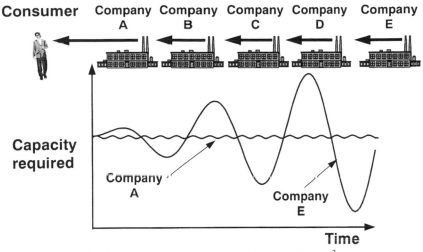

Fig. 4.1 *Supply chain demand amplification*[3]

ordering more. The reorder quantity may be based upon many things including bulk discounts from the supplier, warehouse space and expected sales. If the supplier then sees a change in ordering pattern it may revise its forecast, but may not understand the reason for the change resulting in excess or insufficient stock. As the first-tier supplier's schedule is based on its fluctuating forecasted demand, it gives orders to its suppliers to build components to this fluctuating schedule. This will be distorted by the supplier's stocking and purchasing policies. In turn the second-tier supplier has difficulty forecasting the needs of its customer and so holds additional stock. The fluctuations in demand are amplified by each element of the supply chain as demand passes from company to company, back to the raw material supplier, making life more and more difficult for each successive tier of supply.

So, what appears to be an acceptable ripple of a few per cent in Company A can tend to reach approximately plus or minus 60 per cent in Company E resulting in an upstream demand amplification of at least 20 to 1. So, within this scenario, the capacity-planning problem for Company E becomes thoroughly unmanageable.[4] The costs of taking on and laying off factory capacity to cope with the fluctuations in demand also add to the costs of the supply chain as a whole and are ultimately borne by the end consumer.

Unfortunately, businesses in the nineties are much more complex than that modelled by these theorists, therefore their systems are

considerably more unstable. Generally, companies attempt to overcome this by making to forecast. However, forecasting is extremely
unreliable and any risk tends to be reduced by holding large levels of
finished goods stock to protect against forecasting error. This also
results in longer lead-times due to the effects of making extra goods
for safety stock. These inventories continue to further distort
demand, leading to the Forrester Effect becoming more pronounced.
In effect, a vicious circle is in action, displayed in Figure 4.2.

Where demand is higher than forecasted demand, there is a time
lag between the situation being realized and the required product
being produced, that is, its lead-time. During this period of time sales
will be lost. Where demand is lower than forecasted demand there
will be excess inventory which will incur a working capital charge.
This inventory may become obsolete if the nature of the product
changes and the cost of writing off obsolete stock can be significant. If
dumped on the market it can damage margins on the mainstream
product by undercutting its price, or even impact negatively on
market share.

All of these above factors make supply chain dynamics the
inherently most complex element to successful management and control of the total supply chain. Although many companies experience
the effects of fluctuations in stocks and production rates, resulting in
immense costs and manufacturing disruptions, the root causes are

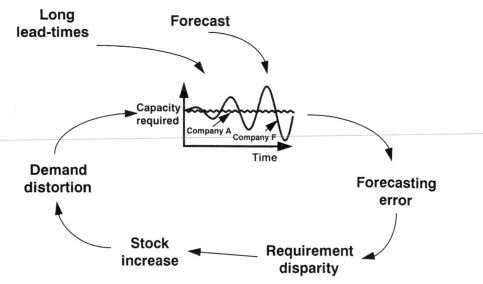

Fig. 4.2 *The effect of forecasting on demand*

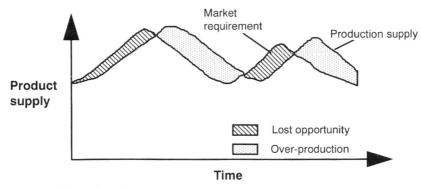

Fig. 4.3   *The consequence of not meeting requirements*

seldom understood, but are typically self-induced through ill-conceived management practices.[5] The decision-makers within the supply chain all too often apply similar patterns of behaviour which may well be internally efficient, but prove detrimental to the other players in the chain, through the focus upon the segment of the chain which is under the ownership of an individual proprietor.

APPROACHES TO SOLVING THESE ISSUES

By now you have probably realized the effect that poor supply chain design has on your business. You may also be asking yourself how you can improve the situation, particularly if you are a supplier organization. Unfortunately it is no easy task, although moving in the right direction has benefits to individual businesses even if they are within a less than perfect supply chain. There have been a number of excellent books published in recent years on such techniques. These are listed in the section on suggested reading. The objective of this discussion is to provide an introduction to the key concepts these books provide, leaving the detailed solutions for their originators to explain.

Full supply chain integration is the optimum strategy for reducing the Forrester Effect and the poor performance that it brings. The basis of this is to have a supply chain that has free access feedback to end-user demand patterns as well as access to all of the logistical information contained within the system. This will enable inventory to be held and managed in a coordinated way. Principally this means that the structure of the supply chain through the application of Time Compression and the principle of inventory positioning enables the minimization of stock points and stocking levels. As a result, amplification is reduced because there are fewer stock points and quicker response times through simultaneous demand feedback. However, because there are so many causes of poor supply chain dynamics which vary from situation to situation, it is unlikely that dynamic behaviour can be totally eliminated from a supply chain.

Despite this, it is clear that the most value from Time Compression can be obtained by taking the holistic approach, looking at an entire supply chain to eliminate system dynamics and improve the performance of the chain as a whole. There are however few individuals or organizations that have sufficient power to take such action. Therefore, the question for many of businesses is how can the optimization of an individual company contribute to the optimization of an uncoordinated supply chain.

The best place to start is by describing the ideal solution. This is a well-known concept called 'Just-in-Time' (JIT). Whilst it is ideal it is not equally applicable to all environments; for example, it would be difficult to utilize when building a one-off product like a skyscraper. Even so there may be parts of the process of building a one-off to which it is applicable and which might result in Time Compression of the entire project, for example, administrative processes or supply of standard components.

The Just-in-Time philosophy was first developed as the Toyota Production System as a means to provide minimum waste and factory size. One of the key elements of waste it seeks to minimize is time. The ultimate goal of the system is to level the flows of production and goods. According to its inventors, Ohno and Mito,[6] the JIT production system works on the principle that:

- The customer provides the information of what is to be made and when, with each individual order being responded to on an individual basis
- Information on what is to be made is passed from one production stage to another using small cards called '*kanbans*'. This is known as a 'pull' system
- Materials are delivered from suppliers only in the exact quantities required and the exact times to meet the material production schedule
- Equipment is arranged in the order that value is added to the product
- Automation with stopping devices to stop waste is readily utilized[6]

The close coordination between customer and supplier required for effective JIT systems requires a different approach to supplier relationships than the traditional adversarial relationship. The complexity of managing the supply chain can be decreased by reducing the number of suppliers a company has. This in turn reduces the overhead costs associated with dealing with suppliers. JIT requires that reliable information and schedules are passed on to suppliers for them to be able to make reliable deliveries of the correct parts. The close working relationship required between companies to make this philosophy succeed requires a high degree of trust.[7] This is often a major problem after years of adversarial purchasing negotiations.

So, the ultimate aim must be to develop a long-term mutually trusting relationship between the customer and supplier. Price is no longer the most important factor; lead-times, quality and other capabilities, such as design ability, must now be considered

TIME-BASED SUPPLY CHAINS

Most supply chains have the form they do as a result of management practices which did not consider the whole picture, for example, through actions such as least cost, bulk purchasing or inaccurate forecasts. These supply chains need to be engineered in a way that recognizes that the success of any supply chain system relies upon the success of all players within that chain. Time-based supply chains operate differently from the traditional chains within which most businesses operate. There are a number of guidelines for using Time Compression to increase supply chain performance which include:

- Reducing the lead-times of all players in the supply chain to allow faster throughput of products to the end consumer. Merely concentrating on an individual business is likely to have little effect on the overall lead-time; products will typically reside at a stocking point further down in the supply system.
- Removing all duplicate stocks throughout the chain. These stocks are unnecessary, raise carrying costs and distort the actual end consumer demand to the other supply chain members. They also disguise the real problems.
- Holding inventory at the lowest possible stage in the supply chain and late configuring products to order to provide increased

product variety. Many companies hold finished goods stock which is not only expensive, but a proportion is inclined to be sold at discounted prices due to over-supply.

- Limiting the percentage change in the size of successive orders to reduce the effects of demand amplification throughout the chain. This stabilizes demand to all players. Typically, companies show little regard for their suppliers, demanding whatever order size they need.
- Sending consumer order information for products to suppliers throughout the entire supply chain, as opposed to the first-tier supplier only. Withholding information from the supply chain increases forecasting error.
- Working with their customers and suppliers on a partnership basis to resolve supply chain issues, removing obstacles to performance and slashing lead-times throughout all businesses in the chain. The supply chain is only as strong as the weakest link.
- Using capacity within the business to add value only when the customer actually needs it. Attempting to fill capacity of equipment to avoid poor utilization measures results in the capacity being full when important orders need to be made. The chance occurrence of redundant stock is also greatly increased.

OPTIMIZING INDIVIDUAL COMPANIES

The first place to start in optimizing the supply chain is in your own business. In essence, it acts like a mini supply chain with different functions supplying components and information to each other. When interpreted in terms of business processes, it can be controlled and managed in exactly the same manner. It does, however, have to work with the constraints placed on it by its customers and suppliers as well as the external drivers that affect the supply chain. The benefits of time-compressing your internal supply chain towards the ideal can be realized by your own company, even if you are not part of a supply chain which is pursuing Time Compression. As your performance improves, your company will become more attractive as a supplier to those supply chains which are compressing time in pursuit of competitive advantage.

Typically, the manufacturing company's operations involve the movement, storage and transformation of materials and products from the point of origin to ultimate consumption. The primary activities that must be managed efficiently and effectively to carry out these processes include manufacturing operations and supply together with distribution activities. Unfortunately, many organizations continue to compartmentalize the management of these activities by placing responsibility for them under different functional areas – production is considered as one area while transportation and warehousing are considered another. By separating management decision-making responsibility for these activities, coordination difficulties emerge that detract from the company's ability to compete on a value-added basis.

Overcoming the inertia created by functional thinking will enable the organization to reduce the sub-optimization that occurs within the company and throughout the supply chain. To reduce this functional orientation, a strong and focused managerial effort at all levels must be directed at removing both real and perceived barriers between organizational departments. Without organization boundary constraints and the territorial protection measures that accompany them, managers are better able to make critical business decisions.

Traditionally, the complex material flow environment has required convoluted, expensive computer-based scheduling and materials controls to control the complexity. MRP, MRPII and OPT installations have become commonplace for companies involved in the manufacture of multi-level assembled products. These systems model the factory in order to optimize production. Unfortunately they often model factories that were designed to create optimization in each of the functional departments, often driven by accounting measures such as utilization. As the barriers between different functions come down the benefits of these types of systems will increase as they are altered to optimize the factory as a set of integrated business processes.

The optimization of the factory and the effectiveness of the business processes within it may entail it being protected from the effects of the outside world. This can be done by holding stocks of materials and finished goods, maintaining excess capacity, and/or coordinating sales and available capacity. If the amount of inventory held and the associated delays are less than what has been removed from the process, then the overall performance of the company and of the supply chain has been improved. As the supply chain as a whole becomes more effective these protective buffers can be gradually removed.

Supplying Multiple Customers

In many of the companies we have worked with, much of the complexity within the manufacturing and distribution processes has occurred because the company is supplying many customers, each with their own individual needs. Factories that based their production processes on the idea of maximizing machine utilization typically make the requirements of each customer on the same set of production machinery. Where there are significant differences between the needs of different customers this can cause considerable difficulties in scheduling, supply of components and meeting quality standards. Trying to push these different requirements on a standardized system leads to sub-optimization in all cases and therefore mediocrity in each aspect of the requirements.

Variety in customer requirements can take the form of:

- Sensitivity to delivery reliability
- Required delivery lead-times
- Quality standards
- The actual design of the product required
- Level of customization of standard products
- Associated paperwork
- Volume of product required

 We have seen many situations where different requirements have been covered by the same business processes, usually resulting in performance approaching the lowest common denominator or, worse, widespread fire-fighting to overcome this. An alternative solution is to separate different groups of requirements into different business processes, in effect untangling them. In manufacturing this is often called 'cellular manufacturing', in distribution it is referred to as 'distribution channels'. Setting up different business processes for customers with different product requirements and different sensitivities to lead-time allows those requirements to be focused on. It also has an effect on the remaining business processes as sources of turbulence and causes of fire-fighting are removed, allowing them to operate more effectively. Colocation of manufacturing functions in a 'cell' also makes inefficiencies between these functions visible and encourages their removal, enhancing the overall performance of the business process.

Late Configuration

There is one type of solution which can provide both the benefits of large batches and high machine utilization, and the ability to deliver products to the exact requirements of customers. This is late configuration. Products are designed such that the changes required for different customers or different end products are made at the last possible stage of production. In this way large production runs of the standardized, base components can be made. These are then converted to meet customers' exact needs when orders arrive. As the components are standardized the overall stocking level and risk are lowered and production costs reduced.

One company that made a major breakthrough using this principle was Avro, the aircraft manufacturer. To secure orders Avro must tailor certain parts of their aircraft precisely to customer requirements, typically galley fittings, avionics or fuel capacity options. Subsequent to the manufacture of the base aircraft, the company used to allocate additional design and production time to ensure the aircraft could be reworked to order, typically involving a rebuild of the basic airframe and then a total refitting of the galley and associated equipment. This created an immense amount of non-value-adding time in the form of rework, whilst more critically preventing Avro delivering aircraft within the time-scales that customers required. The company also had to pay increased premiums for additional working hours incurred whilst trying to meet customer requirement dates.

Avro utilized Time Compression techniques to reduce product lead-times from point of order to point of delivery. Obviously it was impossible to build every entire aircraft from scratch in just a few weeks, so late configuring each aircraft, from a standardized 'white tail' state was the ideal solution. Avro set about redesigning their basic aircraft to build in a number of standard building points. The build points were created to enable any configuration of galley, avionics or fuel options to be added without changing the basic aircraft. So the need to redesign the basic aircraft for every customer was eliminated. The aircraft could be configured exactly to suit customer orders in a few weeks.

OPTIMIZING THE SUPPLY CHAIN

Once you have sorted out these key issues within your business it is possible to provide assistance to your customers and suppliers to deliver benefits to all players within the supply chain. For example, Coats Viyella, a textile manufacturer, helps its suppliers to shorten the time it takes to provide yarn to its business units. This helps them compete against lower-priced imports by shortening the time the retailer has to wait to fulfil orders. As imports typically involve excessive lead-times, retailers are willing to pay higher prices to the company who delivers more quickly, especially for higher-priced fashion items. Another example is C. J. Fox, a fastener supplier to the aerospace industry, who have driven a 'full service' supply initiative into their customer base. By delivering Just-in-Time and taking responsibility for stock replenishment at customer site, the need for customer order processing, and thus wasted time, is eliminated. Both these companies recognize the importance of reducing the time it takes for products to pass through each player in the supply chain.

Our experience has shown there are a number of strategies to improve supply chain performance which, whilst highly effective throughout the total supply chain, prove just as beneficial across any supplier–customer association. That could be between companies, business units, departments, or even between cells. Each can be tackled in a very similar manner, while using the same approach.

Controlling Demand

One big problem with Just-in-Time in a supply chain is that it requires a relatively steady demand. If the demand your customer is generating is uneven there is little that can be done to cope with the fluctuations except keeping excess capacity on line or holding stocks. Every player in the chain then uses buffer stock and as variety increases in line with customer needs, more styles, sizes and colours need to be stocked. These additional reserves require additional overhead in terms of management and control, expediters and additional scheduling capabilities. Each of these attributes cost money which will ultimately be reflected in the price the customer pays for the product. It is worth remembering that if you are generating uneven demands for your suppliers, it will be costing you money.

This dependence upon steady customer demand means that the nearer to the end consumer a company is, the more effect it can have upon the supply chain through its ordering policies. Admittedly some industries have extremely seasonal demands from the end consumer. In such cases it is wiser for the retailers to forecast and manage demand within the entire supply chain based on their close knowledge of the customer, than for each supply chain echelon to forecast independently based on distorted information from their immediate customers.

Information Sharing

A principal element of successful management of the supply chain is effective information flow, communication and integration. This permits organizations to optimize the flow of goods along the chain, through sharing information about markets, materials requirement forecasts, inventory levels and production and delivery schedules. As a mechanism to improve supply chain performance it offers potential for efficiency improvements due to the availability of complete, timely and accurate information. This arrangement may permeate the total supply chain, from point of origin to final consumer, and is heralded as providing a speedier and improved product or service to the customer. However, there is yet more to be done. Companies such as the retailer Marks & Spencer are considering new ways in which they can share more than just information; ideas abound for adapting and evolving traditional business processes and even for sharing information and inventory between organizations on a much wider basis.

The main benefit of efficient information flow is a company which is both flexible and can rapidly respond to the market-place as required: whilst inventory needs to be used as an instrument of competitive advantage rather than to cover inefficiencies; control systems consequently must encourage integration and not traditional functional barriers. Besides the routine exchange of information, relationships between companies can be strengthened by meetings between managers responsible for similar functions to resolve issues and to explore alternative methods of operation.

Electronic data interchange (EDI) systems represent an opportunity to speed up total supply chain response time by using direct and rapid links to suppliers, with up-to-date demands and build rates. The ongoing development of EDI systems, coupled with the rationalization and partner development of supplier networks, has already led to direct scheduling within the supply base, where the demands of the ultimate consumer are directly relayed to each supply chain element rather than being filtered and corrupted through the chain progression – like the Chinese whisper.

However, there are a number of problems which have made the introduction of effective supply chain cooperation harder. The most frequently reported constraint is the inadequacy and incompatibility of computer systems and the need for investment in this area to achieve long-term benefits. Data is often unrecognizable, incomplete or inaccurate and problems arise because of differences of definition and timing. To ensure that links with suppliers are feasible, technological solutions are now a major area of consideration within vendor rating systems, which question a supplier's ability to invest in new technology for the purpose of future integration.

Echelon Removal

A further strategic element of supply chains relates to the removal of functional echelons or levels/tiers of companies within the supply chain, for example a wholesaler. This is a form of Time Compression whereby the value-adding activity performed by one level is integrated into another existing level of the chain at the same time as being compressed. This allows that echelon of the supply chain to be removed. The removal of a level from the supply chain will usually remove at least one stocking point and also enable faster and more accurate communication of the demand with the lower echelons in the supply chain. These two factors will have the result of reducing the effect of supply chain dynamics. In order to perform this type of Time Compression the rules surrounding the principle of vertical integration will have to be observed in order to ensure that the most value-adding solution is achieved.

A recent project with, a manufacturer of consumer durables, emphasized the benefits of removing an echelon. Historically, the supply chain from this company to the retail market was serviced through a network of wholesalers fed from a factory warehouse. The wholesaler no longer served the interests of the supplying company, generally declining to hold the appropriate stock. Unbeknown to this manufacturer, the wholesaler tended to use their strong brand name as a loss leader to attract customers to their premises. They would then persuade them to purchase products from foreign competitors, on the basis that product was available immediately, as opposed to the seven-day lead-time. The tactics were obviously incompatible with any concept of attempting to serve the end user, especially because it was in the wholesaler's interest not to share information relating to what was happening in the market-place. In this situation, the wholesaler echelon had to be eliminated from the chain, reducing the overall lead-time to the retailer and reducing the overall stock. It also provided more accurate market information to the manufacturer.

Cooperation

The only method to compress overall supply chain cycle time is to work with the companies with which your business interacts to assist them in competing more effectively. It is clear that companies which buy and sell from each other are far better at managing the supply chain through setting mutual capacity, production and inventory levels. For example, time and cost can be directly eliminated from the chain if suppliers immediately know the capacity, lead-times and usage rates of customer companies, rather than wait to receive orders from purchasing departments. If information systems are developed to serve all players within the chain effectively, as opposed to individual component systems, benefits in time will again be delivered. However, the reduction of time is not the only possible objective of closer cooperation. In our experience, many companies report benefits in improved customer service, reductions in delivery failures, improved product availability, reductions in order cycle time and the ability to respond faster to changing circumstances.

Manufacturers such as the Rover Group currently have a number of teams established across the business to work with the companies with which they do business to seek out joint opportunities for improvement. With more than 70 per cent of the cost of any vehicle bought in, Rover recognize more than most the importance of their suppliers on the overall success of their products. Using supplier development initiatives, the Rover Group brings together suppliers to guide them through time-based strategies, teach tools and techniques such as process mapping, and offer resource assistance. By focusing efforts upon Time Compression and the removal of waste, these groups of companies are able to achieve massive increases in the effectiveness of the entire supply chain.

Reducing Supply Chain Complexity

The longer and more complex the supply chain, the worse the performance of that chain is likely to be. The complexity of managing the supply chain can be decreased by reducing the number of suppliers a company has. This in turn reduces the overhead costs associated with dealing with suppliers. Leading companies tend to deal directly with only a small number of first-tier suppliers rather than have their own businesses supplemented by purchases from a plethora of independent suppliers. Many manufacturers overcome this by developing suppliers with the capability to build subsystems. For example, a supplier of car dashboards may act as the first-tier supplier to a vehicle manufacturer. They may then use the suppliers of odometers, tachometers, switches, vents and so on to build a complete subsystem and supply the assembly direct to the vehicle manufacturer. This simplifies the supply chain, distributing the responsibility more evenly to the other players in the chain.

A further opportunity exists by customer and suppliers working in parallel as opposed to in series. In traditional assembly processes, each stage of production must be complete before advancing to the next phase. For example, structural assembly must be completed before the systems installation can proceed. Hence production is finalized within each production stage prior to being passed to the next. The purpose of modern approaches to manufacturing such as simultaneous engineering is to overlap the functional activities. This not only reduces the lead-time by the length of the overlap, but also allows the product assembly process to be carried out more effectively.

Late Configuration

Late configuration in the supply chain operates in exactly the same manner as within the individual manufacturing company. Components are designed such that the changes required for different customers or different end products are made at the last possible stage of production. This way standardized base components can be made by the supply base. As the components are standardized the overall stocking levels, demand amplification and risk are lowered and production costs reduced.

Benetton revolutionized the knitwear business through this philosophy by creating the ability to replenish the shelves of their retailers with a made-to-order garment direct from Italy in just three weeks. Before this, Italian imported knitwear had a lead-time of around three months. The company traditionally used to manufacture knitted garments from dyed yarn. Unfortunately, they also suffered the consequences of excessive lead-times on yarn production and had to forecast garment sales in style, size and colour and continue to hold appropriate stocks of coloured yarn and finished garments to buffer demand. Benetton did an excellent job of reducing the product lead-time. By using a base natural-coloured yarn, the garments could be knitted to size and held as semi-finished products, ready to dye to order as complete items. By getting order information immediately back to Italy and organizing the dye houses to work on fast turnaround, small batch sizes, Benetton was able to keep its retail shelves full of the colour and styles that were currently selling without carrying piles of inventory in its pipeline.[8]

Aligning Capacities

To avoid excessive lead-times and high inventories, flexibility has to be designed across the supply chain system. By aligning manufacturing capacities between each player in the chain, planning and scheduling systems are simplified. Stalk and Hout[9] originally showed how the synchronization of lead-times and capacities smoothes fluctuations in demand.[8] This automatically eliminates time spent by every company in the supply chain recalculating schedules and capacities to align their own manufacturing systems with demand. The process is a non-value-adding task and its elimination reduces the amounts of rework in the chain.

Each stage within the chain has to be flexible and have the ability to respond to changes in product mix and volume. If any one player · creates a bottleneck within their internal supply chain, then any additional changes to mix and volume are going to accumulate as work in progress within that player. Hence, the throughput of the total supply chain is damaged. Companies such as the Rover Group look for imbalances in capacity throughout their supply chains and work with the suppliers to help eliminate the problems. This could be through direct assistance, for example implementing customer-specific cells, or changes to the methods by which Rover supply information.

However, aligning capacities requires further cooperation between all players in the system, especially the end manufacturer. The majority of bottlenecks in the supply chain occur because the company at the end of the chain fails to pass updated order information down to its suppliers. Companies in the chain are typically unaware that their customers' priorities have changed and continue to make the previous week's requirements. However, aligning capacities does not involve building more capacity; it means understanding the current capacities of each player in the chain and using the information intelligently. By passing information to suppliers earlier, suppliers have more time to plan their effective use of capacity.

SUPPLYING NEW PRODUCTS

Many of these supply chain strategies have had to be deployed to reduce the effects of poor supply chain design. The effectiveness of the total supply process depends on competent design and adequate control, just as the effectiveness of each company depends upon these practices. Yet, little effort has been applied to existing supply chains to improve the situation, mainly because the inefficiencies are the outcome of long-standing products, systems and relationships. Introducing new products often provides a further opportunity to design the supply chain to alleviate many of the problems we have discussed.

Suggested Reading

M. Christopher, *Logistics and Supply Chain Management: Strategies for Reducing Costs and Improving Services* (London, Pitman, 1992).

R. C. Lamming, *Beyond Partnership: Strategies for Innovation and Lean Supply* (London, Prentice-Hall, 1993).

M. Sako, *Prices, Quality and Trust – Interfirm Relations in Britain and Japan* (Cambridge University Press, 1992).

M. Saunders, *Strategic Purchasing and Supply Chain Management* (London, Pitman, 1994).

CASE STUDY – SHORT BROTHERS

The Company

Short Brothers plc is the European Group of Bombardier Aerospace and competes in the world aviation and defence markets. Shorts employs some 9500 personnel world-wide and operates across four main sectors – Aircraft, Nacelle Systems, Defence Systems and Support Services.

To date, their products are in service with over 200 customers in 75 countries and close working relationships have been made with customers throughout the world. The customer base includes Bombardier Aerospace companies – Canadiar, de Havilland and Learjet – together with Boeing, Rolls-Royce, British Aerospace, Gamesa, Hurel–Dubois, International Aero Engines, Rohr, Lockheed Martin, Thomson–CSF, and national and international defence forces.

Strategic Drivers

The aerospace industry world-wide is trying to recover from a recession which eliminated all the profits made by the industry from its origins almost 60 years ago – these losses equate to in excess of $15 billion (US). Now, the biggest threat facing the aerospace industry is the rise of the Far East. Taiwan Aerospace is in talks with Boeing over possible joint development of a 100 seat regional jet. The proposed collaboration could also involve the Chinese aircraft industry as well as Japan. Air traffic volumes in the Far East have risen by 20 to 30 per cent in recent years. It is by far the largest growth market and aircraft manufacturers need to be accessible and world class if they are to achieve a market share that will allow them to grow and to survive.

At present over 1000 excess aircraft are 'mothballed' throughout the world because many airlines were unable to cancel contracted deliveries. Airlines spare capacity over the past three years represents the equivalent of 400 empty jumbo jets flying each day between London and New York. The financial burden on airlines means that the return to reasonable profit may not be seen for some years. The industry's financial performance over the last few years has made it extremely difficult for many carriers to finance the purchase of new aircraft. The airlines need \$850 billion to pay for the 12 000 aircraft due in service within 25 years. As the airline operations prepare to re-equip their fleets to meet many new rules and regulations and to improve efficiency of the business they are demanding 20–30 per cent price reductions for the aircraft. These demands are being passed onto the suppliers. As a result, aircraft manufacturers like Shorts have to be innovative and radical so as to ensure continued competitiveness.

The Programme of Change

As part of their efforts to achieve 'world class' status, Shorts have recognised the importance of working with their suppliers through their Supplier Development and joint improvement initiatives.

Shorts previously had no supplier development strategy and purchasing operated on an ad hoc basis. It had to deal with 7500 suppliers. Supplier relationships were adversarial and supply contracts were awarded based solely on price. This policy and relationship with suppliers led to a high supplier turnover which resulted in a great amount of effort wasted in 'breaking in' new suppliers. The complexity of the situation meant that Shorts had a poor payment record. To summarise Shorts gave no visibility of their strategy to their suppliers. As a result, Shorts introduced a Supplier Development strategy focusing on seven key success factors: customer focus, non-recurring cost, time to market, recurring costs, lead-times, utilised assets, quality and research and technology with the aim of radically improving their situation.

The main objective of the Supplier Development strategy was to rationalise the supply base from 7500 suppliers to 1500 suppliers. This was instantly reduced by 1200 suppliers through removing dormant suppliers from the data base, that is those who had not provided items for a notable period of time. More significantly, suppliers whose performance was poor were disengaged. This formed the basis for creating a tiered supply base that aimed for world class standards in terms of schedule, quality, cost, delivery lead times and customer satisfaction and is totally dedicated to the success of Short Brothers and its products.

The aerospace industry and associated industries operate to a system where demands by the customer are placed on the supplier usually without due regard to the consequences. This is a failing not only of the suppliers, but also the short-termism of the customer. Shorts was not alone in overlooking the supply chain as a business process; however they were at the stage where they were able to learn from the mistakes of competitors and capitalise upon them. They realised that suppliers and customers are able to tailor their service to that which best suits the overall supply chain. For Shorts this meant the dedication of people, plant and equipment. This investment required significant return for both the supplier and Shorts, typically in terms of expertise. The improvements were expected to generate greater volumes of business with new projects, to such an extent that other smaller customers of the suppliers would not be able to attract similar levels of service, effectively locking the destiny of the suppliers into that of Shorts.

The first phase of the Supplier Development programme was to select and evaluate around 100 suppliers with which long-term relationships were to be developed. These were named 'preferred suppliers'. The purchasing managers within the various divisions of Shorts nominated their strategic long-term suppliers to the Supplier Development team and together they worked on building the relationships between Shorts and its supply base.

The following project was part of the Supplier Development programme and it focused on six preferred suppliers to Shorts, three manufacturers and three distributors of fasteners.

Fastener Management

Shorts recognised the need for Time Compression in the area of fastener control. Unlike many competitors and best practice companies, Shorts operated a 'blue-card' manual system of stock controlling fasteners, described in detail below. The result of this was that Shorts were holding in excess of ten times the volume of fasteners that were actually required. This was felt to be unacceptable.

The project began with an examination of Shorts previous method of fastener control. Shorts favoured re-order level control as it provided confidence as to the availability of stock whilst the re-order and re-supply process took its course. In general terms it means that at any one time Shorts was holding between six and nine months' stock of high volume, low value fasteners (in excess of £6 million).

This decentralisation policy meant that each line business unit purchased their own fastener requirements. In areas of common usage the highest user assumed purchasing responsibility.

Former Fastener Supply Strategy

Historically, the organisation's fasteners had been treated with disdain. The amount spent on this commodity represented less than five per cent of the total, distributed across over 500 companies. Consequently little attention had been paid to the purchasing policy associated with the commodity since the 1950s, when the ethos was to carry large volumes of stock as insulation from short-term supply shortages.

Parts were typically brought into the company in large quantities, usually representing approximately three to six months usage, a value of around £6 million. The quantities estimated were a considered opinion on behalf of the buyer based on purchase history, knowledge of build rates and the frequency of the blue cards appearance. The average lead-time for manufacture of fasteners was 12 to 16 weeks.

The parts were inspected on every receipt and one in five cases were sent to the company laboratories for physical and chemical testing. Once inspected the parts were then distributed to the store locations. Here they used to be counted to verify the quantity received was the quantity ordered. The material would then be stored, a small quantity of three to six months usage placed in a reserve location along with the Blue Card, the remainder placed in an open stock location, and any surplus placed in an over flow location. The stock would then be exhausted until the reserve stock was breached, whereupon this stock was placed in the open stock location and the Blue Card passed to the buyer for re-order.

Although this traditional supply policy provided the advantage of affluent buffer stock, the disadvantages were endless: no accurate

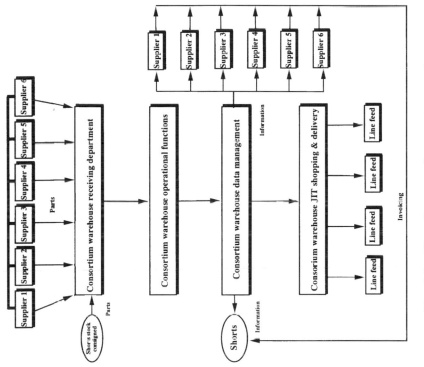

Fig. 4.4 *Flow diagram of consortium service*

stock levels, reduced service levels, large volume obsolescence, frequent shortages, incorrect stock profiles, poor forecasts, no accountability, overhead costs, etc. This situation was further compounded by the fact that Shorts, under Bombardier's guidance, created a de-centralised environment. Therefore all line business units were responsible for purchasing their own fastener requirements. Commonality of parts and suppliers led to many duplicated activities.

Whilst the rest of the company advanced and adopted new manufacturing principles, hardware was left to cope with the antiquated 'blue-card' system of re-order level.

The New Hardware Strategy

Given that any strategy needed to be in line with the company's overall goals, the short-termism of the strategies employed elsewhere, and the opportunities that existed within the market place it was decided to adopt the Japanese concept of the Keiretsu, or group. The key concept was to bring together a group of companies, all working together for the mutual benefit of the supply chain. This group needed to be reasonably small, yet encompass all current fastener requirements and possible new areas. Shorts concentration in the fields of Nacelles, Composites and Fuselage helped shape the criteria for selection, the main areas being:

- Expertise/Advantage in specific commodities
- Past experience with Shorts – delivery and quality performance
- Technical assistance
- Potential for growth

Three manufacturers and three distributors of fasteners were chosen. A number of Supplier Development meetings were held where the concept of the Keiretsu was explained along with the criteria for selection and the other parties selected. After initial scepticism at these early meetings, all six companies agreed to work together for their mutual benefit. They did this by jointly establishing and running a local warehouse, supplying Shorts with all its fastener requirements, direct to the line on a JIT, pay as used basis.

Time Compression Results

Through the introduction of this initiative, the new fastener system brought substantial cost savings to Shorts plus a lead-time reduction from 16 weeks to two days.

There were also a number of additional benefits:

- Movement away from the non-value added sales-buyer interface, towards designer-engineer and operations-stores interface
- Early involvement in design-build teams leading to early identification and manufacture of parts
- Identification and possible resale of surplus and redundant stocks
- 400 part numbers removed
- Improved Bill of Material accuracy
- Accurate information system
- Commitment to Open Book and Negative Pricing
- Large savings from current system, i.e. freeing of 7000 sq. ft of space with its associated costs and removal of £3.5 million of existing stocks
- JIT delivery of 3 million worth of parts allowing manufacture to become leaner
- Suppliers are responsible for delivery performance. Distributors order as required from manufacture
- Possible expansion to sister companies
- Hardware cost reduction

Learning Points

- Creation of strategic alliances and working with a core supply base as partners provides benefits to both parties. These took the form of immediate operational benefits and improved design for benefits to occur as new products are brought on line.

- It is possible for competing suppliers to work together for the mutual benefit of all.

5 Time and New Product Development

In the last chapter we covered the business processes of manufacturing and of the supply chain which encompass the processes of many companies. Within any company there are many other business processes to which exactly the same principles apply. A commercial business process like finance or purchasing may involve the processing of pieces of paper rather than steel. The only differences are in scale – in-trays replace warehouses, briefcases replace trucks. One of the most important business processes is that of designing and developing new products, which for the purposes of this book we will call the 'new product process', although it is commonly known by other names such as design or product development. The Time Compression of this process provides the focus for this chapter.

CHARACTERISTICS OF THE NEW PRODUCT PROCESS

The new product process is unusual in that it turns creative thinking into tangible results through combining the processing of paper (drawings, data), IT systems (CAD) and materials (prototyping). The final result is not only a product but a manufacturing process to produce it. The new product process is also unusual in that it requires the input of almost all functions of the business. The techniques we describe in this chapter are applicable to the development of any new product. A 'new product' can be anything from a minor engineering change to an entirely new product and manufacturing process. Minor engineering changes to existing products tend to be very similar in process to those in firms with a very high turnover of new products, for example fashion industries like jewellery. The principles can be applied to any type of new product. The 'new product process' may also be the process of customization which occurs in companies where each product they produce has some unique design element. This design time can be a critical element in the overall delivery lead-time.

79

The new product process is complex, largely because of its multi-functional nature and the iterative nature of much of the learning that goes on within it. This learning does not become complete until the product is physically realized, fully tested and launched on the market. In most traditional companies the new product is passed from function to function, but the people who work on it are not, resulting in much of the benefit of this learning being lost through failing to reconcile actions and their downstream results.

Despite the complexity of the new product process, it is a business process. A set of ideas are accumulated, tested and ultimately shaped into a physical product or service. For this reason the product development process suffers from the problems of other business processes such as the supply chain, for example system dynamics effects similar to those identified by Forrester. It is just that the manifestations of the problems are slightly different. The tendency to load the work of engineers in excess of capacity, delays in recruiting/laying off engineers to flex capacity and poor communication throughout the supply chain lead to oscillating demand on the new product process.

THE RISK OF FORECASTING PRODUCT SPECIFICATION

The new product process has a demand for its output from customers. The demand is for the right product in the right place at the right time. Forecasting the exact nature of this demand is difficult. Until the product is launched on the market there is uncertainty as to exactly what features are required, what promotion is required and which sales outlets are best. The further from the launch date these requirements are made, the more uncertainty surrounds them and the more likely they are to be wrong. In effect short lead-times reduce the risk of not meeting customer requirements. Even if the specification of the product is initially what the customer requires, the longer the lead-time, the greater the chance that those requirements will change. The changing of customer requirements usually manifests itself as specification changes. If the change affects the project early then it may be quite easy to alter the design to fit. If it occurs when the project is near completion the degree of change can be significant with considerable detailed redesign and changes to tooling (which may already exist) will be required. These changes will eat up valuable engineering time and

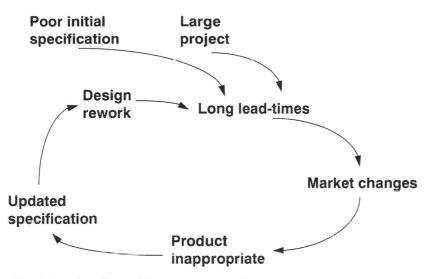

Fig. 5.1 *The effect of large projects and poor specification on lead-time*

delay the project. Delaying the project means its lead-time is longer, inviting yet more specification changes and further delay, a vicious circle as depicted in Figure 5.1.

The changing of customer requirements may also manifest itself as changes in priorities of different projects. Every time energy is diverted from one project to another there is a changeover time as the engineers get up to speed on the new project. Many changes in priority tend to mean that the overall amount of value-adding work undertaken falls and much of the energy expended is not capitalized on in the market-place. This is compounded by the effects of late projects which top management expedites by throwing resources at them. Where one project is speeded up, others are starved of resources and so are delayed. Ultimately they have to be expedited, resulting in other projects being delayed and the risk of them not meeting customer requirements being increased. This vicious circle also results in design costs that spiral upwards.

PROJECT OVERLOAD

Every product development organization we have encountered in our research has had a group of partially completed projects within its process, waiting for somebody to find the time to finish them. Some projects have been superseded by other changes and so represent purely wasted effort. In many of the organizations we have worked with this situation has been exacerbated by projects being loaded onto the development resources with no consideration of the existing load and overall capacity of those resources. The continual shifting of resources from project to project in response to immediate priorities inevitably results in product development programmes becoming the arena for policy resolution as the different projects fight for scarce resources. This undesirable state of affairs results in delays to project execution whilst these policy decisions are resolved.[1] Ultimately none of the projects get to completion as fast as they could.

The situation described is uncannily similar to the problems faced in the manufacturing function of businesses in the past. This was due to the prevalence of 'push'-type manufacturing systems where orders were pushed into the system without regard for capacity and pulled through by teams of expediters chasing the most important orders. The result was unreliable delivery performance, excess inventory and low productivity, the same outcomes that we have seen from the new product process. Most companies would not allow this performance in manufacturing, yet they allow it in product development. Would you? In our new product example incomplete projects are analogous to work in progress on the factory floor and superseded projects can be likened to obsolete inventory that has to be scrapped. Both of these waste time and cost money.

Our research on new product processes identified 'project overload' as the most frequent cause of underperformance The phenomenon was seen to be common in the USA both by Wheelwright and Clark[2] and by Smith and Reinertsen[3] who generated the term. Project overload has a number of effects which explain why it leads to poor performance of the new product process. These are:

- Having engineers working on several projects results in their commitment to a given project being reduced. Delays may occur where there is a conflict in the engineers' time between two or more urgent projects. This tends to be another vicious circle as delays in the project mean that extra projects are launched to keep the engineers busy.
- Having a large number of active projects distracts engineers from the important projects. Queries, paperwork or meetings on projects that engineers are not currently involved in distracts them from working on their immediate task. We have also seen

engineers who have spent considerable amounts of their time helping solve immediate fire-fighting problems in production resulting in the neglect of long-term design work. The effects of these distractions on engineering productivity can be considerable; for example, Nayak showed that engineers spent only 35 per cent of their time on value-adding work.[4]

- Without clear priorities on which projects are to be done first, engineers may 'cherrypick' interesting projects in preference to less interesting but more important projects.
- It is difficult to cope with unanticipated projects in an overloaded system. Another project would need to be pushed aside to make way for the important new addition.

APPROACHES TO SOLVING THESE ISSUES

When the manufacturing function of companies suffered from the problems of overload, a number of different solutions were developed. The best known of these were MRPII and Just-in-Time manufacture. It is now time for the new product process to be treated with similar techniques. A number of excellent books have been published on such techniques. These are listed in the section on suggested reading. The objective of this discussion is to provide an introduction to the key concepts these books provide, leaving the detailed solutions for their originators to explain.

The main weakness identified by our work on the new product process was that companies failed to take a view of the system as a whole. Many of the companies we worked with had sophisticated procedures and tools for managing individual projects. What these tools failed to take into account was the knock-on effect to other projects and other activities within the organization. Our research has shown us that there is considerable benefit to be gained by spending time to understand the management of the new product function, its portfolio of projects and the interaction of the new product process with the company as a whole.

There are a number of fundamental elements to consider when time-compressing the new product process:

- Control: Using product strategy to ensure that there is a close match between the projects being worked on, resources available to do them and company strategy

Integrate
Compress

- Spending time at the beginning of the project to clarify the specification, ensure early involvement of all functions in concept design and in doing so reduce the scope for downstream delays
- Improving flows of information within the process
- Speeding up the learning cycle
- Reducing delays in associated processes

Product Development Strategy

Control

Our findings, that many of the problems of the new product process are partially a result of project overload, raises the question as to how the demand on the process and resources available can be matched. There are two ways in which this issue can be handled: controlling the number of projects in the new product process, or controlling the level of resources. It is also possible to optimize the throughput of multiple projects using detailed project planning. This approach is relatively complex compared to the others and is still severely limited if there is a mismatch between projects and resources.

Control

The simplest answer is found in effective filtering and prioritization of new product ideas, thereby controlling the number of projects in

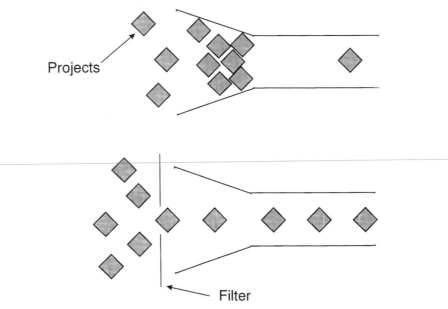

Fig. 5.2 *Effect of a product filter on 'project overload'*

the process. Many of the companies we have worked with permitted any worthwhile project into their new product process because they were just that, worthwhile new products. However, few reconciled the number and size of projects against the number of development staff available to undertake them. By asking the question as to which projects most closely matched the company's strategy, giving these priority and holding back less important projects, we found that the effectiveness of the new product process can be improved enormously. This is clearly illustrated in the Jetstream Aircraft case study at the end of this chapter.

There are a number of different approaches by which performance improvements can be made when you are confronted by this issue. Figure 5.3 shows how focusing on a single project at a time results in it getting to market quicker. If several projects are undertaken and resources split between them they will take longer. This difference occurs because engineers do not have to wait for tasks to be done on another project before they can start their task and because there is effectively a changeover time for an engineer switching between projects. If these waiting and changeover times are reduced then the combined time for two projects done sequentially will be shorter than for the same two projects done simultaneously. The longer a

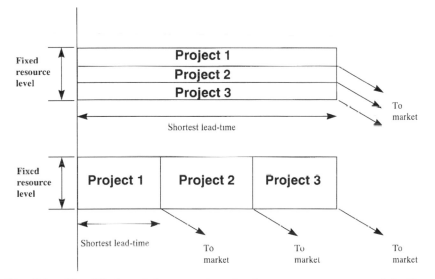

Fig. 5.3 *Simplified model contrasting simultaneous versus sequential effort on three projects*

project takes the more likely it is that it will fail to meet customer
needs or have specification changes part-way through to adapt to
changing customer needs. In addition the specification for project two
in Figure 5.3 need not be finalized until project one is complete and
the specification for project three need not be finalized until project
two is completed. Thus the projects are more likely to be more
successful in the market-place. In many companies it may be possible
to work on more than one project at a time so long as resources are
not split between different projects.[5]

Another approach to solving this problem is incremental innovation which is followed by many successful companies, for example
Sony, and advocated by a number of academics. This is the idea that
instead of choosing to do large, high-risk projects, it is better to do
many smaller, incremental projects. Wheelwright and Clark discuss
incremental innovation in their concept of the aggregate product
plan, whereby incremental, derivative projects are built on to larger,
platform projects which form the basis of each new product generation.[6] Incremental innovation is very effective for developing existing
product concepts. There is still a need to run larger projects to
develop new platforms upon which further incremental innovations
can be built. In addition larger projects may need to be run to develop
products to create entirely new markets or to develop new process
technologies.

The small projects of an incremental innovation-type approach
have many advantages over big projects:

- It is much easier to be flexible in scheduling small projects. They
  do not take too long so it is relatively easy to make way for an
  unexpected, important project or to react to a change in company
  strategy. In the same way it is easy to make way for the inevitable
  delays that occur when the unexpected strikes a project. They can
  also be slotted more easily into gaps in an existing schedule. In
  this respect the use of small projects is analogous to small batch
  sizes in manufacturing and results in the same benefits, better
  delivery reliability, shorter lead-time and lower cost.
- Small projects have shorter lead-times so the forecasting horizon
  is much closer, leading to a greater likelihood of meeting
  customer needs.
- Small projects cost less to develop and so risks are smaller. This
  allows products to be tried and dropped if they fail, with minimal
  cost penalties.

The 'Fuzzy Front End'

An example of one of the most common areas of non-value-adding time in product development was provided by Smith and Reinertsen in their idea of 'the fuzzy front end'.[7] They point out that enormous amounts of time, sometimes running into years, are lost because product ideas are not managed in between their conception and the start-up of a team to exploit them. They suggest that the lack of management attention on the front end of the new product process is due to the relatively small amount of money spent on it. However the impact of the front end on all issues of product success is considerable. For example, research has shown that the design phase for a product resulted in 60 per cent of the cost gap between a company and its best competitor and was responsible for two-thirds of sources of customer dissatisfaction.[8] It is during the new product process that all of the key decisions on the characteristics of a product are made. Once these decisions are taken, the manufacturing process has limited scope to reduce cost and improve quality.

The decisions made in the initial specification and concept design stages are key points of leverage within the process. A few hours of management time spent on these decisions can make a substantial impact on both the performance of the development process and the competitive parameters of the end product which ultimately determine company performance.

Specification

The setting of the specification of a new product is an important activity that warrants far more management attention than it typically receives. In some companies we have found that the specifications are set by marketing departments in terms which are too vague for serious design work to be done. For example, in one company which manufactured a decorative product, the marketer wrote down a description of what customers wanted. This was then turned into a picture of what the designer thought the written specification meant. As the old saying 'a picture is worth a thousand words' suggests, the written specification did not contain anywhere near enough information to convey the customer's exact needs to the designer, resulting in the design not meeting customer needs and having to be repeated. In this case there were effectively two specifications, the written one and the drawing which were very different in content. We have seen similar problems occur between marketing departments and technical engineering functions.

If done well, the setting of the specification provides an opportunity to gain ownership of the product within the company and to reach consensus on trade-offs at an early and therefore inexpensive stage of the new product process.

The objective of the specification-setting stage is to provide a broad and consistent understanding of the purpose of a new product, its expected customers and competitors, and the value and benefits which customers will derive from it. A broad and consistent understanding across functions, and if possible across customers and suppliers, will allow trade-offs between different product functions to be made throughout the project. Thus the specification focuses on the what and not the how. In contrast, a specification that emphasizes the how, as many we have seen do, can restrict design options and remove focus from the critical elements of the design, leading to a less than optimum product. It is also best to think in terms of customer benefits and not product functions. Emphasis on functions alone can add complexity and therefore adds cost and time to the project.[9]

Once a broad understanding of the need for a new product and its specification have been gained, the understanding can be used to begin to specify key parameters. Typically these will include target cost, sales price and expected volume, potential for the development of the product in the future and key functional performance parameters, for example accuracy or reliability. These should provide an unambiguous guide as the project enters the concept design stage.

The need to gain a broad consensus on the need for the product and its customer benefits dictates that the specification be written in a multi-functional meeting. Only this way can consensus be attained. Even then it is likely that there will be some conflict when trade-offs need to be made. If these trade-offs are not satisfactorily resolved at the specification stage they will resurface downstream, usually with considerably more impact on time and cost. Reaching a consensus may require the help of an impartial facilitator. Another approach that some companies have found useful is Quality Function Deployment (QFD), a tool that provides a matrix in which the critical linkages between different product features are exposed and can therefore be resolved.[10]

Since one of the potential benefits of setting the specification jointly is in gaining ownership of the product within the organization, it is important to make sure that the people who are involved in setting the specification are those who will be involved in working on the project. Thus their understanding of the purpose of the product will be carried through all the stages of the new product process, allowing trade-offs to be made without altering the product's ability to meet its objective.

As we have already discussed, specification changes are a major contributor to delay in projects. In the ideal world they would not exist, however in practice they are something that needs to be dealt with. The need for specification changes can be reduced by shortening the lead-time of the project. If the lead-time is short, it is less likely that the market will shift. Also if there is a constant flow of new products, then it may be possible to incorporate a new technology or functions into the next product a few months down the line, rather than delay the current project. Specification changes may have different effects on the design process. Changing a small detail on the design can be relatively easy; changing a fundamental element of the product architecture is expensive. Thus the effect of changes can be minimized by designing the product architecture to take account of the risks, both market and technical, inherent in the product.[11]

Concept Design

Once the specification has been set, the project proceeds to the concept design stage. At this point different concepts will be derived and evaluated, ultimately ending up with one design. This is a key point of leverage within the new product process. At this stage in the design process decisions are made which will determine the nature of the product, its cost, ease of manufacture, quality and development time. Design decisions made after this point will have little effect on the overall performance of the product. It is during the concept design process that the customer benefits and trade-offs agreed within the specification process are embodied in the new product. The end result of the concept design process will be a realistic framework for designing the detail of the product and its supporting processes which represents the needs identified within the specification. Such an early emphasis on overall design and function will allow for a relatively simple design which will make downstream processes easier.

Whilst an effective specification process may have resolved many of the trade-offs inherent in the product, the concept design process will most likely bring others to light. Thus in order to gain maximum benefit from the concept design stages it is important to involve all functions involved in the new product process. Since this stage is the cheapest and fastest point to change the design of the product, it is better to spend time to reach a consensus here, rather than incur costly rework at a later stage in the project. By involving all functions, including manufacturing and customer support, it is possible to take account of their perspective, thereby ensuring that all aspects of the project are feasible. This can be further enhanced by the involvement of suppliers. It is also advisable to use the same core project team which devised the specification as these people will understand the purpose of the product and the trade-offs made, thereby allowing further consistency in developing the desired product.

Product architecture
The question of product architecture is key to speeding up the design process. If a design can be split into two independent modules, then their design can be done simultaneously and so reduce the design process. Modularity also allows a design to be updated without having to redesign the entire unit, a feature that promotes incremental innovation. Similarly a modular approach may promote a wide range of different product models that can be introduced or updated over time. Modularization also has some disadvantages which need to be weighed up against these benefits. Modularity can add to product cost through the use of fasteners or electrical connectors. It is also common for the interfaces between the modules to be weak links in the product.

There are a number of key architectural decisions which need to be answered during the concept design phase:[12]

- To what degree should functionality be modularized?
- In which modules should functionality be placed?
- How much reserve performance should be put in each module?
- What type of interfaces should be used between modules?
- How much technical risk should be taken in each module?

A good example of the use of modularity in product design is the personal computer. The speed with which PC technology progresses has meant that the only easy way to keep up is to have a modular design. The hard drive, floppy disk, CD-ROM and processor cards are all modular units. They allow customers to specify their exact needs and upgrade their systems. The manufacturers and retailers can achieve this without holding a huge number of variants of PC and thus avoid many of the problems of obsolete stock. The different modular units can be developed independently of each other, thereby allowing rapid development of the overall product.

There are several issues to consider when designing in a modular fashion:[13]

- Careful location of product functions within modules so as to allow easy development and control of the number and types of interface
- Using generous design margins to reduce the risk of having to redesign a module. This needs to be balanced against the cost of providing extra margin and effects on product performance
- Having interfaces between modules that are fixed early and not changed
- Keeping interfaces simple with standard interfaces
- Concentrating risky technology within one module. This reduces the risk of the product as a whole failing to work. It also allows a small number of the most talented people to be focused on the one, small area of work and for management to monitor it closely

Improving Information Flows

Within the new product process the idea of improving information flows is not a new one. The idea of using multi-functional teams in engineering has been popular as part of the idea of concurrent engineering. Information flows have also been addressed through the advent of CAD/CAM systems and their associated electronic data management packages.

In traditional product introduction processes each stage of development must be complete before advancing into the next phase. Product design, for example, must be completed before the manufacturing process can be designed and built. Hence product information is finalized within each functional department before being passed to the next. The purpose of modern approaches to development such as concurrent engineering is to overlap the functional activities. This not only reduces the lead-time by the length of the overlap, but also allows the new product process to be carried out more effectively. Close, working-level integration of the people involved in a development project results in interfunctional issues being raised and resolved early in the project and rapid solution of later problems. Achieving close, working-level integration is not as straightforward as its simplicity might suggest. The most common approach is the setting up of a co-located, multi-functional team.

Multi-functional teams

The topic of multi-functional teams has been discussed widely in the product development literature. For example, Smith and Reinertsen suggest that teams should consist of:

- Ten or fewer members
- Volunteers
- Members who serve on the team from product concept to production
- Members who are assigned to the team full-time
- Members reporting solely to the team leader
- Members from the key functions involved
- Members who are co-located within conversational distance of each other[14]

Wheelwright and Clark proposed a number of different structures for development teams.[15] They suggested that the most appropriate type of team for larger projects was the heavyweight team. This is distinguished by the team leader being powerful within the organization relative to the functional heads who supply resources. The resources are thus assigned full-time to the team and are under the project manager's full control.

In our work we have seen many of these rules broken with significant effects on the development process. In one organization the dedicated, co-located team consisted of a large number of people who were in actual fact part-time and had two desks, one in their functional department and one in the team room. This was exacerbated by the team room being an old, windowless area away from the plush office accommodation elsewhere in the company. This caused problems in communication between different parts of the team and allowed team members to be easily side-tracked by their functional managers. The poor environment reduced the importance of the project in the eyes of the team. In another organization the co-located team was about thirty strong. Engineers sat with other engineers, the commercial functions sat together. No single person, including the team leader, knew everyone and what they were doing. Co-location alone is not sufficient; the team members need to have a strong incentive to communicate and work together. This can be achieved through the presence of a powerful project manager and attractive rewards, be they financial or prestige. The team environment must also be able to break down the barriers created by different functional cultures and their individual sets of terminology and norms.

In contrast the team environment at companies with world-class development processes is very different. For example, at Nissan, dedicated teams are also used. These are staffed from the very beginning of the project to its end by a group of people from three major groups, design, development and manufacturing. The design group is responsible for achieving design specification, the development group focuses on the production of models to the required quality, cost and delivery targets, and the manufacturing group focuses on the volume production of the model. The engineers involved are brought together on a temporary basis for the duration of the project. The development staff and some of the design staff are typically based at the manufacturing facilities and are seconded to the design facility to form the team. As the development work nears completion the team moves back to the plants where they assume day-to-day responsibility for the new model. Thus staff from the plants work on a particular model throughout its life, from setting the specification to the point where production ceases. This generates ownership of the vehicle, its tools and manufacturing processes and provides continuity of objectives for the entire product life. Each of the groups involved work to the same common objectives and milestones which ultimately lead to a focused and cohesive team. The team is fully empowered to make design or other changes by themselves in their efforts to meet the targets. Change decisions are authorized by consensus, not through compromise, so that the team fully owns them.

Bit players

One of the key elements of a team approach is to have all of the participants in a development project dedicated to the project. One common cause of delay is where specialists who are not on the team delay a project because that project is not at the top of their priority list of things to do. Inevitably such specialists become a bottleneck in the process. One way of reducing this dependency on specialists is through increasing the skill set of staff so that specialists are only required for the most difficult problems. Another is to code the most commonly used specialist knowledge within a CAD system, thereby reducing the dependency upon the specialist. A similar approach is taken within 'design for'-type systems (for example, design for manufacture and assembly (DFMA)).

Another group which has a similar delaying effect is senior management. This commonly manifests itself as a decision-making delay. Many companies' new product processes include financial gates which must be passed through. These may include inclusion in annual budgets, referral for capital expenditure on items such as tooling and referral for fit against strategic objectives and investment criteria. It is common for such decisions to take considerable amounts of time as the paperwork rises then falls through the hierarchy and meetings of senior management are called. In some cases the decision is so critical that the engineers at the sharp end may not be able to wait for the decision and will just continue with the development process. In this case the decision is ineffective from the points of view of both senior management and the engineers working on the project. This issue can be solved either by speeding up the decision-making process or by empowering lower-level managers and engineers to take key technical decisions without upward reference.

At one company with which we worked it was found that the time to pass capital expenditure decisions for tooling was twelve weeks. The engineers completed the necessary paperwork and then continued with the development process whilst awaiting a decision. Our investigations found that such capital expenditure requests were always approved so the risk in the engineers proceeding with the project was minimal. This decision was thus completely ineffective from the point of view of management controlling the project and from the point of view of engineers working on the project. Top management were enthusiastically promoting the need to reduce lead-time. By reducing their decision-making time to one week they were able to demonstrate their commitment to the project by action and not just by words.

Content of information

Another issue connected with the discussion of information flows is the nature of the information passed on. Different functional departments have different requirements of a product, different terminology, and different understandings of the process. This often results in one department receiving what it perceives as inadequate information, yet the providing department sees it as essentially complete. Alternatively a department may commit a downstream department to objectives which cannot be achieved, for example, impossible delivery dates for a new product. Such misunderstandings of requirements or capability typically result in either rework or compromise, neither of which helps to satisfy customer needs. One solution to this problem is multi-functional teams as already discussed. Another which is more appropriate in some organizations is to educate upstream departments about downstream capabilities and information needs, and to educate downstream departments about the uncertainties faced by upstream departments.[16]

At one company we worked with which made a customized product, the sales people, estimators, purchasing staff and manufacturing staff did not understand each other's information requirements. The sales people would allow customers to choose products outside the capability of the company to make them. The estimators would use one supplier in quoting a price, the procurement people would use a different supplier to buy the item. This resulted in many products which did not make a profit. A workshop was run involving representatives from these departments. They decided to run product awareness training for the sales team and to establish a central purchasing function to overcome these problems. This resulted in a reduction in the time to design and process an order from two weeks to two days.

Another example of the importance of correctly phased information flows was shown in automotive press-tooling, where the casting to make the tool from is a long-lead-time item. Often the designers are reluctant to release the tool to manufacturing until it is complete. This means that manufacturing cannot order the casting, putting its lead-time on the critical path. By releasing enough information to manufacturing to determine the size of the casting, and allowing a little extra to guard against risk, it is possible to order the casting much earlier, thereby reducing the critical path. Our benchmarking activity showed that this resulted in a difference of around 40 per cent between the fastest and slowest press tool manufacturer's critical path. This understanding of the importance of staged information release was applied to a tooling design and procurement process stretching across ten departments in two companies. The early interface of casting suppliers with the design and planning activities of the press tool makers allowed the process of transporting the

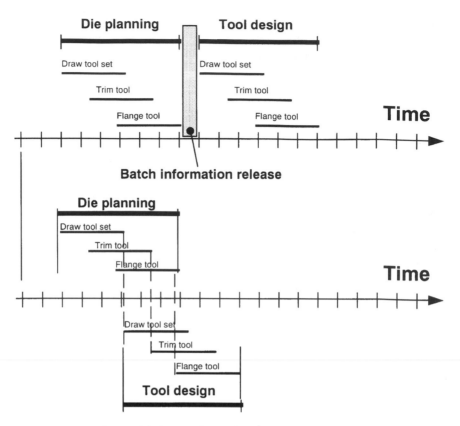

Staged information release

Fig. 5.4 *The effect of staged information release on press tool lead-time*

pattern, scheduling, manufacturing and transporting the required casting to occur in an organized and uninterrupted manner. An inconsistent lead-time of between six and nine weeks was reduced to three weeks. Further improvements in the interface between designers in the foundries and the press tool designers reduced changes at the casting manufacture stage, reducing the lead-time by a further week.

Using technology to transfer information

The evolution of information technology, CNC machine tools and similar technologies over recent years has been a source of many attempts at reducing the development time of new products. Some of these attempts have been extremely successful, others less so. The onward march of technology means that systems are increasingly good at what they do and have become easier to use. Despite this the use of technology in the new product process is littered with pitfalls, usually very expensive ones. The main problem is that a suboptimal process may be automated. Many of the new product processes we have time-compressed had existing CAD systems, yet we were still able to reduce the lead-times enormously through changing the management approach, not the CAD system. CAD systems tend to focus on the value-adding activities within the new product process, which make up a tiny proportion of the overall development time.

In summary, we believe that whilst technology has an extremely important part to play in the new product process, a role that will become more important as time passes, it is not the best place to start when trying to compress time. It is better to take time to understand the management of the process as a whole, and only invest in technology when an effective process exists. In general, management solutions provide considerably better results for a given investment than do technological ones.

SPEEDING UP THE LEARNING CYCLE

The new product process is by definition a learning process. The newness of the product means that not everything needed to build it is known or tested. This has many implications for the new product process. In particular it means that not everything will be right first time and that there will be unexpected problems which may require additional resources. Whilst learning is unavoidable, it is possible to move it towards the front of the process and address the key risks, thereby reducing downstream risk. The principal mechanism for such early learning is prototyping, either physical or computer-based.

The learning required to build a new product is generated through design–build–test cycles. By speeding up these cycles it is possible to bring an action and its effect closer together in time. We suggest that as much as possible of the learning required to build new products is acquired early in the process. This way uncertainty can be reduced in the downstream parts of the process where changes are much more expensive to rectify. One of the key ways of learning within development is through prototyping. This is in effect the 'build' stage of a design–test–build cycle. The building of a physical model reveals many problems, and can be used as a tool to communicate those problems in order to help derive the optimum solution to them. The issues uncovered are often the cross-functional ones that in traditional new product processes do not become apparent until the first production-built prototypes are made. The issue of using prototyping as a means of speeding up the development learning cycle is covered in depth by Bowen *et al.* in their book *The Perpetual Enterprise Machine*.[17]

There are a number of ways of speeding up the design–build–test cycle:

- Removing causes of delay such as queuing, project overload, rework and decision-making by treating the cycle as a business process
- Doing a larger number of smaller prototyping cycles which get specific results faster
- Using modelling and simulation techniques to eliminate some build elements within cycles
- Using rapid prototyping technology such as stereolithography to speed the build element of the cycle
- Using CAD and electronic data management systems for easy changes between iterations of a product

Uncertainty can also be removed by:

- Only incorporating technologies that are robust into a new product
- Focusing risky elements of the design into one area which can be tackled first, thereby assessing the feasibility of the entire project as early as possible
- Using prototyping that covers multi-functional issues so that these are raised at an early stage in the project

The need for learning within the new product process occurs not only within the life of a particular project, but within the process as a whole, that is, learning needs to pass from product to product. Traditionally this was done by grouping people by function. The functional group were co-located and often like-minded, thereby promoting the transfer of knowledge from project to project. In the multi-functional team environment this is much harder to achieve. In addition there is a need to transfer learning on how to manage projects and integrate functions which the traditional structure did not account for. It is this learning from project to project which is the mechanism by which companies can build up strategically important core competencies, be they in product development or in specific technologies.

Learning is a reaction to taking an action and seeing the outcomes of that action. In many companies the result of an action is disconnected from the action itself, either by distance or by time, thereby making it impossible for employees to connect the two. Speeding up the new product process or the design–build–test cycles within it and having consistency in team membership will make actions and results closer in time, thereby increasing the chances that learning will occur. The use of multi-functional teams will bring actions and results closer together in spatial terms and so increase learning. The learning developed by employees involved in projects will be taken to subsequent projects they are involved in. By utilizing 'incremental innovation' type strategies with small projects, that learning will be put to use quickly and will be built upon and spread further through the company. Another approach is to have a formal project review. Many companies' procedures incorporate these, yet it is rare for them to be carried out fully and rarer still for the learning to be utilized. This is usually because of the day-to-day pressures placed upon people, with reflection and learning low on the priority list. As with any activity that is low on priority lists, the only way to get it done is to raise its priority, and ultimately it is the responsibility of senior management to do so through their own actions and expectations.[18]

REDUCTION OF DELAYS

Just as the ideas of value-adding and non-value-adding time can be used to identify the causes of wasted time in a supply chain or manufacturing facility, the same techniques can be used to identify delays in product development.

The least obvious, yet least expensive way to remove sources of delay is at the 'fuzzy front end' of the project where delays are common between the identification of a need for the product and setting up a team to exploit that need. Another common area of non-value-adding time is between functions. In some of the companies we have worked with, design completes the functional design, waits for all of the drawings to be completed such that any changes can be made without affecting any other department, and then passes on the drawings to manufacturing. This results in the drawings queuing to be passed on to manufacturing, thereby increasing the lead-time of the project.

Another very common source of delay in the new product development process is in administration. An example of this was seen in one company which took 29 weeks to design and procure a vital component with a supplier's lead-time of ten weeks. This time was taken up by a combination of factors, including waiting for decisions to purchase (despite having preferred suppliers) and waiting for a slot in the supplier's production schedule.

TIME-COMPRESSING PROJECTS

These techniques have proven to be extremely effective in time-compressing projects in the new product process. We have also found that some of the techniques are applicable to projects to change the company as a whole. In the following chapters on the subject of change we will show you how.

Suggested Reading

J. P. Deschamps and P. R. Nayak, *Product Juggernauts: How Companies Mobilize to Generate a Stream of Market Winners* (Boston, Mass., Harvard Business School Press, 1995).

P. G. Smith and D. G. Reinertsen, *Developing Products in Half The Time* (New York, Van Nostrand Reinhold, 1991).

S. C. Wheelwright and K. B. Clark, *Revolutionizing Product Development: Quantum Leaps in Speed, Efficiency and Quality* (New York, The Free Press, 1992).

CASE STUDY – JETSTREAM AIRCRAFT

The Company

Jetstream Aircraft Limited is a subsidiary of British Aerospace plc (BAe). It designs, markets and manufactures the Jetstream range of turboprop aircraft. There are three models, the J31, J41 and the J61 ATP which differ in size. These are tailored to the exact specifications of individual customers. It has around 2000 employees and a turnover of £113 million (1994).

Strategic Drivers

The aircraft industry is an extremely competitive one. In recent years, the losses incurred by many airlines, coupled with mergers and acquisitions, resulted in an industry which is extremely competitive in terms of cost and customer service. As a result the airlines have become increasingly demanding on suppliers of aircraft to deliver their exact requirements at lowest cost in short lead-times. This is a fact of life even for the largest aircraft manufacturers as illustrated by Boeing's commitment to achieving the six-month aircraft. In doing this they are using the idea of late configuration to ensure that customer requirements and the associated manufacturing processes do not have to be finalized until six months before delivery. In the case of Jetstream, customization of the aircraft can include changes to fittings like galleys and seating arrangements, or engineering changes to make the aircraft viable on new routes, perhaps in hostile climates such as those found in developing countries. Overcapacity within the aircraft manufacturing sector combined with new entrants has raised the level of competition to win these orders. Besides the ability to offer customization, order-winning criteria also include the delivery time for the aircraft. As the market becomes more competitive these are becoming order-qualifying criteria.

The changes within the industry have had major repercussions for Jetstream. They can no longer guarantee a steady order book and the level of customization required makes it difficult to speculatively hold finished aircraft. Time Compression was seen as a potential solution to this problem in that it could be used to allow aircraft to be built and customized more quickly, thereby making Jetstream more responsive to its customers without increasing its level of risk.

Profit from Time

The Programme of Change

The project was part of the measures taken by Jetstream to improve
the performance of their design, manufacturing and supply chain
activities to make them more responsive to delivering customized
aircraft more quickly at a profit to the company.

Diagnostic stage 1

Our initial analysis took an overview of the entire process from the
sales function initiating a product change to its embodiment in the
aircraft. We used Time-Based Process Mapping to identify the best
opportunities for Time Compression. Typical lead-times within the
engineering change process at Jetstream, prior to the project, are
shown in Table 5.1. We found that the lead-time to deliver an agreed
package of customer modifications was excessively long and
extremely variable between one order and the next as illustrated by
the large difference in lead-times between the best, worst and notional
lead-times.

Even allowing for the difference in work content between one order
and another, this analysis suggested that the process of establishing
the full specification of the finished product was not geared to speedy
response. This resulted in last-minute 'fire-fighting' to ensure that the
aircraft was built to the correct specification.

Our ongoing discussions with management during the TBPM
analysis highlighted the key role played by the Engineering Change
Process in coordinating the engineering and embodiment of modifications to the aircraft. A reduction in the length and variability
of cycle time of this process would be expected to result in more

Table 5.1 *Lead-times within the Engineering Change Process at Jetstream*

Task	Notional time-scale	Worst time-scale	Best time-scale	Most recent case
Change approval	<1 week	3 months	<1 day	2 days
Raise modification sheet	1 week	3 months	<1 day	3 days
Approve mod. (Air worthiness by CAA)	<1 month	6 months	Telephone	2.5 weeks
Production embodiment	2 months	1 year	2 weeks	2.5 months
Issue all drawings	1–3 months	8 months	1 month	2.5 months
Sign off mod. approval	1 day	>1 week	<1 day	3 days

responsiveness and better control throughout the process. This would be seen as an improvement in the accuracy of embodiment of modifications to the aircraft. It was therefore decided that the Engineering Change Process and its interface with the customer-driven modification process would be investigated in detail. Our analysis and discussions with managers showed that this process involved a number of key managerial decisions and that inadequate information at some of these resulted in unsatisfactory performance of the process. Decision Node Analysis (DNA) was chosen as the most suitable tool to provide a framework for this type of analysis.

Diagnostic stage 2
At this point in the project a manager was assigned to manage the improvements to the engineering change process on a full-time basis. He was a very experienced and competent technical manager who had written many of the engineering process procedures and had used them in his previous roles. This experience made him a superb choice as the change agent and project champion.

Fifteen managers involved in the engineering change and customer-driven change processes were identified as key fact holders in the process. They were interviewed individually using the framework provided by the DNA methodology. Throughout the interview process we discussed our findings, suspicions, the theory behind them and our intended direction with the project champion.

Five key decisions were highlighted:

1. The customer's decision on what is required.
2. The decision to offer the customer a requested option.
3. Filtering modification requests and prioritizing them.
4. Deciding which aircraft a modification would first appear upon.
5. The sign-off of the engineering drawing after the design is complete.

The diagnostic process revealed that the second, third and fourth of these decisions were, to a large extent, ineffective. We discuss these below.

The decision to offer the customer a requested option
In order to make this decision, a request was sent from Customer Engineering, who liaised with the customers, to the other functional departments involved in the change. The information required was

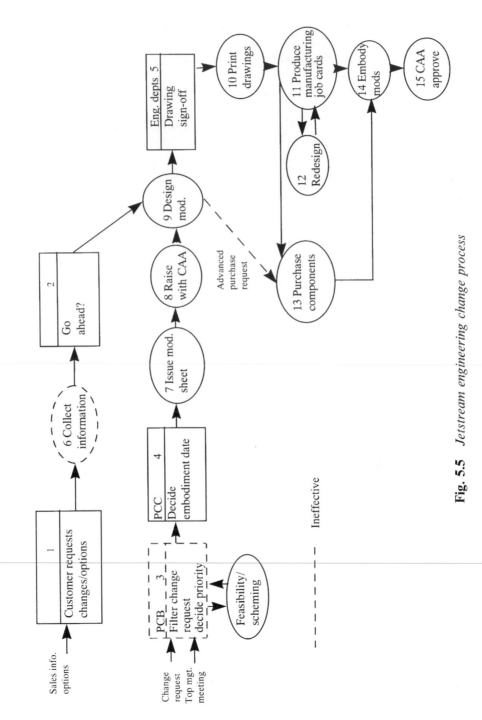

Fig. 5.5 *Jetstream engineering change process*

fed back slowly, sometimes too slowly to be included in the decision, and was occasionally incomplete. This resulted in offers being made to customers based on incomplete or inaccurate information which caused problems in meeting customer requirements to the agreed time-scales and costs. These delays in collecting information were usually due to conflicting priorities for the engineers involved.

Filtering modification requests and prioritizing them
Requests for modifications to the aircraft could come from any part of the organization. The requests were scrutinized by a committee of senior managers, predominantly from technical functions. This committee looked at the justification for projects and categorized them according to their importance in terms of safety, aircraft performance and handling of the aircraft or rejected them. In practice it was rare for a modification to be rejected. Some modifications were approved without the availability of full information regarding their financial justification. The categorization system was very good at identifying critical changes for safety reasons. However changes for commercial reasons, for example, reductions in the cost of the Bill of Material of the aircraft, were typically given low priority categorization. This meant that most embodied changes to the aircraft were related to its safety and functional performance. The failure to filter and prioritize engineering changes meant that there were a large number of low priority projects within the engineering change system which were rarely worked upon. This was shown by the queue of changes in progress which, despite effort to reduce its size, remained large and constant. These are symptoms of a state of 'project overload'. The absence of clear prioritization meant that the process often became confused by the demands of ever shifting operational priorities.

Deciding the aircraft on which a modification would first appear
Once a request for modification had been approved, responsibility for it passed to a second committee. The first task of this committee was to decide which aircraft a modification would first appear on. This was known as the embodiment aircraft. The committee members were expected to input their department's requirements in agreeing the embodiment aircraft. In practice the committee was poorly attended and many of the attendees did not have the information required. As a result, target embodiment aircraft were sometimes set on incomplete information. Ultimately this meant that some of the targets set were missed or only achieved through 'fire-fighting'.

Additional issues identified

The existence of more than one process by which a change could be instituted caused confusion as to the planned configuration of a given aircraft. This meant that some aircraft were not initially built to the configuration promised to the customer, resulting in expensive rework or retrofitting of changes. Also the sequential nature of the development process, combined with the problems related to setting embodiment dates, resulted in considerable difficulties for down-stream departments such as Manufacturing Engineering.

Generation of Solutions

At the end of the diagnostic stage the conclusions of the analysis were drawn up by the researchers working together with the project champion. Relevant theory, options for solutions and examples of their usage were identified and discussed until we arrived at a common view of the issues and a number of alternative solutions based on the project champion's expertise of the company environment and the researcher's experience. The project champion took these ideas and used his influence, supported by the data collected and relevant theory, to persuade his colleagues at all levels of the need to make changes to the process. The changes suggested were each quite small, and so could be implemented as a series of alterations to procedures, paperwork and the activities of existing committees. This, combined with the background of the project champion and a common understanding of the need to improve the process, resulted in negligible resistance to change. The changes were made over a period of six months, a pace dictated by the changing understanding and perceptions of the different stakeholders in the process.

The Decision Node Analysis showed that the decision 'filtering modification requests and prioritizing them' was a point of weakness within the process. This resulted in a number of solutions being discussed. The following solutions were implemented:

- The name 'Engineering Change Process' was changed to 'Product Change Process' in order to remove any 'engineering only' connotations from the process. This, at a stroke, reoriented the various stakeholders into accepting the problems of change management as a 'company-wide' challenge.
- The project champion explained the importance of the change process and the decisions made within it to all of the functions

Control

who had a stake in the process. The importance of full attendance at the committee meetings in order to make consensus decisions was explained. This resulted in more widespread and representative attendance. The attendance of the Finance department representative alone reduced the lead-time by four weeks.

- The change request forms were redesigned to be more meaningful and to contain all of the information required to help make effective decisions.
- The project champion encouraged greater discipline in the decision-making process by the improved cost justification and rationale for the modification. Those modifications that tied in with the company's strategy or that resulted from safety issues were given priority. Those modifications that were worthwhile, but were not priorities in terms of the company strategy were put on a waiting list. Previously they too would have been made active projects. This was facilitated by using the data collected and background theory to explain the effect of certain actions.
- The product change committee sent as many as 50 per cent of all modification requests for further evaluation before a decision on them was made. This resulted in improved estimates of cost and time-scales and made the approval decision more objective.
- A second categorization system was developed by which non-safety critical issues could be classified. Each project was categorized depending on its benefits in terms of cost savings, production easement, weight saving, dispatch reliability or product improvement.
- The process was purged of obsolete or low priority modifications. The number of modifications in the system was reduced from 400 to 150. Sixty-five of those were active and the remainder were placed on the waiting list. This process was done by committee members working as a team.

In effect these measures controlled the demand upon the engineers working within the engineering change process.

The Decision Node Analysis also showed that the point in the process where the decision of which aircraft a modification would first appear upon was made was an area of weakness. The following improvements were made there:

- The importance of the decision, the committee and the repercussions of a poor decision were explained to all relevant departments by the project champion. They were successfully encouraged to attend the newly constituted committee.

- Senior management were persuaded to consolidate the engineering and customization change processes into a single process under the control of this committee.
- The procedure was altered so that the initial target embodiment aircraft set was treated as a flexible estimate. Committee members were encouraged to check the feasibility of the target within their departments or with suppliers prior to a firm target embodiment aircraft being set.
- Non-urgent modifications were targeted at existing batch breaks in the aircraft's production. This reduced confusion by consolidating changes.
- The minutes of the meeting were changed from a list of project statuses to meaningful prose, thereby increasing communication to both those on the committee and those who were not.

These actions were designed to ensure that the targets being set were realistic and therefore could be achieved by all departments involved. In gaining participation in the setting of targets the likelihood of departments meeting them was increased.

Results

The implementation of the measures identified resulted in the following improvements to the process:

- The lead-time of the engineering change process from a modification being requested to a firm target embodiment aircraft being fixed has been reduced by 75 per cent. This has been achieved despite the introduction of an additional stage in the process.
- The frequency with which modifications were embodied on the aircraft as originally targeted has increased from under 50 per cent to 95 per cent. Of the remaining five per cent, most have been embodied earlier than originally planned without incurring any penalty.
- There has been an increase in productivity amongst the engineering departments through reduced time spent on administrative activities. This is evidenced by the drastic reduction of 'pending work'.

- There is now a strong direct linkage between the company's strategic objectives and the priorities for modifications to aircraft. This is expected to show significant benefits in the medium to long term through improvements made to the aircraft's competitive position.
- It is anticipated that the improved performance in delivering aircraft to the customer's exact specification, on time and within cost, will boost the company's competitive position.
- The use of the new procedure in a multi-functional context has had a dramatic benefit on resource planning in engineering, manufacturing and customization.

Learning Points

The learning points from this project were:

- That taking effective decisions upon priorities for projects can remove a state of 'project overload' very quickly with major benefits to lead-time, delivery reliability and productivity. In effect this decision is a point of leverage.
- That full participation in setting targets for projects increases the likelihood of those targets being achieved.
- That a single project champion coached in the framework of Time Compression can be very effective in carrying out this type of change activity. This is highly dependent upon the nature of the project champion who should have sufficient experience, ability and process knowledge to be able to influence his peers into taking action.

6　Time Compression and Change

The concept of time-compressing a business process is of little use unless it can be turned into realized improvements to company performance. Our research suggests that the implementation process is where the success of the project will be determined. This chapter introduces some of the key issues in initiating organizational change and explains how Time Compression can help the change process.

Changing an organization has never been easy. The business press is littered with examples of failed change initiatives. To take an example, Michael Hammer, the populist of Business Process Re-engineering, estimated that 70 per cent of BPR projects have failed to deliver the benefits they originally promised.[1] Within the companies we have worked with we have frequently seen a trail of failed change initiatives. These produced considerable cynicism within the company which made change even harder to achieve.

The root causes of this failure tend to derive from two distinct sources. The first is that change initiatives are rarely put into a context that the whole organization can understand. Therefore a great percentage of the change effort is directed into translating the initiative into a meaningful form for each distinct element of the organization. The second is that people like stability and routine. Why should managers and employees embrace an attempt to modify their practices? Poor implementation of change programmes tends to increase resistance to change. Failure encourages employees to think that the old way was better after all, making further change more likely to be rejected. Thus, the more a company tries and fails to change, the harder it has to try. The way out of this situation is not to try harder, it is to work smarter. In other words, if you always do what you always did, then you always get what you always got.

We have found that a Time Compression approach smoothes the change process due to the fact that everyone understands the notion of time, facilitating ease of communication of objectives and the approach to achieving them. It also forces the issues down to a physical level, helping those people actually changing the process to identify what can be done and how that relates to the bigger picture.

This is because it is easy for employees to understand issues such as the faster the time to the customer, the less likely the customer is going to get impatient and look for other sources of supply. Most employees have experienced the annoyance of delay both at work and as consumers outside the workplace.

During our Time Compression projects we have been faced with many issues to overcome in the pursuit of success. The most common of these typically appear in the form:

- Initiating change because 'it must be good for the company', rather than because it fits with the company's strategic priorities, otherwise known as 'fad surfing'.
- Inadequate and ambiguous definition of change project requirements leading to changes in specification of deliverables as the project progresses.
- Unforeseen events that significantly alter the vision for a project, or render it obsolete. Sometimes these are related to changes in the external environment and are essentially beyond the control of the company. More commonly they are related to changes in the priorities of senior management, for example, the adoption of a new 'buzzword' or the ideas of a new manager. These are within the control of the company.
- Failure to identify an effective project champion or project sponsor resulting in responsibility being passed around when decisive action needs to be taken.
- Trying to change too many things at once. In some companies change teams have been set up for a number of different schemes, yet each team has drawn upon the same set of people, particularly line managers, thereby creating conflict between different projects.
- Talking change but not backing it up with action.
- Setting expectations too high so that failure is felt even though some progress has been made.
- Poor performance in estimating time-scales and resource requirements. When asking someone for a time estimate the answer is typically 'it depends'. Estimating time and resources is very difficult due to poor specification of programmes, commercial pressure to underestimate, and having little capability to estimate the effects of interconnected programmes and other organizational tasks, typically outside the control of the change team.
- Failure to balance the needs of different functional departments. If one function dominates, its requirements for change tend to

dominate also. Typically this results in solutions which are not optimal for the company as a whole.

- Failure to balance technology, process and human elements of a change. Sometimes change focuses on installing a new process or new machine and neglects the human element. Sometimes change focuses on 'culture change', 'teamwork' or some other human issue, yet neglects to tie it in to the needs of the business. Each of these imbalances leads to failure.

TRADITIONAL APPROACHES TO CHANGE

Many of these issues are a result of the approaches to change that have been developed since the Industrial Revolution. Whilst these approaches have been valuable in developing our industrial base, they are now inadequate as each fails to balance the strategic, technical and human issues of change which our research shows is crucial to success. We have identified two major approaches to change.[2]

Task-Oriented Approach

This focuses on 'hard' tangible issues such as the implementation of new business processes, machines or other technologies. The approach stems from the 'Scientific Management' school of management thinking originated by the work of Frederick Taylor. Research has shown that projects taking this approach tend to fail due to not taking account of human and organizational issues.[3]

Process-Oriented Approach

This focuses on the 'soft' human and organizational issues. This originates from the 'behavioural' school of management which emanates from the work of people including Elton Mayo, Douglas McGregor and Frederick Herzberg. It has become increasingly popular in recent years and is often known as 'Organizational Development' or 'Culture Change'. A common feature is its use of change programmes, focused on one human resources issue and imposed by senior management. This approach tends to fail because it pays insufficient attention to connecting change to the specific performance targets required of the business.[4]

MAKING CHANGE WORK

There is only one element of a company which can create change and that is people. Products cannot change themselves. Processes cannot change themselves. Nothing can change unless it is changed by people. Similarly the company will only change if its people are carefully directed as to what they need to change. Without this direction, change will be chaotic and ineffective to business performance. Thus successful change must involve targeting motivated people at a specific task. However this is somewhat easier said than done.

A time-based approach can help provide a clear set of objectives for change and target motivation in the right direction. Setting an objective of, for example, 'reducing delivery lead-time from A to B by 50 per cent' is easy to understand from anyone's perspective. It is clear that the change will benefit customers and so make the company's products more attractive. It is also easy to understand what sort of changes will achieve this. The only question remaining is that of how to do it.

Motivating people is not easy, especially when it involves them moving from a position of stability to one of uncertainty. This problem usually manifests itself as 'resistance to change'. Such resistance is only to be expected. In a change project we are asking people to change the things they do at work. We are expecting them to use new procedures, take on new roles and responsibilities, organize themselves differently and possibly adopt a completely new approach to their work. Everyone becomes a stakeholder in the project and their fears and aspirations need to be catered for.

The Time Compression Programme's approach to projects has been focused on anticipating such resistance and taking steps to ensure that it does not occur in the first place. Despite this some resistance usually occurs as it is impossible to anticipate every eventuality. We find it helpful to believe resistance is a sign that we have missed something important, and so look to ease it rather than fight it. We can do this through building feedback loops within the change process and through initiating learning opportunities.

There are many reasons why someone may not be happy with a proposed change, including:

- **Uncertainty** – What is going to happen to me? Will my role change? Will jobs be lost as a result of the change?

- **Confidence** – I'm not sure if I can do this, I've never tried before. How will failure look on my record?
- **Competence** – I've not been trained how to do this, I might get it wrong. Will the company train me?
- **Misunderstanding** – I can't see why they are doing this. I think they should be doing something else.
- **Lack of trust** – They always mess up changes, why should this one be any different?
- **Self-interest** – If this change occurs I will lose my privileges and power.
- **Conflicting messages** – They are only paying lip service to this change, anyone can see that you only get credit for maintaining the status quo.
- **Ambiguity** – What exactly do they want me to do?

Resistance to change is seen as something that afflicts people who are being changed. Any person whose role will be altered in any way is a stakeholder in the process, and can therefore be a source of resistance or support. In our experience resistance to change can also stem from those people who are commonly seen as initiating the change, top management. It affects both their approach to initiating change, and their reaction to changes that involve changing themselves. Unlike resistance to change lower in the organization it is very difficult to overcome resistance in the boardroom. Such resistance usually manifests itself as lack of commitment to change.

Every publication on change we have ever seen highlights the importance of top management commitment. This implies that top management commitment is not often present, a sure sign of resistance to change within the boardroom. Without top management commitment, change will not occur. True top management commitment is shown by spending time helping the change teams below them to overcome the organizational boundaries and policies that they come up against. In doing so the board sets up the environment for change within the company.

GAINING COMMITMENT

I hear and I forget, I read and I remember, I do and I understand

Confucius, who delivered this pearl of wisdom, way back in ancient China, clearly understood that the best way to gain people's understanding, and therefore their commitment, is to get them involved in the activity. The Time Compression approach involves all stakeholders in the diagnostic and solution generation phases of the project. Through this they gain a clear and shared understanding of their objectives, of the current situation and of what is required to improve it. This leads to successful and swift implementation of improvements, which are accepted into the day-to-day activities of the company. It is unlikely that someone who has been involved in the design of a solution will resist its implementation. Other research has shown this too. For example, one study of 163 organizations' change initiatives[5] showed that those using edict or persuasion as a means of encouraging change resulted in a failure rate of 50 per cent, those using token participation resulted in a failure rate of 25 per cent and those using complete participation resulted in complete success. A participative approach to solution generation has been shown to generate complete commitment to those solutions[6] and is a key element of an ideal approach to change.

THE IDEAL CHANGE

Our experience of change suggests that the ideal organizational change is trying to achieve:

- Benefits aligned with the organization's strategic priorities and therefore good return on the investment in time and money committed to the change
- Ownership of the change process from employees at all levels
- Self-sustaining change, that is, change becomes a way of life

These points are often described in the management literature although in reality the ideal change is rare. However we have seen organizations who possess these traits and they are very successful. They also had to start down the road to excellence at some point in their history. At first there were mistakes made and lessons learnt. As more and more of the organization learnt how to change things effectively the pace of change increased and change became the norm rather than the exception. In effect the process of change has been time-compressed.

The first step in this long journey is to look at a road map to see where you are going and the different routes to get there. There are always many routes, some long and tortuous, others direct and risky.

However since every company and every situation is essentially unique it is impossible to generalize a route suitable for every change in every organization.

There are many models in existence which attempt to describe the ideal route for a change. The important thing is that the model addresses the issues we have raised in this chapter and that it suits the existing culture of your organization. We have come across some organizations which have a prescribed change model for every eventuality. We have seen this constrain the change process to a route which is neither the shortest nor the easiest of those available. This is compounded by the fact that as more change is experienced the ability to pick the best route improves. Therefore as the culture of your organization changes, so must your change model.

THE TCP CHANGE MODEL

If you have never experienced successful change before you may feel that you do not have enough experience to choose the best route for a change. We have developed a simple model which we use as a guide

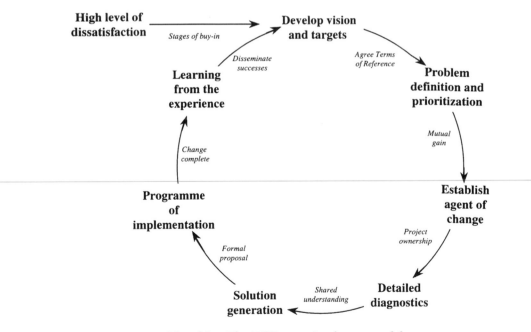

Fig. 6.1 *The TCP generic change model*

to our route-planning process throughout a Time Compression project. Like any change model this is not suitable for every situation although we have found that it works very well for the Time Compression approach and can be easily tailored to the situation in any company. We hope that it will help you to understand our train of thought and assist you in developing a change model for the route required in your own particular circumstances. It consists of a number of major steps which we have found help to overcome all of the issues we have raised in this chapter. It also incorporates many of the fundamentals of Time Compression so as to speed up the process of change.

High-level Dissatisfaction

The first requirement for successful change is that there is dissatisfaction with a company's performance at the top of the organization. Such dissatisfaction may occur as a result of poor performance figures, pressure from customers, competitors' performance, the opening of new markets or seeing 'world-class' companies at first hand. Once such dissatisfaction is present, top management will be supportive of improvement.

Creating a Vision and Targets

Having become dissatisfied with existing performance company management will look for ways of improving performance. At this stage there is a danger of grasping at solutions to the many problems that the company is seen to have. It is often easy for people to say what they do not want, but not so easy for them to define exactly what they do want. The objective of this stage is to generate a vision of what a company wants to become and what it needs to do to get there. This will need to be aligned with the external influences upon the company and what it sees as its core competencies. The vision should include targets for performance in key parameters of its business. Such a vision can then be used as the basis for deciding upon the priority of the issues to be tackled and to provide a direction with which to align change throughout the company. This consistency of vision and the focus of change that it engenders leads to Time Compression in the change process. It ensures that all change takes the company in the direction that the vision dictates.

Problem Definition and Prioritization

Having identified the key parameters of performance it is possible to identify which business processes contribute to the meeting of that performance target. The vision will provide guidance as to which processes should be tackled first. If the process is large it may be appropriate to do some high-level diagnosis to target a particular part of the process. The amount of resources needed to carry out projects needs to be estimated so as not to launch too much change at once. This process ensures that there is no state of 'change project overload'. In doing so it removes sources of possible delay and time-compresses the change process.

Setting up a Change Agent

Having decided what to tackle first, the people involved in the process are identified, that is, the stakeholders. A change agent is created either by the appointment of a carefully chosen project champion or by bringing the stakeholders together as a project team. This allows clear ownership of the change process to be gained which will ensure that the project is driven towards its goal as quickly as possible.

Detailed Diagnosis

The project team will carry out or monitor the task of mapping the business processes targeted. This stage also allows the team to build a consistent language and understanding, thereby overcoming many of the functional differences between its members. This is facilitated by keeping the mapping process simple and short. This helps to identify opportunities and anticipate problems, thereby reducing delays later in the process.

Solution Generation

The project team turn their shared understanding of the problems and their detailed knowledge of the existing process into a solution, using the data they have collected to keep the discussion focused on the key issues. The solutions are turned into a number of prioritized implementation projects. If the original process examined was large it may be necessary to carry out another even more detailed diagnosis and solution generation stage with sub-project teams and then pull these solutions together to ensure they fit together as a whole. The involvement of all stakeholders in generating solutions facilitates gaining their commitment. This ensures that the implementation phase can be as short as possible.

Implementation

The implementation projects are carried out, which is one of the most complex tasks of the change process. However, if the previous stages have been carried out effectively, involving all of the key players and stakeholders of the business, this stage should go smoothly and quickly.

Learning from the Experience

Change processes such as these never work perfectly. It is wise to learn from the mistakes made and incorporate them into the process for future changes. Using these learning points will provide further Time Compression in the change process.

TAKING THE FIRST STEP

In this chapter we have raised many issues which you might recognize in your company. The task ahead might seem gargantuan. Don't worry! Everything has to start somewhere. The first steps on the road to excellence are:

- Be clear about the need to change (read the next chapter).
- Do not get hooked up on model selection. Time Compression offers a flexible approach.
- **Just do it!!!**

Suggested Reading

C. Argyris, *Overcoming Organizational Defenses* (Needham Heights, Mass., Allyn Bacon, 1990).

W. C. Byham and J. Cox, *Zapp! The Lightning of Empowerment* (London, Century Business, 1991).

C. Handy, *Understanding Organizations* (London, Penguin Books, 1993).

J. Janov, *The Inventive Organization: Hope and Daring at Work* (San Francisco, Jossey-Bass, 1994).

CASE STUDY – ROVER BODY AND PRESSINGS

The Company

The Engineering section of Rover Body and Pressings (RBP) designs and manufactures the press tools required for the development of vehicles by Rover Group and some other European motor manufacturers. RBP also produces and supplies panels and sub-assembled units to Rover and other local auto makers.

The Engineering section of RBP encompasses process engineering, tool design, pattern manufacture, machine shop and try-out facilities. The tool design and development facilities are spread over two sites at Swindon and Cowley and have a capacity of more than 200 major tool sets per year.

Strategic Drivers

The world automotive industry has a considerably greater production capacity than the present demand both regionally and globally. This has led to severe international competition between manufacturers in terms of price, service and ownership experience. Increasingly demanding customers mean that value for money, quality and reliability are taken for granted and new sources of compettitive advantage are being introduced by different manufacturers. These include aspects of design, performance, environmental considerations, safety and technological features which must all be delivered in increasingly short periods of time and reduced cost.

Time to market is one of the most important sources of competitive advantage in the car industry. This, combined with ever decreasing product life-cycles and increasing product development costs, has resulted in major restructuring of the industry worldwide. Alliances, mergers and acquisitions have been reshaping the landscape of the industry over the last fifteen years. The process of new model introduction is at the epicentre of this battle and affects every aspect of the business and its performance at this early but crucial stage of the life of a vehicle.

Across the world, the Body in White (BIW) design and development constitutes the longest lead-time element of a total car development. It varies between three and seven years for the fastest and slowest vehicle manufacturers. World-class companies, predominantly Japanese, design and develop their press tooling, from style freeze to production-ready full set of tools in just under 80 weeks. This is the single most time-consuming activity of a new model development cycle. The benchmark of the fastest three manufacturers in the world at stands at 40, 38, and 32 months. Auto makers do not solely rely on their captive suppliers of press tooling, but also source major segments of the BIW tooling from independent players. The most critical issue in this industry is universally agreed to be the lead-time of supply. For RBP, achieving Time Compression is therefore a prime source of competitiveness and a matter of survival.

Programme of Change

The Time Compression project was initiated in line with other measures taken by RBP to improve the lead-time to design and develop the tooling which makes up the critical path of new model introduction. The process from style freeze to panel production used to take 104 weeks which compares with a best-in-class 80 weeks. It involves complex interaction and iteration of information to transform a total surface model of a car into some 200–300 panels, each requiring a set of press tools to be produced and assembled together to achieve the intended engineering and aesthetic requirements.

This Time Compression project combined with other initiatives, had the objective of providing lead-time reductions of 20 per cent.

Programme of Change

Phase One: Diagnostics

The first step was the formation of a team consisting of members of the Warwick Manufacturing Group's Time Compression team and a number of executives from RBP's Engineering section. An extensive interview programme and analysis of the company's procedures and documentation was set up to develop an accurate process map of the design and manufacturing activities and information flow analysis of the interface between the numerous departments involved. The processes and performance of a number of major world-class players were also analysed against that of RBP, forming the basis of an extensive competitive benchmarking exercise.

A high level process flow diagram of a typical tooling development programme is shown in Figure 6.2.

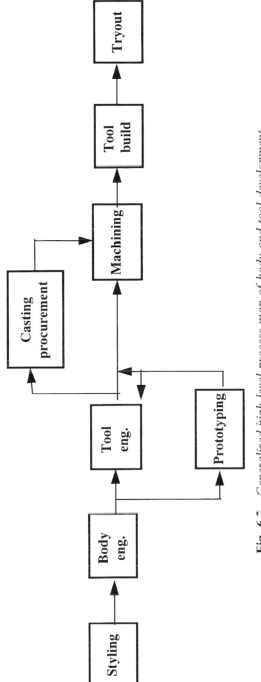

Fig. 6.2 *Generalized high-level process map of body and tool development*

The results of this investigation pointed to the areas of work where major gains were possible for Time Compression.

The results of the information flow analysis also pointed to deficiencies of integration between design and manufacture. An example of the information flow is shown in Figure 6.3.

The results of an extensive benchmarking exercise, encompassing a close examination of major Japanese motor manufacturers and tooling suppliers as well as best-in-class European companies revealed important differences in strategy, approach and methods of work with respect to new product introduction processes.

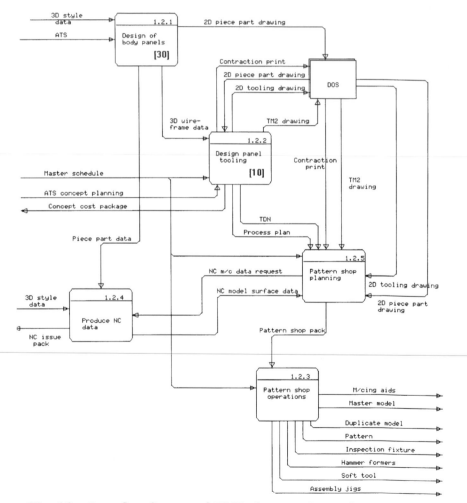

Fig. 6.3 *Data flow diagram of RBP's design and manufacture interface*

The tooling development lead-times of the leading companies showed an advantage for the Japanese companies over their European counterparts. The high-level performance benchmarks, measured in lead-time, are shown in Table 6.1.

A comparison of the lead-times at various activities revealed detailed differences between RBP and best practice in a number of areas. The initial findings were later confirmed and coincided with the major findings of a manufacturing strategy study being done concurrently with the objective of devising better working practices to improve the internal performance of the tool manufacturing function.

These studies prioritised the following areas for initial improvement:

- Rationalization of manufacturing facilities into small, medium and large tools
- Improved engineering interface between design and manufacturing functions
  Clearer lines of communication and greater integration of upstream and downstream processes

Upon analysing these requirements, two independent areas showed major gaps compared to world-class standards. Phase II of the Time Compression work focused on these issues which were:

- Casting supply
- Tool marshalling and try-out process

Table 6.1 *Lead-time comparison for tool design and development.*

	Rover Body & Panels	Japanese Manuf. 1	Japanese Manuf. 2	Japanese Manuf. 3	Euro. Tool Supplier	Japanese Tool Supplier
			[Time in Weeks]			
Tool design	10	7	10	10	10	10
Pattern making	6	–	–	–	3	–
Foundry	5	8	8	–	6	7
Machining	5	6	6	–	9	5–6
Tool build	10	12	11	16	11	6–7
T1 to T2	26	9	–	10	9	–
T2 to T3	7	7	18	14	6	20
Total	69	49	53	50	54	48–50

Phase Two: Re-engineering the processes for greater integration

The work on casting supply concentrated on the modelling and optimization of this supply chain, making use of Rover's RG2000 supplier development initiative and the principles of supplier partnership. We visited and analysed local and world-class casting suppliers and the processes they employed. Significant improvements were shown to be possible.

The best of the local suppliers and managers from the relevant functions within Rover Group were brought together to work jointly to exploit Time Compression opportunities. Over a series of workshops and follow on meetings, it was agreed that the casting suppliers would become involved in the early stages of the tooling design. This early interface allowed them to understand the critical aspects of the casting and increase its manufacturability. This permitted synchronised scheduling of pattern manufacture by RBP and casting by the foundry with no time wasted in between. This resulted in a reduction in lead-time from a variable six to eight weeks to a consistent three weeks lead-time for the casting.

A second element of the Time Compression project concentrated on re-organization of various activities in order to simplify the lines of communication, as well as removing some of the non-essential practices that obstructed the clear and easy passage of long lead-time items. Distinct areas of improvement were in:

- Establishment of a clear stage-gate process to bring a greater influence from the manufacturing activities into the design stage
- Increasing the influence of the project team by using heavyweight project managers
- Greater emphasis on design to reduce engineering changes at manufacture
- Simplification of the planning activity
- Streamlined tool marshalling and try-out activities

These changes were achieved by company management changing procedures to integrate the new stage-gate process into the existing quality system and working procedures. The formal changes were supported by a number of presentations and informal discussions where the reasoning behind the changes was explained and discussed. The changes were then introduced by using a current tooling project as a pilot implementation project. The power of the heavyweight project manager ensured the success of this.

Results

The implementation of the measures identified above, together with the previously mentioned internal initiatives, have brought about significant Time Compression in the overall lead-time of tool design and manufacture by more than 30 per cent.

The current lead-times of tool design and development, measured from the start of process and tool design to the delivery of production-ready tools, is now around 50 weeks, a significant achievement.

Learning Points

The learning points from this project are summarized below:

- Time Compression requires the participation of and the acceptance of all relevant parts of the organization.
- Putting the emphasis on the up-stream processes of design yields the greatest benefits in time with less rework and higher quality of final product (tools in this case).
- Cooperative communication in team structures is essential for rapid development of tools.
- Simplicity is the key to the design of processes and procedures.
- Focusing on Time Compression does indeed benefit the quality of work and reduces the costs of development.

7 Creating the Environment for Change

In this chapter we will look at the first couple of steps in our change model, creating a high-level dissatisfaction and developing a vision and targets. These are key to maintaining the consistency of approach and focus which will allow successful change and its Time Compression.

Within the business community it is widely felt that the pace of change has increased. Whereas once companies could remain the same for year after year without serious problems, they must now continually improve and change to survive. The objective of a change programme is not just to change the company once. What is required is the development of a capability to change increasingly quickly, and at an increased frequency. That way the company will be able to constantly react to its environment and in doing so increase its chances of survival. Our experience has shown that developing an effective change capability takes time, especially in companies where it is unusual for anyone other than top management to take the initiative. However, once successful change is experienced, the company will find change to be more acceptable, will learn from its successes and mistakes, and hence generate further successes and benefits to the business. As the old adage goes: 'Success breeds success.'

CHANGE AND ITS BAGGAGE

How many change initiatives has your company tried in the past decade: MRP, Total Quality Management, Just-in-Time, Business Process Re-engineering, Activity-Based Costing? How many have been successful? Many companies tend to fall into a succession of different approaches to change. They try an approach. After a year or so it does not deliver the expected results and is deemed to have failed, so they try a different approach, often replacing or shuffling top management in the process. The same happens again and so the approach is changed again.

From the shop floor this appears to be 'fad surfing'. Senior management are seen to try to impose a change. Junior managers assess what it is they need to do, work out what they need and put their suggestions forward in terms of plans and budgets to be approved. These may not be approved because the priorities of the business change, or may be approved but with the caveat 'this was too expensive, you'll have to do it for less'. Either way it is seen that the change was not that important anyway. Everyone involved with the project feels disenchanted because all of their effort has come to nothing and vows not to bother putting in the effort next time senior management has a brainwave. The end result is that the company does not change, and the capability developed from the exercise becomes the ability to side-step change, not the ability to implement it. Developing the ability to side-step change does not add value to the change process, it is just a delay that slows down the process of change and prevents the company from responding to its customer's needs. Removing this non-value adding activity is a way of time-compressing the change process.

Time-compressing change relies on it being treated as a serious activity within the business and resourced adequately with good people who are rewarded for changing things and not for maintaining the status quo. It also requires that there should be consistency of approach, objectives and their communication. In a quickly changing business world this seems to be an impossible task, yet we believe that it is both fundamental and possible.

THE ROLE OF SENIOR MANAGEMENT

Change of any kind, including Time Compression, will occur most easily in an environment which is supportive of change. Creating such an environment relies on balancing the disciplines required to align changes to company strategy and the space needed for employees to become involved in designing the changes they will implement. Perhaps more importantly it involves the management of a company coming together to actively support a long-term game plan, even when short-term performance may be reduced. That way the long-term plan will be achieved sooner and its benefits will reach the bottom line sooner. This can only be facilitated by senior management.

The role of senior management is to determine the why and the what of the approach, but not the how. In order to maximize the likelihood of success, the determining of exactly how to change the company needs to be left in the hands of those who will have to implement the changes and live with them in the future. However senior management do need to create the environment for this to happen.

CREATING DISSATISFACTION

The first task is to have senior management who are dissatisfied with the status quo. We have found that this occurs in a number of ways:

- Customers complain or provide performance measures for their suppliers.
- Performance becomes so poor that management has to do something about it.
- A new perspective on company performance is developed and shows how poor that aspect of performance is. This can be done through the use of tools such as Time-Based Process Mapping.
- Senior managers visit 'world-class' factories and realize how far behind they are.
- Senior managers meet managers from more developed companies.
- Senior managers see or read the views of a visionary 'guru' and are persuaded that there is better to be had.
- New managers see how far behind the company is compared to their previous employers.

Having become dissatisfied, senior management need to decide what to do about their position. Inevitably this will include changing things. Some managers will tend to take immediate action. We suggest it is wiser to stand back, look at the business as a whole, assess the company's objectives and strategy (remember Chapter 2) and then spend time solving the underlying problems that are key to implementing that strategy.

Typically we find that many managers within the business already possess a high level of dissatisfaction; they just require an approach to verify the rationale behind that condition. An example of this was provided through a project with a subsidiary of LucasVarity. Top management within the business were already convinced that they were not providing products to their customers in the most economic manner. To assess this theory, a project team was established to confirm the problem through time-based analysis of the distribution system and through a direct comparison with competitors. The results of the analysis confirmed the situation, and a change team was tasked with rectifying the situation. In this case, the generation of the dissatisfaction came from both internal and external sources.

In other situations we are approached by middle and junior managers who are aware of the difficulties facing their business, yet feel that their senior management are not doing anything about it. This is a difficult position to be in as change from below can occasionally be seen as mutiny. In such cases, the first step is to create dissatisfaction and awareness amongst senior management in a similar manner as previously described. However, the key is to use a mechanism which best articulates your concerns in a language that senior management will understand. Time Compression offers a perspective that management recognize as a fundamental business performance measure.

PROVIDING A REASON TO CHANGE

Once senior management have decided to change things their first public task is to create dissatisfaction with the status quo amongst the company as a whole. This may already exist and so can be built upon. However it may need to be actively provoked, especially if the company perceives itself as being successful.

The strategic opportunities or difficulties presented by the environment external to your business unit may provide opportunities to facilitate change. Take-over threats, big losses, new entrants to a market or substitute products can all provide clear indicators of the need to change, and often result in effective change occurring very quickly as all employees align to fight the common threat to their livelihoods. Waiting for a catastrophe to happen is not a very attractive way to initiate change. A new top manager can also be used to catalyse significant changes. Pettigrew showed how aligning internal change to these disruptions in the company environment can be effective.[1] However these issues are often visible to outwardly looking senior management long before most employees become aware of them. Effective communication and leadership can be used to preempt problems by raising awareness of the issues involved to catalyse change.

Creating dissatisfaction is a dangerous task which needs to be carefully managed. Just as it takes time for senior management to take on board the need to change, employees will need to be led to the same conclusion through real, convincing data and be allowed time to assimilate them. Similarly, different groups of employees may need differing methods of communication. Again time facilitates a common understanding. Having become dissatisfied, employees will want to do something about the threat to their livelihoods. It is vital that this newly found creative tension is directed before it has time to dissipate, leaving the workforce anxious and demotivated. This energy is best directed by creating a vision and a number of prioritized performance objectives.

In our experience, employees are more likely to accept a vision generated by other employees, rather than trying to accept 'yet another management initiative'. This proved true in the LucasVarity case mentioned earlier. By encouraging an internal project team to initiate the diagnostics, analysis and vision, rather than relying on management to force the issue, change throughout the business was more easily accepted. Employees tend to be content with employee-driven initiatives. Ideally the whole workforce should be involved in determining the vision, thereby gaining internalization of that vision from all employees. We accept that this is a difficult proposition in large companies, but in smaller companies or business units it may prove to be a viable approach which will lead to a solid basis for the process of change that will follow it.

There has been much discussion in the management literature of the idea of creating a vision. That vision should be determined by your business and be relevant to its future. Development needs should play a part in determining the vision. For example a vision of 'maximizing shareholder value' may not inspire employees, especially if they are not shareholders. However a vision like that of Caterpillar, 'to supply any replacement part anywhere in the globe within 24 hours' proved to be inspirational and extremely successful. The overall vision should be supplemented by prioritized operational performance targets such as quality levels, costs or lead-times on key business processes which will provide a means of turning the vision into reality. It is these targets which will provide the tasks on which the attention of employees will be focused. Chapter 2 explained more about how to determine a strategy for your business, how to determine the key business processes and how to set targets for them, especially with respect to time-based strategies.

CONSISTENCY OF APPROACH

At the beginning of this chapter we described how inconsistency in approach led to non-value-adding change activities. In order to time-compress the change process it is important to remove these activities by maintaining a consistency of approach for long enough for real results to be achieved. Some companies have maintained this consistency of approach and gained enormous benefits, for example, Motorola have followed their six sigma quality target since 1987.[2]

By an approach to change we mean the perspective that the change uses for people to see opportunities to improve the business in line with its strategic priorities. Time Compression has certain attributes which we have found make it an extremely effective approach:

- A Time Compression approach is flexible enough to allow many different perspectives to be used within it, allowing consistency to be maintained.
- Time Compression is a perspective which has largely been ignored in recent years and so tends to yield big opportunities.
- The idea of time is easy to understand and interpret as it is common in everyday life.
- The approach focuses on the product or process, not on the individual, and so is usually felt to be non-threatening.
- Time Compression is easy to focus on business objectives.
- Performance measures are easily set and understood.

Our experience has shown that having consistency of approach is more important than the actual approach to change used, both for Time Compression and the likelihood of success of a project. It is very difficult for employees to determine exactly how and what they are going to change when the reasons for change and the objectives of the change are frequently altered. There are many reasons why inconsistent messages may be received from management. Managers may change positions and so change the direction of existing change efforts. Managers may not have reached a consensus on the direction of change and so may undermine the existing direction, either through their words or through their actions. The existing approach may be perceived to be not working due to poor upward communication and so is replaced. All are liable to undermine existing efforts to change.

It is interesting to compare the factories of Nissan, Toyota and Honda. It can be seen that historically these companies have taken different approaches to developing their businesses. Nissan used empowerment of the employees, Toyota used Lean Production and Honda used Total Quality Management. Yet each of the companies is decidedly similar. There are many ways of approaching change, and because all of the parameters of a business are interlinked the company will tend to develop in much the same way. To take an example let us look at the treatment of inventory under a number of different approaches.

No matter which of these approaches to change is taken, the result will be the same, the inventory will be managed better and reduced. The main differences between the approaches is the priority of such an issue. In Time Compression inventory is typically one of the first

Table 7.1 *Comparison of approaches to inventory*

Approach	Approach to dealing with inventory
Time Compression	The product is queuing before an operation which is adding to its lead-time. This non-value-adding time should be removed
Total Quality Management	Inventory may get damaged, may deteriorate, and wastes effort in double handling and storage
Safety	Inventory can cause a hazard because it may cause accidents if not stored carefully. Double handling gives ground for repetitive strain injuries
Lean Production	Inventory is waste and should be removed
Cost	Inventory requires working capital which costs us interest which reduces our profit

things to be dealt with. This is because of the effect on non-value-adding time. Inventory adds immense costs to products without providing any value to the end customer. In a Total Quality approach, inventory may be seen as secondary to rework in order of priority.

Time Compression and Other Approaches

Whilst Time Compression provides an exceptional consistency of approach, we have also found that most specific issues can be tackled effectively from any of a number of perspectives, for example Lean Production or Total Quality Management. We have also used the Time Compression perspective within other approaches so as to maintain consistency of approach to avoid encouragement of 'fad surfing'; this time-compresses the change process itself. For example it can be argued that time is a kind of waste which allows Time Compression to fit within any approach that focuses on the reduction of waste including Total Quality Management and Lean Production. Similarly at one company we ran quality projects under an overall Time Compression approach. Careful selection of an approach will allow other perspectives on improvement to be used within it, thereby allowing a great deal of flexibility in the management of the change process without undermining the overall objectives of the change.

Within the overall approach to change it is possible to use any number of techniques to achieve the change, for example Business Process Re-engineering, teamwork, or continuous improvement. We believe that these techniques do not make good approaches in themselves as they do not provide direction. For example, using Business Process Re-engineering as a banner advocates 'start from scratch', but does not say what the objective is. It also leads to inflexibility as in some parts of the business a more incremental approach such as continuous improvement may be a far more sensible method for improvement, yet this appears inconsistent with the overall banner. However these techniques are valuable tools for use within other approaches and have been used extremely successfully within a Time Compression approach.

Choosing an Approach

In choosing an approach it is important to look at your business and its history. What are your strategic priorities? Which approach will deliver these? Which approaches have been tried before? Is there any historical baggage associated with these? What is the usual perspective within your business? Which perspectives will yield most benefit? Which approach will be most acceptable within the company? How adaptable does the approach need to be?

In general we have found that most benefits are gained by taking a perspective that has not been used before, and by adopting a perspective that is easy for employees to understand and non-threatening. Time Compression fits these requirements extremely well. The attitude of the people involved in change is a major factor in selection of an approach. Change is hard enough to initiate without creating unnecessary insecurity through a poor choice of approach. Ask yourself how employees will react to an approach to change. If the workforce see cost-cutting programmes as a way to line the pockets of managers and shareholders at the expense of their jobs they are unlikely to be enthusiastic about the programme.

COMMUNICATING THE VISION AND OBJECTIVES

A vision and approach to change are unlikely to succeed if those employees expected to deliver them do not know the rationale behind them and are unaware of what is expected of them. Many of the ills of change efforts are attributed to poor communication. These may take the form of misunderstandings or contradictions which result in the wrong things being changed which are non-value-adding to the business. Their removal will help to time-compress the change process, getting the most value from the least resource expenditure.

> **I know you think you heard what I said and understood what I meant. But what you don't realize is that what you heard was not what I said, and what you understood was not what I meant.**

Communication is not what is said but is what the recipient understands as having been communicated. Many managers also forget that words form only a small fraction of what is communicated, perhaps best thought of as 'actions speak louder than words'. For example, we have already suggested that consistency in approach to change is vital. This is because changing approaches communicates lack of commitment to the change process and fickle management. Coyle and Page identified other commonly used assumptions for change and how they are interpreted by employees.[3]

When communicating verbally ask who your audience are. What sort of experiences do they have which can reinforce your arguments? What sort of language do they use? What will be their reaction to what you are saying? What questions will they want answers to?

Despite the common sense behind these questions and their answers we still meet employees who return from information meetings about the latest round of changes shaking their heads and wondering what they have been told. Giving a speech that requires use of a dictionary for your audience to interpret is poor communication. Raising questions that are not answered or skirting around the key issues only leads to speculation and rumours. Contradicting previous messages requires explanation. Think about what makes your employees the way they are. What newspapers do they read? What do they do in their spare time? What interests them? What frustrates them? Talk to some of them and see what they think of your ideas.

One area of communication often misunderstood is that of communicating performance measures. The performance targets for the board may quite legitimately be increasing return on assets or share price. Sometimes these are communicated as the stated performance targets to the company. How many of your employees know what return on assets is and how they can affect it? Do your employees care whether the share price goes up or not? We would suggest that these are not appropriate operational performance measures. These high-level financial targets need to be turned into measures of lead-time, delivery time, quality level, delivery reliability or cost appropriate to each business or part of business.

In the Time Compression approach we focus on operational performance measures which are based upon time. We have found that measures of time are especially valuable because:

- Everyone instinctively understands the units of time
- There is little scope for misinterpreting a time-based measure, especially when compared to the vagaries of cost accounting
- Time-based measures can be decomposed easily from business process to activity to sub-activity and so on. It is effectively a fractal measure
- Time-based measures drive activity to an actual physical level

We find that time-based measures aid the communication process by providing clarity of objectives and an easily measurable way of

Table 7.2   *Assumptions for change and their effects*

Assumption	Effect
Change must start at the top We, the board, should work with a task force of consultants to define their corporate purpose, vision, values, strategy and change agenda. The troops should accept leadership from us, the generals. If the direction is right, we should win people's hearts and minds	Change is first experienced by others in the company as being predetermined, imposed and distant from them
Rushing will help speed up change We might have taken time for ourselves to explore, debate and unite around change. But change is urgent. Now we should simply explain our decision. Other people should understand and follow	A programme is rushed through and pushed out on to others. It is disconnected from other people's internal reality, it is a bolt-on job, not integrated. Early polarization manifests itself in supporters and resisters, positions become entrenched. Rushing change slows progress and increases resistance
Top people must behave as role models Individuals, particularly top managers, should demonstrate loyalty and support for the change. You should do this even if you are not sure about it yourself	Role models lack conviction. The implicit message from role models is that the company expects you to disconnect yourself from your true feelings. Hearts and minds are being lost, not won. Motivation and energy are dissipated
Reward and reinforcement should be aligned If people support change they should gain survival and reward. If they resist change they should experience disapproval and negative consequences	Experienced people pretend support and commitment when in reality they feel rushed, confused or opposed. Resistance is driven underground. Commitment is replaced by compliance. A hidden, but more real, life arises from above the surface. Meetings become like a Woody Allen film where the speech and the feelings subtext are disconnected and in opposition

Table 7.2 (*continued*)

Assumption	Effect
News will filter through if there is a problem If you have an open door policy your finger should be on the pulse of the company, and you should soon find about any problems that exist	Top managers assume they are in touch, but in a driven, forced change programme become progressively more detached from the true feelings of the staff. Resistance remains hidden. People act as if they are committed or open-minded, but hide their feelings. Management decisions become progressively more inappropriate and disconnected from the motivations, needs and values of staff
Resistance should be fought If change moves slowly that means there is resistance, and performance is suffering	Resistance increases
A new approach can be bolted on if needed If all else fails you should try calling in the facilitators and consultants but only as a last resort	The facilitation or consultancy methods are received cynically as dishonest and manipulative: change by the back door. Experienced people learn how much to disclose to the facilitators/consultants and how much to keep hidden. The full potential of facilitation/ consultancy methods remains untapped. Facilitators/ consultants and their clients become disappointed. The board feels a loss of control. The change programme hits the rocks. Board members resign and are replaced. The cycle begins again. The company sails forward unchanged into oblivion

Source: Coyle and Page, 1995.

achieving them. This clarity of purpose helps reduce non-value-adding activities within the change process and therefore time-compresses it.

TURNING WISHES INTO ACTIONS

Generating wishes is easy. We all vision improvements to the business. There are plenty of people, for example consultants and academics, who will preach on what can be achieved in the hope of getting your business. The hard task is turning these into action and successfully implemented solutions. The first step in this process is to communicate the vision, strategy, prioritized performance objectives and an approach to the change process that you have agreed upon. Then it is necessary to direct the creative tension developed at specific targets. The next chapter looks at how to target the priorities for change and improve the likelihood of a rapid and successful outcome.

Suggested Reading

J. Janov, *The Inventive Organization: Hope and Daring at Work* (San Francisco, Jossey Bass, 1994).

P. M. Senge, *The Fifth Discipline Fieldbook – Strategies and Tools for Building a Learning Organisation* (London, Nicholas Brealy, 1996).

CASE STUDY – LUCAS WIRING SYSTEMS

The Company

With an annual turnover of £200 million and around 5000 employees, the Lucas wiring companies have grown to become the largest supplier of automotive wiring systems in the UK and a leading player in Europe. The company offers European vehicle manufacturers a supply capability for power, signal distribution and circuit protection systems – providing cable, components and assembling wiring harnesses and fuse boxes for over 1 million vehicles per annum for a customer base including Rover, Honda, Toyota, Rolls-Royce and Nippondenso.

Strategic Drivers

Trading conditions in Europe's automotive components industry are changing rapidly as competition and pressure to cut costs force widespread rationalization. Vehicle manufacturers continue to target cuts in outsourcing costs and shift greater levels of technology development, assembly and sub-supplier development responsibility to their first-tier suppliers. Many first-tier component suppliers from outside Europe, particularly from the USA and Japan, have been increasing their presence in Europe as part of offensive strategies to expand their global operations. This is in line with efforts across the industry to enhance economies of scale and develop a greater ability to offer clients the benefits of sourcing from a more focused, global supply network. For suppliers, the pressure to reduce costs has never been greater, contrasting sharply with the need to invest in R&D and improve manufacturing efficiency. In addition, many of the costs associated with rising raw material prices have been absorbed by the component manufacturers, as many suppliers have been unable to pass these rises on to the vehicle manufacturers.

The vehicle manufacturers are increasingly moving towards global manufacturing of cars and light commercial vehicles, each focusing more and more on vehicle assembly and preferring to outsource large subsystems. This trend is being accompanied by a significant reduction in the number of companies which directly supply the car manufacturers. Similarly, most of the major systems suppliers are focusing on their core product/technology areas and reducing the size of their own supplier lists. Together, these trends are having a significant impact on the structure of the supply base, which is going through a period of radical restructuring. The transformation of the components supply industry now touches almost every aspect of a supplier's business from production to organizational structure, financial resources, marketing, sales and distribution.

These changes within the industry have had major repercussions for Lucas. All of their customers are becoming increasingly sophisticated in their requirements for a flexible and rapid response. Minimum order quantities are described throughout the industry sector as, too high. Weekly MRP scheduling needs to be replaced by daily JIT style deliveries, against a background of increasing complexity in terms of non-standard size, colour and conductor combinations. Time Compression was recognized as a potential solution to these problems.

The Programme of Change

The existing harness production system (from raw material to finished component) was conceived over seven years ago under quite different market conditions. During that time the majority of cable was supplied to a single on-site customer, who delivered harnesses to as few as four vehicle manufacturers. High volume and low variety were representative of a market attempting to reduce cost through economies of scale.

In the 1990s the complexity of vehicles is increasing and end customers are demanding a greater proportion of vehicles built exactly to customer order. Hence a significant rise in demand volume and variety is present from all automotive wiring harness manufacturers. The future undoubtedly worsens the situation:

- The trend to move toward increased business units, typically satellite operations in areas with reduced labour rates
- External customers move toward build to order and requirements, for responsiveness, such as Rover Group's Personal Production initiative
- Further increase in demand for cable, especially in greater variety and reduced volumes
- Product complexity will remain, while new requirements are emerging in packaging
- Smaller batch size requirements to minimise stock holding
- More frequent deliveries, conceivably several per day

In order to meet these challenging demands of the external customers, combined with internal objectives to reduce inventory and improve service levels throughout Lucas wiring companies, several attempts to resolve the situation had been tried and had failed. Despite the general consensus that the current system was not the best and most cost effective means of manufacturing harnesses, a practical solution was lacking. Time Compression was identified as a mechanism to provide this practical strategy.

Diagnostics

Our initial analysis took an overview of the entire process from the raw material receipt for cable manufacturing through to despatch of the finished wiring harness to the vehicle manufacturer. We used Time Based Process Mapping to identify the best opportunities for Time Compression. Gaining a high level overview of the major issues involved in this business process was obtained from interviews with the key personnel throughout the entire supply chain, including customers, enabling a comprehensive diagnosis of the business to be generated.

The main issues to arise from the process mapping exercise were;

- The overall lead-time was 45 days, far in excess of any manager's understanding of the total process lead-time.
- The value adding portion of the cable supply process averaged five per cent.
- Four categories of stock exist across the entire chain, totalling over £5 million in value.
- Very few parallel activities were present within the chain. The production of cable was achieved through a range of sequential processes.
- Although cable was manufactured to one MRP run, cable was cut and assembled to a subsequent MRP run signifying an inability to synchronise production rates.

Although the Time Based Process Maps provided an excellent high level view of the total supply process they failed to accommodate specific detail around a number of dynamic issues, in particular the weekly scheduling system, production profile, inventory statement and the constant occurrence of shortages. Each of these concerns required further analysis. Various tools and techniques were available for the investigation of such situations, each of which were only as accurate as the data validity. In this instance, a combination of interviewing techniques and extraction of raw data (i.e. prior to interference) from the MRP systems proved adequate. The detailed analysis follows.

Scheduling system

The scheduling system throughout the Lucas wiring companies was programmed weekly via an MRP run for delivery of cable to the customer the following week. Although demand was very erratic by conductor, size and colour, the total volume remained at a theoretically constant level. This was exemplified through vehicle manufacturers providing reasonably steady and accurate schedules to Lucas. However, the weekly MRP time lags and uncertainties that existed within the internal supply chain caused these capacities and inventories to respond in a way that exceeds the original required demand. Consequently, the demand became amplified as it progressed down the supply chain, and as a result caused waste and confusion throughou the chain. The longer the delay in information getting from the marketplace to the factory, the more distorted the company's view of demand became.

The effects upon the cable business unit at the end of the supply chain were detrimental, leading to a combination of immense stocks in the products which were not required and significant shortages in the products which were. Subsequently, the planning and scheduling approach should have protected manufacturing economics, however, the conventional MRP planning logic falls short in this respect.

Production profile

A simple runner, repeater, stranger analysis of the orders for cable flowing through the cable business unit identified classical Pareto inference. Figure 7.1 illustrates that 80 per cent of the volume of cable evolved from only 20 per cent of the part numbers – high volume, low variety (runners). Correspondingly, 80 per cent of the part numbers accounted for only 20 per cent of the volume – low volumes, high variety (strangers).

This determined that the current method of treating all cable in a uniform manner was counter-productive and generated waste. Analysis also indicated that up to 30 per cent of parts with small

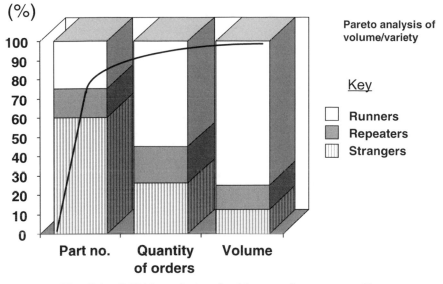

Fig. 7.1 *R/R/S analysis of cable manufacturing profile*

volumes were common to all sites and could be manufactured economically in large quantities and independently distributed.

Inventory profile
Analysis of the inventory profile accentuated the damaging effects of the imposed minimum order quantities. Cable customers consuming large volumes of cable observed lesser effects of order quantities because their order sizes were typically in excess of the MOQ. However, the majority of customers who consume high variety and low volume classes of cable attribute over 80 percent of the stock holding to the MOQ.

Primarily this denoted that forcing minimum order quantities upon each individual customer, whilst declining the ability to combine order quantities across sites, resulted in a total stock holding situation well above the basic requirement. Furthermore, the chance occurrence of obsolescence was increased which corresponded to inventory lead-times.

Shortage analysis
The combined effects of weekly scheduling, demand amplification and inventory holding produced a volatile demand in raw cable requirements upon the cable business unit. As every activity in the

supply chain relied on the receipt of cable, widespread fire-fighting had become commonplace to react to absent cables for customer harness orders which had become urgent.

Results of Diagnostics

The results of the investigation revealed the obvious need for radical change to the existing cable supply system in line with the strategic direction of Lucas. However, despite the many problems identified across the Lucas supply chain, the majority of these could be addressed by eliminating the root cause issues.

- Excessive stock caused by making to forecast, not to order, combined with the lack of MRP synchronization and imposed large minimum order quantities
- Excessive fluctuations in demand at Cable Business Unit level caused through the inability to maintain a level schedule through lack of vision resulted in capacity problems, shortages, additional transportation requirements and inefficiencies within cable manufacture
- Analysis also indicated that up to 36 per cent of parts with small volumes was common to all sites and could be manufactured economically and independently distributed
- Uneconomic cable manufacturing
- Deficient communication throughout the supply chain, typically using incompatible media

Generation of Solutions

Once a complete diagnosis of the production system had been completed, a series of workshops were organized with key managers spanning the entirety of the process under analysis, including customers and suppliers. This allowed open forum for potential solutions between the people that would actually be involved in the 'new process' directly or otherwise. The shared vision of the team coupled with their common understanding of the process analysis enabled an agreed solution to be developed. This ensured that an effective result was achieved, that was a company wide solution as opposed to a local departmental quick fix. The focus of the workshops included relevant theory, options for solutions and examples of their usage which were identified and discussed. A common view of the issues resulted, together with a number of alternative solutions based on the project teams expertise. Several potential solutions were developed, however two were seen to provide the most benefit.

In order to meet the challenging demands of external customers, combined with internal initiatives to reduce inventory and improve service levels throughout Lucas, the following solutions were implemented.

- Customer orders for cable were supplied to order, the minimum order quantity being reduced to appropriate box size with no detrimental effect to the existing pricing policy.
- Segmentation by runners, repeaters and strangers provided an essential foundation. It delivered an opportunity to tailor planning and scheduling approaches for optimum performance. It allowed runners and repeaters to be produced with outstanding cable manufacturing economics, focusing the stranger stream on cost reduction and minimising obsolescence.
- The cable manufacture scheduling week was changed to synchronize with customer schedules. This provided the ability for the CBU to operate from the most accurate information available, that is the data generated from the MRP run that defined the cutting programme and generated the cutting run, eliminating distortion.
- When operating in a 'supply to order' environment, future demand requirements could be analysed to enable small volumes to be collated to enhance cable manufacturing economics, reducing change-over, scrap and other non-value adding activities. Conversely, to protect against obsolescence, it was possible to manufacture extremely low volumes exactly to order.
- The great majority of cable inventory was moved to a central location adjacent to the CBU and managed, controlled and owned entirely by the CBU. The assembly business's CST areas also now hold an agreed level of buffer based upon the time elapsed between placing an order and the cable being available for cutting.
- Since customers operated in weekly buckets, daily schedules were unable to be produced in a practical manner. Therefore, the most appropriate solution was to operate daily delivery upon a *kanban*

Simplify / Compress

Co-ordinate

Control

basis. The requirement will be generated utilizing a bar-code on the transport box, returned to the customer storage area to generate an electronic message to the CBU to replace stock if actually required.

Results

The project required a significant degree of analysis giving Lucas wiring companies an excellent view of the key strategic directions in which they needed to develop to become increasingly competitive in the future. The business has developed new processes and a new organizational structure that focuses on the process of delivering products to the customer rather than meeting individual functional goals. It has also developed new goals and measures and a clearer understanding of where its key strengths lie for serving the market.

The effect of all these activities showed improvements in performance throughout the Lucas wiring companies, specifically and not surprisingly in the Cable Business Unit. Much of this improvement is as a result of the greater understanding of the entire supply chain process and its performance.

- Cable lead-times reduced 75 per cent of cable supplied with 24 hour lead-time, the balance within 7 days
- Cable inventory reduction by 50 percent throughout the Lucas wiring companies.
- Obsolescence of stock reduced
- Provides the flexibility/responsiveness to react to customer changes
- Enhanced cable manufacturing economics
- Increased service levels

Learning Points

- Change project overload is a common reality. Several other improvement initiatives existed during the latter phases of this project. Without prioritization, project managers fight for appropriate resources, whilst employees caught in the cross-fire experience confusion and frustration. Applying filtering systems to classify the relative importance of projects overcomes this predicament.

- The importance of using a team to generate solutions is absolutely paramount, not only to ensure that an effective and global solution is produced but also for ease of implementation. If a team of people have been involved in solution generation, that is the output is literally their work, it is highly likely that they will have more ownership of and more commitment to the successful implementation of their ideas.

8 Wishes to Actions

In each of the organizations we have worked with there have been numerous opportunities to improve the performance of the business. Indeed in most there have been more opportunities than could be coped with at any one time. This chapter is about deciding which of these opportunities to exploit, based upon the company vision and strategy you have developed for your business, and about setting up the mechanisms to exploit them.

The idea of appraising business improvement projects is not new. Capital investment appraisal systems have been part of the finance function's systems for many years. However these typically fail to hit the real resource constraint which is not money. Many of the Time Compression projects we have been through have had relatively low levels of capital expenditure for a relatively large impact on performance. The key constraint we have identified is the time of employees, particularly managers. The participative approach, that we suggest is the key to success, requires that the employees who actually work within a process are involved in its improvement. By definition these people have a full-time job working on the process. In order to take part in improving the process they have to be released from doing something else. Their managers will typically also have a full-time job managing, yet are also expected to actively support each of the development projects. If a manager has several improvement projects in his area he will be expected to cope with them all. Our research has shown that this leads to insufficient attention to any of them, ultimately alienating those working on them at the detail level. In some of the less developed companies we have worked in the senior managers have been the only group with experience of changing things and their spending time to coach less experienced managers was vital to the success of projects.

In order to overcome these resource constraints to time-compressing the change process, it is necessary to focus that resource on the key business objectives and critical business processes. It is also important to ensure that the project workload equates to the amount of resources available to do it and that day-to-day problems do not take energy away from longer-term development activities. Doing so means either keeping active project portfolios small enough or finding more resources to do more projects.

The need to free up people for improvement work means that something must get worse before it gets better. It may be production output, quality or lead-time. The aim is therefore to use this investment in people's time wisely to ensure that it reduces the effects of resource constraints and gain benefits as quickly as possible. Fortunately it is possible to prioritize projects in such a way as to increase the amount of resources available to do them. Ultimately everyone in the company will develop the capability to undertake change, thereby providing maximum flexibility and speed in changing the business.

PRIORITIZING PROJECTS

There are two key factors to consider in prioritizing projects:

- The ability of a project to produce the maximum benefit required by the company's strategic priorities for the level of critical resource required
- The ability of a project to produce more of the constraining critical resource, thereby increasing the number of future improvement projects that can be handled

The balance between these two factors depends upon the need to gain immediate strategic benefit and the need for longer-term strategic benefit which the growth of constraining resource facilitates. We suggest that the easiest way to handle this balance is to start a few small projects in line with overall objectives, fully resource them, bring them to completion and start a few more. The company gets strategic benefit from completing the project in the shortest possible time and the people involved in the projects can be used to start more projects, accelerating the change process. This approach requires a strong and disciplined focus to ensure that the largest strategic opportunities are capitalized on as early as possible.

The prioritization of projects may have to take place more than once. It may be necessary to prioritize a process area and then prioritize specific activities within that area. The same techniques for prioritizing changes may be applied iteratively until projects are small enough to handle.

MAXIMIZING BENEFIT FOR INVESTMENT OF RESOURCES

The first step is to take the business process identified as most important and look at the opportunities within it. If you are not sure which this is see Chapter 3 which looks at identifying critical business processes. If you manage a department, not a company, imagine that your department is a little company with internal customers and apply the same principles. It is important that effort is focused on the critical business process only and aimed at the top priority operational objective. Projects on less critical areas of the business will take up time and energy which could be better spent on improving the critical areas. Projects aimed primarily at meeting less important operating objectives may take energy away from meeting the most important ones. Either way the process of change will be slowed down.[1]

A quick analysis of the business process you have identified as critical will reveal the best opportunities for easy improvements. This type of analysis does not take long as accuracy is not required. The idea is to identify the two or three largest opportunities. Once identified these can be analysed in more detail to look for the causes of the delays and possible solutions. Here are the frameworks we usually use to identify these opportunities.

Using Time-Based Process Mapping (TBPM)

The objective of Time Compression is to reduce the amount of non-value-adding time. Some parts of a process have more non-value-adding time than others. Time-Based Process Mapping (discussed in Chapters 10 and 11) can be used to quickly identify these. By targeting resources at these large chunks of non-value-adding time, large improvements in lead-time can be made for relatively little effort. An example of this we have found quite commonly is that managers ask us to look at their manufacturing processes. A quick overview sometimes shows us that the time consumed by the manufacturing process is insignificant compared to the distribution, ordering and administration systems and that these would prove more effective targets for lead-time reduction. This is common because manufacturing is expensive in accounting terms and so has had significant management attention over the years.

Points of Leverage

One of the key tenets of the Systems Thinking[2] school of management is the idea of points of leverage. This is the idea that a small and carefully placed intervention can have enormous effects on an overall system. Our research has identified a number of potential points of leverage within business processes. The clearest of these is at the 'fuzzy front end' of the new product process. Creating a good development strategy, product architecture and filtering system has been shown to have an enormous effect on development lead-time. In the supply chain, purchasing policy provides significant leverage over the benefits to be gained from the chain. Also linking sales outlets up to the factory scheduling system such that orders are slotted into the schedule in front of the customer will help to flatten demand and remove scheduling uncertainty, thereby making manufacturing activity much simpler.

Spotting points of leverage is not easy or guaranteed. We do however suggest that the following are good places to look:

- **Where major decisions are taken.** These will be decisions on things that happen downstream, for example, decisions on priorities, product design, process design or company policy.
- **Early in a business process.** Since the points of leverage create impact on downstream activities they will tend to be early in the business process.
- **At or near functional or company boundaries.** In Time Compression, many of the biggest mismatches between what exists and what is required occur across functional or business boundaries due to lack of communication. These often have decision-making on the interfaces and so make very easy targets for change.

REPRODUCING THE CONSTRAINING RESOURCES

The Time Compression approach aims to deliver a capability to change, not just a single change. The ability to change is dependent upon an adequate supply of key resources, specifically people capable of making the change happen, time of employees including managers, and cash to invest in changes. By prioritizing projects so as to replicate the constraining resource, the company will eventually reach the level often described in the management press where the whole of the company is capable of initiating and successfully implementing change. Here are a number of strategies we have identified for reproducing constraining resources.

Increasing Experience of Managing Change

In many of the companies we have worked with the resource constraint has been the number of people with experience of running and taking part in improvement projects. By using a project team with a mixture of experienced and inexperienced change agents the ability to partake in change can be spread, bit by bit, throughout the organization. It helps if these projects are successful so pick easy projects initially and ensure there are enough experienced people to guarantee success. It may also be possible to use staff employees or outsiders to coach the team through the change process, thereby passing on their skills.

Increasing Resources

In some companies it has proved difficult to free up line resources. It is possible to pick the first project which will result in fewer people being required on a process. Instead of making the spare people redundant they can be trained in the skills required for change during the project and then used as facilitators for further projects. This was done with great effect in one company where an employee was freed up through a process change, taken off-line and coached in quality techniques whilst running an improvement project. After about two months he was put in a team leader's position in a quality blackspot which was causing delays throughout the process. He used his new-found skills to great effect.

Buying in Resources

Since the long-term objective of our approach to the change process is to generate a wider capability for change we do not suggest the use of temporary resources for improvement work. The exceptions to this are using them in a coaching role or to cover for full-time employees who can be transferred to improvement work.

Generating Cash

If the resource constraint is money then one way to generate it is to carry out a project which will result in the freeing up of working capital or assets. An example of this is inventory reduction. The cash can then be invested in other improvement projects.

Generating Enthusiasm

In some companies there is fear of the change process and fear of failing. The best way to overcome this is to show tangible examples of success within the company which often show employees what is possible. By picking projects which are both important and relatively simple, and by careful management to ensure their success, it is possible to reproduce the sense of enthusiasm this generates.

CREATING THE INFRASTRUCTURE FOR CHANGE

Having decided upon which issues are to be tackled first it is time to set up the infrastructure for the change process. The first task is to identify a suitable change agent and a project sponsor. The change agent is responsible for managing the day-to-day change process. Typically it will consist of either a project champion or a project team. The project sponsor is ideally a senior manager who will support the project by persuading senior management to tackle those issues that only they can solve and which stand in the way of success. Clear ownership of the project by employees who are in positions to make or influence key decisions will allow the change process to progress quickly and smoothly, thereby time-compressing it.

Project Sponsor

Most change projects come across barriers to change which are determined by company policy. These may be reporting procedures, performance measures, capital expenditure control methods, or personnel policies. Often it takes senior management power to help the project team to remove such barriers. The project sponsor is the change agent's principal point of contact within senior management. It is the project sponsor to whom they will go if they require support.

Thus the project sponsor needs to be able to influence his peers to take appropriate actions, and to explain to the project team the limits of what can be changed. Our research has shown that in order to fulfil this role the project sponsor should:

- Have a clear understanding of the project objectives and be enthusiastic about championing it
- Have a detailed understanding of the internal and external environment of the company
- Be able to influence or control the resources available to carry out the project
- Be able to influence or control other projects which may have an effect on the project in question
- Have good interpersonal skills to allow them to work closely with the project champion, project team and their peers

Change Agent

The change agent is the person or group of people who are responsible for actually carrying out a change. The choice of the change agent is key to the likely success of the project. Deciding whether to use a team or a single person is dependent upon the size and scope of project and the culture of the company. We have had successful projects where there has not been an explicit project team, for example at Jetstream Aircraft where the project champion had all of the knowledge, experience and influence to develop the project within the normal working structure of the company. We have also had successful projects where a team approach has been used, for example, Coats Viyella used a multi-functional, multi-level project team. Fairey Hydraulics utilized a team of super-generalists and in the Rover Group a team of over 20 people was established to develop suppliers.

For the project to be successful the change agent, be it a team or an individual, needs the following attributes:

- They should be bought into the need for the project and be enthusiastic about championing it
- They should have a detailed understanding of the internal and external environment of the company
- They should have the ability to gain the respect of peers through their experience and knowledge

- They should have time available to focus on the project
- They should have good interpersonal skills to allow them to work closely with the project sponsor, their peers and team members and help persuade colleagues of the course of action required
- They should have a detailed understanding of current processes and procedures
- They should possess the full range of perspectives on the objective and performance of the process, for example, those of the major functional departments involved
- They should possess decision-making power over the whole process and the resources involved within it. In some cases it may not be possible to have decision-making power over the whole process. In these situations the project sponsor is relied upon to gain the necessary commitment

Gaining all of these attributes in one person can be difficult, which is why we have tended to use project teams. The make-up of the team can be used to overcome potential areas of resistance. By using stakeholder analysis it is possible to identify those employees who perceive that they have most to lose from the forthcoming changes. Getting them involved in the team can be a powerful way to overcome their potential resistance. It is also possible to identify those people whose commitment is crucial for the success of the project and who should be involved. These may be key decision-makers or may be leaders of opinion. It is also important to have people who will gain from the change and will help to drive it forward. Taking account of these different elements of a team will help time-compress the diagnostic and implementation processes. There will be sufficient expertise within the team to anticipate problems, there will be people to drive the project forward and the team approach will help generate understanding and commitment in those who might have slowed the project down at the implementation stage.

Other things to take account in setting up the team are its size and the characters of the team members. We would suggest that a team of much more than ten people is difficult to coordinate. There is a large amount of academic work available on group dynamics. We find an understanding of this material is useful in balancing team composition.

One question we are often asked about the change agent is whether or not they should be full-time. With employees working full-time on a project team the project will get the attention and focus it deserves.

However the likelihood of success is improved by the active participation of those employees who will have to live with the change. By definition these people will have their day-to-day job to do and so will not be able to work on the project full-time. There are two possible solutions we have used. One is to second line employees to the project team full-time with a brief to involve their colleagues who are still carrying out their day-to-day tasks. The second is to allow time within the working week for the line employees to contribute to the project. In this case it is important to ensure that the priorities of the work to be done in this allotted time are clear. It is often best for some team members to be full-time in order to manage the project as a whole and carry out the implementation, guided by the team as a whole including the part-time team members from the business process being improved.

Consultants

Some companies consider the use of consultants in changing their business. Consultants have a number of roles which they can usefully play:

- They can act as a neutral facilitator in workshops and meetings to help resolve conflict and ensure that everyone's views are heard and balanced
- They can provide an objective view of a company or business process unsullied by the historical and cultural baggage of the company and industry
- They can act as a coach for their specialist skills to managers involved in change
- They may have new tools and perspectives which can be used to raise issues
- They may have easy access to relevant and useful external information sources and benchmarks
- They can be used to ease the communication process in companies where it is a problem
- Their experience may allow common pitfalls to be avoided

The use of consultants has many pitfalls itself:

- Choosing consultants can be a difficult task. First decide in detail what it is you want the consultant to do. The skills required to facilitate a workshop are very different from the skills required to design a solution to a manufacturing problem. A consultant with no knowledge of your industry may be able to provide a more objective viewpoint and highlight more issues than an old-timer from the industry. There are some consultants who are experts in one solution only and that is what they will sell, regardless of how appropriate it is.

• A consultant will never know as much about your company as your employees. After all they work there constantly whereas consultants do not. It is company employees who provide the specific details about the company, its existing processes and how things get done. The role of consultants is to tailor their specialized skills to that environment in conjunction with company employees to bring about results. Thus the effectiveness of consultants is largely determined by their ability to communicate and empathize with company employees at all levels. As such this needs to be high on the list of attributes required.

• Consultants have no power of their own. They rely on directing the power of line managers. Thus they cannot operate without active management support in marshalling and leading the project team. Consultants should not be allowed to lead a project as this will result in reduced company ownership of the issues and of the solutions to be implemented, usually resulting in project failure.

• The least effective approach to consultancy is where the consultant does a few interviews inside the company, writes a report and then leaves the company to implement the findings of the report. This results in no company ownership of the findings, almost always leading to no action being taken.

• It is the responsibility of the project sponsor to make sure that the consultant has been informed of all critical issues. There may be important issues, for example future plans, which are not common knowledge, but which the consultant should be aware of in facilitating the creation of solutions to problems.

DEFINING THE SCOPE OF CHANGE

A key activity of the project sponsor and project champion is the definition of the scope of the project. This is basically a definition of what the project will cover. The process of targeting changes will have identified an approximate area for the change which will have resulted in the appointment of a suitable project champion and project sponsor. This scope needs to be clearly defined through the use of a 'project terms of reference'. This will provide a guide for the change agent and reduce the likelihood of the project scope mushrooming as interconnected issues are found to influence activities.

Project Terms of Reference

The terms of reference of a project are a statement of:

- What area of a process the project will address
- What specific problems need to be addressed
- Performance targets for the process and their priorities so that trade-offs may be made if necessary
- How the project fits into the wider business, its development and overall objectives

They are a statement of the what and the why of the project, but not a statement of the how. The terms of reference will enable the project champion to select the project team and allow selection of an appropriate diagnostic approach. The detailed specification of solutions will not be possible until the diagnostic phase has been completed.

BIG VERSUS SMALL PROJECTS

One of the long-running arguments in change literature is whether to change in one big project[3] or to make many small improvements.[4] Some authors[5] argue that one big change causes so much disruption that it takes just as long to reap the benefits of the change as it does with an equivalent number of small changes.

The pros and cons of these two approaches can be seen from the simple example of an athlete. It is possible for a runner to win a race either by taking longer strides at the same cadence, or to take more strides in a given period of time. Either approach has the same potential for winning the race. If the long-striding runner takes too long a stride he may land badly and lose. If the course changes direction mid-stride then he will not be able to react as he is in mid-air and lose. The short-striding runner does not suffer these risks. His only constraint is how quickly he can move his legs.

Where we have been involved in large projects we have found that the priority of the issue tackled tends to change before the diagnostic phase is complete, let alone before solutions are implemented. Alternatively the project sponsor may have moved on and the replacement has different priorities. Ultimately this results in much wasted time and effort. It is a little like the direction of the runner's course changing whilst the long-striding runner is in mid-air.

In general we have found that many small projects linked to an overall objective provide the best strategy. This is like the short-striding runner's approach to winning the race. This should not be confused with splitting a large project into many stages which would be like the long-striding runner changing his aerial technique. Our approach allows the project to proceed through all stages from initiation to completion as quickly as possible, thereby quickly showing an impact on the bottom line and accelerating the learning process. This approach requires that each project is adequately resourced. When one project finishes the resource is redeployed on further projects. By having small projects it is possible to get results despite the frequent changes of management direction and management personnel we have endured in some companies. It has also meant that the companies can change their tactical direction quickly without wasting the effort they have put into change and alienating their employees.

ACTIONS INTO RESULTS

If you have followed our model this far you should by now have a set of prioritized projects clearly linked to your strategic objectives through the improvement of a critical business process. The next step is to find out what is really going on and come up with some solutions to the problems you find. In the next chapter we will give you some tips on the diagnostic and solution generation process to help you on your way.

Further Reading

M. Beer, R. A. Eisenstat and B. Spector, *The Critical Path to Corporate Renewal* (Boston, Mass., Harvard Business School Press, 1990).
R. H. Schaffer and H. A. Thompson, 'Successful Change Programmes Begin with Results', *Harvard Business Review*, January–February (1992), pp. 80–9.

CASE STUDY – MASSEY FERGUSON

The Company

Massey Ferguson is a global supplier of farm machinery. This case study records the work done with the Coventry plant of Massey Ferguson which employs 1500 people. The plant had a 1994 turnover of £270 million, manufacturing 22 000 built-up tractors and 29 000 tractor kits. Over 90 per cent of production is exported to in excess of 140 countries. The business operates on an assembly-to-order basis. It can be split into four main areas: machine shops, major sub-assembly, tractor assembly and knock-down kit packaging. Massey Ferguson is a subsidiary of the AGCO Corporation.

Strategic Drivers

Tractor manufacturing has traditionally been about seeking to meet demand with standard products. Over the past two decades the contraction of the global market for tractors combined with an increase in competition has altered the nature of the market. Increasingly tractor manufacturers must gain competitive advantage through providing a wide range of options without incurring penalties in delivery reliability, cost, quality or lead-time.

The growth in options has resulted in the number of possible specifications mushrooming, which has put considerable strain on the current systems and processes. The resulting problems in the machining shop, on which our activities were focused, were:

- Arrears in the performance of the system to the schedule
- A shortfall in production capacity
- Difficulty in reacting to changing customer priorities
- High work-in-progress and finished components stocks
- High subcontracting charges

The Programme of Change

The company felt that a time-based perspective upon their machine shop operations would provide a mechanism for the improvement of the ability of the shop to cope with variety. With this in mind they invited us into their plant to examine the feasibility of this approach.

First diagnostic stage

The objective of the first stage of diagnosis was to become familiar with the different cells in the machine shop. Each cell was investigated by interviewing the cell leaders to find out what the major problems were perceived to be. This identified that no single detailed diagnostic process would be sufficient to cover all of the problems experienced. Perhaps most importantly it provided common ground for the researchers and company managers to understand each other's approach and build confidence that the project could result in clear business benefits.

At the end of this diagnostic stage a workshop was held with company staff to identify the way forward. This allowed a suite of diagnostic tools to be put together to meet the needs of the machine shop.

Second diagnostic stage

The diagnostic approach was designed to provide detailed supporting data for the initial analysis. Data were collected on a number of parameters.

- The overall process was investigated using Time-Based Process Mapping
- Each manufacturing cell leader was interviewed to gain an understanding of the characteristics of the cell and to identify sources of turbulence. Cause and effect diagrams were used to capture this data
- Runner, repeater, stranger analysis was carried out on all of the parts in each cell
- Time-based process maps were drawn for a sample of long-lead-time components in cells which experienced turbulence
- The proportion of queuing, process and set-up times for each runner component was calculated

This diagnosis resulted in some key findings:

- Value-adding time was around 1 per cent of the quoted cell lead-time on one item. Forty per cent of time was spent queuing.
- Planners were tending to round lead-times quoted on the MRPII system to the nearest week.

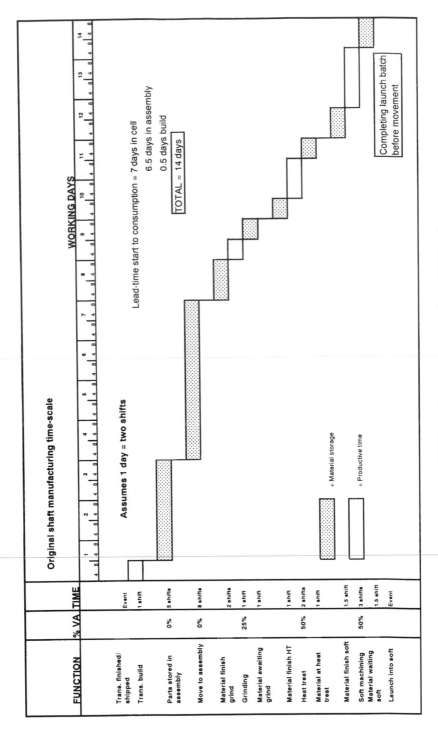

Fig. 8.1 *TBPM displaying process before MLT reduction*

- The variance between planned and actual build at the assembly level was small. At the sub-assembly and component level it was more significant and variable. This showed that turbulence was most prominent at the latter level and was more pronounced in some cells than in others.
- The forms of the schedules given to cells were not appropriate to meet their needs.
- 40 per cent of components constitute only 5 per cent of cell production volume, a high proportion of stranger products with significant implications on the proportion of set-up time.

The use of Time-Based Process Mapping gave the cell leaders a new insight into the manufacturing process. Its focus on the flow of material through the cell clearly highlighted the true monetary value of material tied up in queues and in large machining batches. This insight and understanding of the manufacturing process stimulated the identification of a number of opportunities for improvement:

- Improving the quality and timeliness of scheduling documentation given to cell leaders.
- Reduction of lead-time through removing queues of material between machines, by reducing transfer batch sizes and by reducing set-up times.
- Splitting manufacturing cells up into sub-cells geared to coping with different families of parts produced within the cell.
- Revisiting the make versus buy policy to look at subcontracting stranger parts and bringing in-house those parts that were partially processed by suppliers where possible. This would reduce transportation times for parts, decrease the turbulence caused by stranger parts and lower the cost of unplanned subcontracting.
- Redesigning the supply chain to improve quality and delivery reliability. Failures in these caused turbulence within the manufacturing cells.

These opportunities resulted in one immediate action whereby the cell leaders agreed upon a consolidated set of requirements for the schedule documents which were then used as the basis for improvements to them. Following discussion of the results with the company it was decided to carry out a pilot study for the implementation of Time Compression techniques in one of the manufacturing cells.

Pilot Study

The first step in the pilot study was the choice of a cell. The cell needed to be representative of those in the factory, but perhaps most importantly the cell leader had to be committed to improving the performance of his cell through the use of Time Compression. Finding such a cell was not difficult because of the relationships built up during the earlier diagnostic stage. As this was a pilot project, a 'diary' was set up with the sole intention of capturing the learning points and improvements generated by the project. The project had a duration of two months.

The first step was to set up a template for identifying which improvements should be made. This was done by the researchers in conjunction with the cell leader and the operators. Only the cell operators had the detailed knowledge required to identify the best opportunities for improvement and the commitment to exploiting them. The template was intended to be used by the cell leaders of other cells in the next stage of the project and so had to be generic. In addition the continuously changing mix of components meant that the analysis would have to be completed on a regular basis. The steps decided on for the template were:

1. Runner, repeater, stranger analysis.
2. Analysis to investigate the degree to which the cell was self-contained. This looked at the operations done outside the cell and operations done for parts from other cells, both of which are potential causes of turbulence.
3. Rough-cut Time-Based Process Mapping for runner parts.
4. Assessment of the effect of changes in transfer batch size on the lead-time using the TBPM.
5. Assessment of the effect of implementing *kanban* techniques using the TBPM.
6. Monitoring of the progress of improvements made against established performance measures.
7. Review and improve the process of Time Compression as the population and volumes of the different parts manufactured within a cell change over time.

The analysis was carried out in the pilot cell and the following solutions were identified and implemented. The cell was split into a number of sub-cells, each manufacturing a small number of similar parts on machines organized into dedicated flow lines wherever possible. This worked because there was a significant proportion of 'runner' parts. The researchers and the cell leader worked out optimum transfer batch sizes for the runner parts. The operators were persuaded of the need to diligently count the parts into and out of each machining process and to record the movement of the batches for analysis. This was easily achieved by using the job control card which each pallet of raw material carried with it. The operators only had to add the date and time to the job cards, a small task which they readily accepted. Once these changes had demonstrated predictable and reliable demand and shortened lead-time, the next stage of the project could commence. This was the implementation of a *kanban* system between cells. The *kanban* worked on the basis of the machine shop commencing its operations upon the trigger of an MRP plan and the assembly cell pulling the material through via *kanban* cards. This approach worked well.

Results

The improvements made to the pilot cell resulted in a number of performance gains:

- The setting up of sub-cells resulted in lead-time reductions of an average of 20 per cent for the runner parts
- Material availability for the assembly cell improved dramatically; parts on *kanban* did not run out
- 10 per cent inventory reduction within two months of implementation
- 24 per cent increase in stock-turn ratio
- There was a marked increase in customer–supplier confidence within the internal supply chain

The results were communicated to the management and other cell leaders. This showed that the approach was viable in the environment of the machine shop leading to the techniques being spread to other machining cells. The success of the pilot study also showed to more sceptical cell leaders the benefits to be gained from the approach, leading to its acceptance. Each cell developed its own Time Compression plan. Common principles were tackling runner parts first and putting stranger parts out to contract.

168

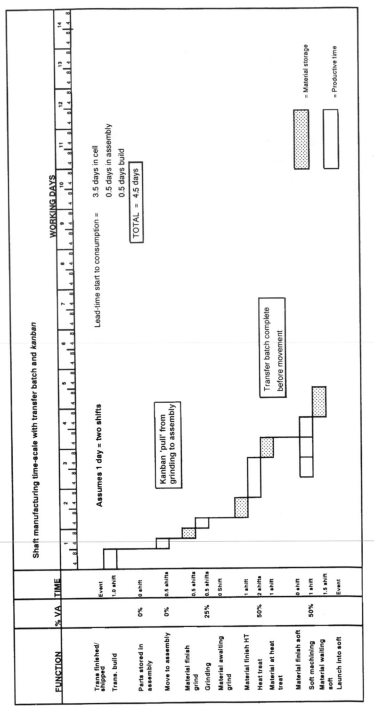

Fig. 8.2 *TBPM displaying process after MLT reduction*

There were some unexpected benefits from the Time Compression exercise. In one case we found that the implementation of *kanban* did not result in the stock-turn benefit expected. It was found that the supplier produced left-handed components for one month, then right-handed components for the next. Identifying and solving this problem resulted in significant savings in component part inventory.

The Time Compression approach gave Massey Ferguson new insight into some areas of its policy. For example, the make–buy decision was seen to be needed to be handled strategically throughout the life of a part due to the effect that stranger parts had on manufacturing effectiveness. In addition Massey Ferguson are now looking at extending the principle of Time Compression into their supply chain to gain further benefits.

Learning Points

- Time Compression is not a one-off thing in cellular manufacturing. It is necessary to continuously revisit the cell design to ensure that the cell is in tune with the requirements of the market-place.
- The idea of using a pilot project to build up the competence and confidence of management in Time Compression techniques was effective. The success of the project was valuable in facilitating the adoption of the techniques throughout the machine shop.

9   Time to Take Action

Making progress to reorganize and restructure your business's operations requires a focused and coordinated effort that is going to be difficult. If you have read the previous three chapters you will by now have decided what issues you are addressing and have set up a team to begin to deal with them. You may also have an idea as to the source of the problems arising from your initial enquiries. The next step in creating change is to generate a fuller understanding of the business process you are investigating.

THE DIAGNOSTIC PROCESS

The diagnostic process is not just about discovering the exact nature of a company's problems. It is a key element of the change process as it is the principal mechanism for building a shared understanding of the process, its objectives and problems, the people involved in it and the politics between them. It also serves to build awareness of the change initiative within the wider company and provides a platform upon which to raise issues and show their importance. It serves to deliver the following:

- **Learning the language of the company.** Every company and every department within a company has its own body of language and cultural norms. This comprises a terminology, often including TLAs (three-letter acronyms) and jargon which are unintelligible to an outsider. If members of different departments are working in a team to change a business process, it helps if they can all communicate effectively in the same language. Few companies would expect an employee to conduct meetings in a foreign language without first training them. In the same way an allowance needs to be made for learning the terminology of different departments. If a consultant or other facilitator is used in the project the diagnostic phase will provide an opportunity for them to learn about the company.

- **Building relationships within the team**. The success of the change project depends upon the team operating as a cohesive unit, so the building of relationships within the team is a crucial issue. The diagnostic process provides a focus for the newly found team. It provides the team with an opportunity for team members to get to know each other. Sometimes we have found that there are already conflicts between team members. The diagnostic process provides an opportunity to explore different views of reality. We believe that this should be encouraged as ultimately consensus will be needed if solutions are to be fully implemented. In cases of likely conflict it is advisable to use a facilitator experienced in group conflict resolution to ensure that the process starts off in the right direction.

- **Building relationships between the team and the outside world**. It is a rare project where everyone who will be affected by a change can be incorporated into the project team. The complexity of the system that comprises an organization usually means that there are many people on the fringes of any changes whose needs must be considered. The diagnostic process provides the opportunity to go and talk to these people, to get to know them and what they do. Our research has shown that listening to the views of all of the people involved in a process and building relationships with them eases the implementation of solutions later in the project.

- **Giving the findings credibility and support**. Some of the people who are not involved in the project team may be key to the acceptance of a solution. They may be decision-makers or opinion-formers. By ensuring that such people are interviewed, the credibility of the results can be enhanced. The people interviewed will feel that their views have been taken into account, and so are more likely to support the conclusions of the diagnostic process, giving weight to the findings.

- **Understanding and prioritizing issues**. The principal purpose of the diagnostic process is to develop a common understanding of a business process and the issues involved in changing it. The collection of valid data helps determine the relative importance of each of the issues identified.

- **Collecting valid, realistic data**. One of the main purposes of the diagnostic process is to produce valid and realistic data. This typically takes the form of a process map agreed by consensus to be realistic. It will also include realistic measures of current performance. The purpose of these data is to provide a starting position for the implementation phase of a project. It also serves to help solve disputes over what actually happens. In some cases we have come across disagreements as to what actually happens in a business process. The availability of data understood to be realistic quickly resolves such disputes. Involving an objective outsider in the collection of data, alongside team members, can help to give further validity to the results.

- **Raising awareness of the issues**. The interviewing activity provides an opportunity to explain to everyone connected with the business process the reasons for the change project, the approach being taken, how the project will be progressed and perhaps some of the theory behind it. The method of using this opportunity needs to be considered carefully. There is a danger of influencing the responses given by the interviewee, thereby distorting the accuracy of the view of the process. This can be avoided by careful interviewing, not revealing anything that may distort information until that information has been collected. In some companies there is also a danger that revealing the issues may cause political conflict, thereby putting the project in jeopardy. In such a company the type of information disseminated will need to be considered carefully.

The Use of a Diagnostic Tool

In all of our projects we have used a number of diagnostic tools, including those in Chapter 2. We have found the use of these extremely beneficial. Diagnostic tools help managers to think of a problem from a different perspective to that which they are accustomed to using. By taking a different perspective it is possible for managers to be able to see what would be clear to an outsider, that is, to see the wood for the trees. A good tool provides a structure to hold those thoughts and facilitates their communication to others. We found that using a tool provided a good focus for directing interviews and collecting of the data we required. A tool also proved to be helpful in persuading people to grant us interviews, as it indicated that we had a definite objective behind our request.

Selecting a Diagnostic Tool

Since the objective of a diagnostic tool is to alter the perspective of its user, the choice of tool depends upon which perspective is desired.

A project looking at Time Compression needs to use a tool that highlights delays to a product passing through a factory, or delays to a development project passing through a new product process. Time-Based Process Mapping (see Chapters 10 and 11) fulfils this role. A project looking at quality problems needs a tool that highlights the reasons behind those problems. A fishbone diagram would be a suitable tool for this purpose.

Our experience has also shown us that simple, visual tools work best. For example, a Time-Based Process Map of a business process covering one side of paper often proved to be very powerful in communicating where the biggest delays were with little explanation. Often we were able to present maps saying, 'the value-adding time in this process is coloured red', where no red bars were visible on the map. The visual power of this statement created some interesting reactions.

The next two chapters of this book have been devoted to discussing the tools we have found useful and their suitability for determining different perspectives.

Deciding the Scope of the Diagnosis

Having decided upon a suitable perspective and tool, the scope of the diagnosis needs to be decided. One variable is determined by the scope of the project which should have formed part of the team's brief. The other variable is the level of detail required in the understanding of the process. The objective of a change project is to change the process, not to analyse the company in extreme detail and reach a state of 'paralysis by analysis', a common industrial condition. Part of the change agent's role is to ensure that the project stays within its defined scope and does not mushroom into a project to cover every issue in the company.

The best way of analysing a large process is to take an overview, highlight the critical parts of the process and then analyse these in more detail and so on. It is always worth bearing in mind Pareto analysis which suggests that 20 per cent of the issues cause 80 per cent of the problems or delays.

APPROACHES TO THE DIAGNOSTIC PROCESS

Within the Time Compression projects we undertook, a number of different approaches to the diagnostic process were taken:

- We facilitated a diagnostic workshop
- We interviewed the relevant employees and reported our conclusions back to the project team
- We trained members of the project team in the use of relevant tools and coached them through the interviewing process
- We interviewed the relevant employees alongside team members and helped them to draw together their conclusions

Whilst we carried out each of these activities in our role of objective outsiders, we believe it is possible to carry out each approach without any outside help. The choice of approach should be determined principally by the culture of the organization and the make-up of the project team.

Diagnostic Workshops

The diagnostic workshop is a technique which can be used successfully to gain an understanding of a process. It is basically a group interview based around a tool used to map the process identified. As an approach it is extremely good at gaining a widespread and shared understanding of the process which becomes invaluable during solution generation. There are, however, a number of significant constraints to the value of the approach.

Advantages

- Gains a widely shared understanding of the process. This is extremely valuable during the solution generation stage.
- Good at building relationships within the entire team.

Disadvantages

- The main constraint of the approach is the number of people that can be easily accommodated. The more people involved in the workshop, the more room there is for disagreement as to what happens in the business process, and the longer the workshop takes. Some attendees may then get frustrated at the amount of time the diagnostic process takes and become disenchanted with it.
- It is very easy to get into a great deal of detail and miss the bigger picture. This can be guarded against by using a facilitator.

- There is no opportunity to collect data to verify a particular point of view. Thus the view of the group as a whole may not represent the true reality. This is often called 'groupthink'.
- Some employees want answers, not talk. They may find the diagnostic process a waste of time. If the solution generation stage is separate from the diagnostic stage it may be difficult to get them to turn up for the solution generation workshop.
- The workshop is prone to the problems of group dynamics. Some people will tend to dominate and others will say little. This can be compensated for by a good facilitator.

In general we would suggest that groups are kept to under ten, that the workshop is held off-site to remove interruptions, that a facilitator is used, and that the diagnostic and solution generation phases are carried out in close proximity where possible.

Face-to-Face Interviews

The face-to-face interview is the other main way of collecting information. It is not as good at gaining a shared understanding as the diagnostic workshop as not everyone can be involved in every interview. However it does have a number of advantages which compensate for this.

Advantages

- The interviews are independent of each other and so any inconsistencies have to be reconciled. Because there is time to collect validating data, it is possible to find out what actually happens, rather than take the prevailing view.
- People can make comments in confidence. This allows them to say things which may not be raised at a group workshop. This is especially valuable if an understanding of the culture of the company needs to be gained.
- The interview process can be used to explain the issues to everyone involved, tailored to their own level of understanding and perspective. It allows interviewees to ask the questions relevant to themselves which may help the team overcome those issues during implementation.

- The face-to-face nature of the interview means that the interviewees feel that they are being listened to and their views and concerns taken into account. This will help give the findings credibility and gain support for them.

Disadvantages

- The interviewers can be perceived as biased in their findings if they do not fit the prevailing view.
- Only the interviewers may have a shared understanding of the process. This needs to be communicated effectively to the remainder of the project team.
- The success of the interview programme is highly dependent upon the interviewers being objective and not loading the findings with their own prejudices.

We believe it is best to have only a few representatives of the team involved in interviewing the employees involved in any one business process. Whilst interviewing we found that we came across contradictions in what different people were saying, which led to issues being uncovered. Spotting such contradictions is very easy if the interviewer has been involved in many related interviews. If different interviewers manage to spot the contradictions it will be necessary to return to the interviewee for more information. It may be possible to split the business process into discrete sections with little overlap of personnel, thereby involving the whole team in interviewing. Alternatively the team need to select representatives to do the interviewing. Since the team will be expected to act upon the findings, the interviewers must be seen to be unbiased and objective. This can be enhanced by using an interview consisting of two people from different departments, or by working with an objective outsider.

Interview Technique

Al Capone, the infamous American gangster, used to say that

More can be achieved with a good word and a gun than with a good word alone

We believe that if you have a gun, or are seen as a threat in any other way, people will become defensive in answering your questions. They may tell you what it is they think you want to hear, or distort reality to protect their jobs and their reputation. Either way the project team will not gain the understanding of the business process that they require. Explaining what you are doing and why will help persuade people to be honest. If you are trying to shed jobs, cooperation is much harder to obtain.

The Time Compression approach can be described in a non-threatening way because it looks at the movement of things, not people. We have found that this tends to reduce people's defensiveness about what it is that they do. However in some factories we have found ourselves confused with 'Time and Motion' people who have historically looked at piecework rates and job times which were used to pressure employees into working harder. In such cases we find that employees are much more wary about what they tell us. Other approaches likely to be seen as a potential threat are initiatives to downsize, remove layers of managed cut costs, increase productivity or outsource. Individuals will tend to associate these with job losses and working harder for less money which have been the historical emphasis put on these approaches.

Using Other Sources of Data

There are other sources of information which are commonly available in most companies.

Systems and procedure manuals

In most companies we have come across, there are a number of folders on every manager's bookshelf which constitute the systems and procedure manuals. These are invariably unused, the dust being cleaned off before every internal audit check. Our experience suggests that procedure manuals tell us what should happen, yet rarely tell us what actually happens. It is best to give them a wide berth unless completely stuck or if there is unquestionable evidence that they are followed to the letter.

Computer systems

Many companies have sophisticated computer systems which record various facts about the business. There is a saying in the computer industry: 'Garbage in, garbage out.' This is usually exactly what happens. Data inaccuracy is rife. When using data from a computer system it is vital to check what it actually represents. Go to where the data is collected and inputted and ask the people who collect and input the data what the information is, how it is collected, and how it is interpreted. It is also wise to check on the accuracy of the data by checking it against reality. Some systems are so poorly designed that the only way to make them work is to take short cuts. Building up an understanding of the process needs to include these short cuts as they are the functional parts of it.

SOLUTION GENERATION WORKSHOPS

When any project enters the solution generation phase of a project, we have found that using workshops is an appropriate and effective approach. The use of a multi-functional team spanning the entirety of the process under analysis allows for an open forum for potential solutions between the people that will actually be involved in the 'new process', directly or otherwise. The shared vision of the team coupled with their common understanding of the process analysis enables an agreed solution or solutions to be developed. This ensures that an effective result is achieved, that is, a company-wide solution as opposed to local departmental quick fixes.

The method of solution generation may well differ depending on the nature of the project at hand. With a large company-wide process, the output may be a number of small projects requiring their own diagnostic and solution generation stages. With a small-scale project, addressing a support process for instance, the output will probably be a new and improved process ready for implementation. Clearly this is not always the case. The main point here is that there is no one prescribed generic outcome. Any change project will possess its own dynamic mix of attributes, culture and people and therefore will procure a different outcome.

When generating solutions in a workshop environment, one approach is to split the group into say three teams of three or four people, provide them all with the same process information, that is, TBPMs, data and so on, and give them different tools to design the solutions. Quite often the solutions are self-explanatory as a result of the diagnosis, however it can prove useful from a creativity standpoint to exercise different techniques. Some tools by de Bono for creative and lateral thinking are quite useful here, such as Creative Challenge, Po and Simple Focus.[1]

More commonly used techniques are brainstorming and the clean sheet approach, where the process analysis is used to highlight current process inefficiencies. A key point here is that solution generation is strongly aimed at providing new processes that have tackled the real root causes to the inefficiencies found in the process, not simply addressing the symptomatic problems. The output from the different teams can then be discussed and rationalized into the best solution for the process under analysis.

In this project team environment the use of a facilitator is highly recommended to guide the team's efforts and to prevent them from straying away from the objectives they have set themselves. Using a facilitator in a workshop environment is also useful particularly for harnessing and catalysing people's enthusiasm and focus, almost to the extent of exciting them about the potential output of their work. Hence, when they have the opportunity to present their work to their peers and superiors, they speak not only from a foundation of knowledge and rigour, but also from one of passion and belief in the task they have been set.

The importance of using a team to generate solutions is absolutely paramount, not only to ensure that an effective and global solution is produced but also for ease of implementation. If a team of people have been involved in solution generation, that is, the output is literally their work, it is highly likely that they will have more ownership of and more commitment to the successful implementation of their ideas.

A good example of this is the project work carried out by Fairey Hydraulics on their goods-inward process. At the start there was clearly some cynicism about the likelihood of achieving anything substantial. Having gone through the processes of having a shared vision and objectives and Time-Based Process Mapping, the group became more comfortable with their task and particularly more motivated about their expectations. A great deal of this was down to their shared and common understanding of what the process actually delivered and how, and what the process needed to deliver. Getting to the 'how' in this scenario became straightforward with the information they had at their disposal as a result of extensive data-gathering. There was a definitive mood shift to one of enthusiasm and energy. This was accompanied by the project team taking clear ownership of their work. Upon completion of the project, the team still met regularly to discuss further opportunities for improvement and have essentially become a self-managed continuous improvement team.

PROVIDING TRAINING AND EDUCATION

How many times have you gone on a training course and then could not remember the material when you actually found a use for it? If the answer is quite often, then perhaps you question the value of that training. Training is a vital activity, but its timing is critical and this is often ignored. The best time to train someone is when they realize that they need a skill. They are committed to the training, and will reinforce it through use immediately, thereby internalizing it. This also means that the training is not wasted as it is used on a particular problem immediately, with a resulting payback.

The role of education is slightly different. Training is learning how to do something specific. Education is learning about what is and what might be done. It is about raising an awareness of issues, what is known about them and what can be done about them. It may point someone in the right direction, but it will usually not result in action on its own. Action needs to be catalysed by bringing the theory and the practical world together. This may be through specific training or through coaching on specific projects towards business objectives. In our Masters degree courses at the Warwick Manufacturing Group we encourage the students who are managers with our partner companies to apply what they have learnt to their work environments in the assignments following each modular course. This is facilitated by a close partnership between ourselves and the companies with which we work. The courses are tailored to the strategic needs of our partner companies, in particular their need to develop future leaders of change within their businesses.

Coaching

Just because someone has been on a course to learn to do something does not mean that they can do it immediately and perfectly. The role of coaching is to provide continuous improvement in the use of those skills. They provide not only feedback, but also the encouragement and support needed to build the trainees' confidence in using their new skill. The best coaches arrive from all aspects of the business. They may be experienced managers. They may be consultants or staff specialists. They may be master craftsmen who have perfected the skill of doing something. These people are the keepers of an organization's learning and are key to propagating their skills throughout the organization.

SETTING PERFORMANCE MEASURES

The method by which performance measures are derived has a direct bearing on the approach to Time Compression projects. They will affect the method of diagnosing the problem, understanding the need for change, and the absolute time-scale of the project. The method by which the measures are generated will also vary as will the approach to gaining buy-in and the resource and speed of implementation. Our research indicates that the use of performance measures is typically ill-defined during the evolution of a project, and tends to fulfil only a subsidiary element among many influencing the advancement of a project. Clearly, there is a strong need to strengthen the method by which measures are utilized as a means of determining the required and actual level of performance.

There is general agreement that all measures utilized must be simple yet effective and must be applicable to the level/division of organization at which they are pitched. The most effective measures in all cases proved to be non-finance-related. The advantage of time is the relative ease by which it can be measured. Management can easily focus upon lead-time, cycle time, time to market, and so on. When time-based measures such as these are integrated into the diagnostics and process maps showing the material and information flows, an extremely strong analytical picture of the business is provided.

As the project progresses, it is possible to begin to quantify the performance improvement the project is positioned to address, allowing determination of whether the current measures are befitting to the project or whether additional/complementary measures have to be administered. Ordinarily, buy-in has to be gained at various points in the project, therefore great attention has to be paid to determining the applicability of measures to the project in hand, that is, the measures are used to bring about real change within the organization, not just to monitor the effects on performance for academic curiosity.

When attempting to analyse project performance, conventional financial-based measures make it difficult to understand whether all the performance improvement (or otherwise) is attributable to the Time Compression project. Some of the companies we have worked with had a multitude of other improvement initiatives in progress. Once again time-based measurement provides the right mechanism to link cause and effect.

Although there really is no fixed set of time-based performance measures which managers should use to gauge business performance, many of the time-related measures we have commonly encountered include: lead-time, inventory, value-adding-time, responsiveness, flexibility, service parameters, delivery, stock turns, stock to sales ratio, set-up times, product profile, arrears/shortages, capacity utilization, supplier performance, WIP, batch sizes, downtime, quality, absenteeism.

COST–BENEFIT ANALYSIS OF SOLUTIONS

In some of the companies we have worked in, financial procedures require that projects are justified in cost–benefit terms. Whilst time-based measures provide a better guide to the benefits of the different opportunities, we accept that the effect on bottom-line profit is vital and needs to be quantified. As Time Compression projects target the non-value-adding spaces between operations, the solutions involved tend to be inexpensive. Many of the benefits are very difficult to quantify in financial terms as they are highly dependent upon the response of customers to the strategic benefits provided. There are some effects of Time Compression which can be quantified in monetary terms more easily and which will often show a strong investment case without relying on the more ambiguous figures. These are as follows:

- A reduction in production lead-time will reduce the amount of work in progress proportionally. It will also reduce the dependency on finished goods inventory. Since inventory absorbs working capital, the working capital has to be paid for in the form of interest. Reducing inventory reduces working capital, freeing the cash for other uses, and reduces interest charges.
- Reduced lead-time to the customer results in less forecasting risk which results in less likelihood of obsolete stock. The scrapping cost of the obsolete stock eradicated can be claimed as a potential saving.
- If forecasting can be removed entirely by making to order, then the administrative costs of the forecasting operation can be claimed.
- The removal of non-value-adding activities in any business process will result in productivity increases which may be realizable by increased throughput or by transferring staff to other opportunities.

- Quality improvements related to faster cycle times can be estimated.
- There may be an enormous cost penalty in lost sales for missing the beginning of a market window for a new product. This can be quantified from past experience.[3]
- Reducing product development lead-time decreases the risk of the product not meeting the market needs with consequent sales penalties and associated costs. This can be quantified from past experience.

And on to Action

In the last four chapters we have covered the issues surrounding changing an organization through Time Compression. Taking account of the factors we have raised will help to speed up the process of successfully implementing Time Compression. The next chapter of this book contains a self-help guide which will help you to take the first step to implementing Time Compression in your business by gaining the commitment and shared understanding available from the diagnostic process.

Suggested Reading

W. C. Byham and J. Cox, *Zapp!, The Lightning of Empowerment* (London, Century Business, 1991).
P. M. Senge, *The Fifth Discipline Fieldbook – Strategies and Tools for Building a Learning Organisation* (London, Nicholas Brealy, 1996).

CASE STUDY – FAIREY HYDRAULICS

The Company

Fairey Hydraulics Limited represents the aerospace and defence interests of Fairey Group plc. The Fairey Group comprises a number of specialist manufacturing companies operating in four sectors: electronics, electrical power, aerospace and defence, and filtration and specialist ceramics. Fairey Hydraulics Limited was formed in 1954 as a subsidiary of the now defunct Fairey Aviation Company to concentrate on the development and manufacture of aircraft hydraulic powered flying controls and systems. Fairey Hydraulics Limited (FHL) is now located in the Bristol area of the UK and produced sales of £27 million in 1996. Business areas now include aircraft flight controls, hydraulic systems and landing gear, guided weapon activation systems, and subsea and sail track control equipment.

The company has developed high quality, traditional manufacturing operation, making most of the critical components such as those for its electro-hydraulic actuation systems, in-house.

The Strategic Drivers

The aerospace industry world-wide is facing increasingly competitive pressures brought about not least by a reduction in demand. As a result, increasing cost effectiveness is a high priority both in the design and manufacturing cycles. All the world's major aircraft manufacturers have programmes aimed at reducing manufacturing lead-times, which are placing increasing demands on their supplier networks to work more efficiently. For those companies also active in the defence field the pressures associated with the changing nature of the market have further increased such competitive demands. Consequently many companies in the defence sector are examining new market areas where their expertise can be further exploited.

The Programme of Change

Our initial Time Based Process Map indicated that the rate at which value was being added during FHL's manufacturing processes was low, being much in line with the industry average of approximately five per cent. This meant that the manufacturing lead-time of products such as the Tornado tail-plane actuator was in the region of 180 days. Fairey's strategic plan has identified a continuous improvement plan which would be a major tool in improving competitiveness. A major aspect of this plan is the compression of lead-times involving all areas of the business.

It was recognized that no single project could hope to address all the areas which have an influence on product lead-time (see Figure 9.1). Hence the Time Compression project was split into a number of distinct but inter-related projects which had the common strategic target of reducing lead-time, as well as more local and immediately achievable objectives. Initial investigation suggested that using time as the underlying driver for improvement would not only develop a more responsive base for production control but would also provide a filter during the analysis of the process. Thus, the factors most critical to improvement, that is those which could remove non-value adding time in the process, could be identified.

The objective of the investigation was to review the factors affecting the flexibility and manufacturing effectiveness of the machine shop, pilot a range of measures aimed at reducing the manufacturing lead-time and develop working practices to allow for continuous improvement in the manufacturing facility. For the purpose of the pilot, it was recommended that two of the key machining centres be used for analysis.

A multi-functional team that spanned the processes in question was set-up to address these objectives. Three key areas were addressed within the project team:

- Lead-time reduction
- Set-up reduction
- Tool management

Three sub-teams were used to tackle these issues.

Lead-time Reduction Project
The lead-time reduction team looked at the overall machining process for opportunities for Time Compression, in particular they looked at;

- Time-Based Process Mapping
- Capacity Modelling
- Working Procedures
- Economic Batch Quantity Model
- Cellular Manufacturing

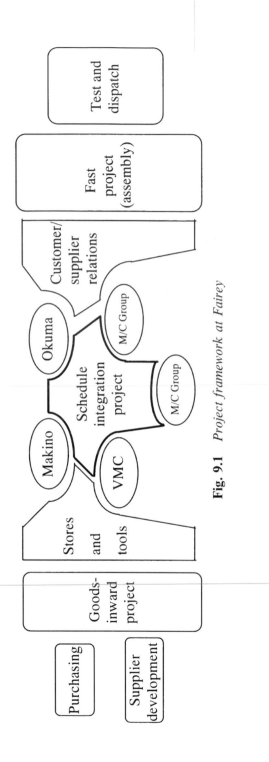

Fig. 9.1 *Project framework at Fairey*

Time-Based Process Mapping was identified as the tool to be used for process diagnostic and analysis work. It was decided that the best approach would be to train key employees in Time Based Process Mapping to allow the application of the tool within FHL. This was done in a workshop with a follow-on session to ensure that the tool had been successfully transferred to the employees. This approach proved to be extremely effective.

Time Based Process Mapping identified the factors which contributed to the long lead-times of machining operations in the company. The maps were used as a basis for highlighting the queues between operations and schedule adherence. A key factor in the long lead-time was the batch sizes being worked by the machines. Large batch sizes result in large cycle times, which occupy the machine beyond an optimum level.

A capacity model was generated using batch size and set-up/cycle time information from the firm's business system. However, the set-up time was not in fact representative of the true machine down time as they included preset hours as well as set-up hours, and as such the capacity plan showed machines to be artificially overloaded. It was suggested that a separate operation be created containing only preset hours for CNC machining, removing these hours from the set-up time and hence showing capacity in its true state.

As soon as the Bill of Routing (BOR) is created, the company business system assumed that the component is suitable for manufacture and once a demand was placed, work orders were raised. If the part was a low level part on the Bill of Material (BOM), and could therefore have a long cumulative lead-time, it would then jump straight to the top of the work-to-list. However, due to a lack of associated manufacturing information (programs, layouts, tolling, etc.) manufacture was unable to begin.

Although this was a clear opportunity for improvement it provided manufacturing with a security buffer for ordering raw materials and creating an effective capacity plan. Hence, it was suggested that the time delay between BOR entry and creation of manufacturing support information be reduced as much as possible.

Set-up Reduction Project

The set-up reduction team concentrated purely on generating ideas to reduce set-up time. A few of these ideas are briefly described here. A high percentage of time taken to set the lathes was due to tool changeover. The use of a magazine of preset tooling reduced this problem. It was suggested that the use and availability of standard gauges at machine side would be a significant saving. During tool validation, first off and setting, time was consumed in the essential task of monitoring tools through the cycle. The time was increased due to the inability to see the tools during cutting because of coolant and swarf spray causing severe abrasions on the viewing window. Spin windows, basically a spinning glass disk, were mounted into the viewing window providing a clear view of the cutting tools, thus reducing the time taken and more importantly, increasing the safety in producing a first off.

Tool Management Project

The tool management team concentrated on understanding problems with current tool management. Some key issues emerged relating to tool rationalization, redundant and sub-contract tooling. There was also reference to tool pre-kitting planning and the feasibility of a formal tool management system. It became evident that this was proving to be an extensive task in itself and the team felt they were going beyond their original remit. It was decided that an investigation into tool management needed to be carried out in its own right, and it was recommended that a team be set up to do so. The team identified the following as being the basis for the lead-time reduction exercise.

- Set-up reduction
- Information and tool marshalling
- Factors forcing large batches

Pilot Implementation

The work of the three teams and other associated activities were collated and co-ordinated into a pilot implementation of the lead-time reduction exercise. The key areas addressed in the implementation were:

- Reduction in batch size
- Work availability list and local scheduling
- Tool and gauge marshalling
- Part programmes and down load offsets
- Additional tool holders

In arriving at solutions the team developed a communication style and working practices which not only supported the machining functions but provided the ability to produce local cutting schedules at the machine group. This not only met production requirements but allowed the machine technicians to optimize machine performance during component changeover.

It was also observed that there was an increase in communication via cross-company, multi-functional teams. This resulted in a greater understanding of the systems involved in manufacturing by more people who are in fact part of the overall process. Performance improved as a result of the project work. There was an increase in the level of unmanned running, the lead-time through the machinery group has reduced and the variance to standard improved. Machine flexibility has improved. Quantities can now be cut that are required for immediate demand rather than cutting for immediate plus future demand and storing the excess.

Results

Trials on one machine group gave:

- Reduction in batch size of 40 per cent
- Reduction in lead-time through machine group of 50 per cent
- Increased flexibility allowed the machine group to deal with 40 per cent more parts
- Increase in performance of 10 per cent

The issues and opportunities raised by these projects resulted in the identification of further Time Compression projects. The first of these were:

- Time to receive material
- Fast track tooling

Time to Receive Material
This project addressed FHL's internal processes that receive goods and make them available for internal customers, for example, production.

The main objective of this project was to reduce the current lead-time of 14 days by 75 per cent. Analysis was undertaken using techniques including Time-Based Process Mapping and brainstorming. This resulted in the identification of several key issues:

- A lack of the right information in the right format when needed
- Poor accessibility to information needed to carry out key elements of the process
- Poor quality information
- Unnecessary administrative activities
- Poor visibility of components within Goods-in
- Goods-in security

These were addressed by the project team to overcome the process and people related issues that incur such an excessive lead-time. The interdepartmental communication and involvement needed to deliver this objective resulted in people across departments understanding the information requirements of the internal supply chain and operating with the minimum amount of paper possible.

Feedback in the form of personal contact and performance measures became a key feature between goods-in, purchasing and production. This enabled the monitoring necessary to assist in continuous improvement after implementation of the new process.

The process lead-time was initially reduced by 50 per cent and then further reduced to four days, significantly better than the original target of 14 days. Other deliverables included less firefighting as a result of prioritized activities from production which were generated by slack lead-times and unresponsiveness.

Fast Track Tooling
The pilot study showed that tool management was a major issue. The Fast Track Tooling project was launched to address the problems related to the excessive lead-times for the internal process that triggered tool order. Using a multi-functional team, the project analysis highlighted four key problems for improvement:

- Extended internal and external procurement lead-times (up to 180 days)
- Excessive tool inventory – value approx. £4.6 million
- Ineffective use of resources
- Ineffective tool management

Through intensive analysis of the system and studying potential solutions, it became apparent that to fully resolve all of the associated problems, a phased approach would be necessary. Therefore the team concluded that the separate phases of implementation identified would each be designed to capitalise on the available resources, budgets and technology, with each phase initiated at the most appropriate time.

The team identified a number of solutions and recommendations which over a project implementation life of 24 months would place the company in a more responsive position. This would allow a number of objectives to be achieved in the FHL Continuous Improvement Plan. Initially, a number of short term actions were suggested that incurred low capital expenditure and resource input, but enabled savings and improvements to be made. These included:

- Initiate supplier partnerships for consumable and durable tool supplies
- Establish single point of contact for procurement approval
- Tool procurement documentation simplification
- Tool rationalization
- Prepare core data for Tool Management element of the replacement business system
- Prepare specification for the tool management element of the replacement business system

The ultimate aim identified by the team for a medium and long term solution was the implementation of a tool management system. As the current business system was due for replacement in 1997, it was approved that a tool management system would be an element of the new business system. Listed below are the major performance measures achieved and planned through the implementation of the project team's recommendations:

- Internal tool procurement non-value added lead-time reduced by 90 per cent
- Reduction in lead-time of perishable tools by 80 per cent
- Cost savings in tool procurement administration of £30 k per annum
- Tooling expenditure reduced by 20 per cent
- Improved product schedule adherence
- Wider use of standard tooling through rationalization
- Introduction of supply chain relationships

Learning Points

- The provision of a common, well communicated and committed top management goal, allows team members to pursue milestones by feeding off the technical knowledge and skills associated with the performance objective
- It can take time for project team members to overcome their initial fears and scepticism, but this can vary depending on the level of familiarity between the people concerned
- The acceptance of change can be accelerated through the use of a facilitator in the project team
- Teams can outperform individuals acting alone or in larger organization groups, especially when their performance requires multiple skills, judgements, analysis and process experienced
- It is important to keep projects small and manageable and to avoid creep in their scope

10 How to Get Started

One of the most troublesome aspects of time-compressing a business process is where exactly to begin. Within any business there never appears to be a static period which permits a clear and directed assault on initiating diagnostics. In this chapter we will show how to use the tool of Time-Based Process Mapping (TBPM)[1] as a means of getting a project moving in the right direction.

The tool was developed by the Time Compression Programme in response to our need to represent the consumption of time in a clear and visually powerful form. Since its inception TBPM has proved to be extremely useful in the Time Compression work we have performed. Thus we advocate its use in your organization. This chapter contains a description of how to use the tool based upon the TCP change model and is supported by the case study of H&R Johnson Tiles Ltd, a Norcros Company. It was our involvement with this ceramic tile manufacturer which advanced the development of Time-Based Process Mapping.[2]

It must be noted that the description of TBPM here has generally been concerned with the value-adding process in dealing with physical artefacts such as products. In the case of mapping information this can be treated in a similar way to a product. For example, pieces of paper passed around an organization with the changes of information upon them relate to value-adding activity. Queuing and inventory are represented by the piles of paper on desks or in in-trays. Electronic transfer could be looked at in terms of the availability of information, thus the frequency of file updates and transfer are factors for consideration.

TBPM is designed to:

- Display the business process in a simple form that represents how it operates in reality
- Display (often uniquely) specific features relating to the business process
- Provide a simple means of understanding what to change
- Provide enough momentum to induce change and overcome any constraints

CREATING A VISION AND TARGETS

The first stage of a Time-Based Process Mapping exercise is to establish the broad strategic view behind the need to change. From this the company strategy, business processes critical to that strategy and a suitable vision and approach for change can be identified. This type of information can be collected from objective interviews with key managers.

PROBLEM DEFINITION AND PRIORITIZATION

This initial stage of the diagnostic process should have identified the critical business processes to be looked at and key customer groups, market segments or products for priority attention. This is the first stage in defining the scope of a Time-Based Process Map.

The scope of the Time-Based Process Mapping must ultimately reach the level where practical action can be taken on the issues that present the best opportunities for performance improvement. It must reach that point as quickly as possible to avoid 'paralysis by analysis'. We have found that the best approach is to carry out Time-Based Process Mapping with increasing focus of scope and increasing levels of detail. This ensures that a holistic approach to process improvement is taken, whilst ensuring that opportunities are identified and exploited quickly. The procedure behind Time-Based Process Mapping is explained. As the scope of analysis decreases, the time units decrease proportionally from months to weeks to days and in turn the level of detail increases. At a high level you might look at how long a product spends in a given factory. For example, as the level of detail increases you may look at how long it spends in a department at the worst performing company, then at a particular machine in the worst performing department. At each level of scope it is important to understand how much detail you require. Collecting too much will result in 'paralysis by analysis', too little will not identify the key issues.

THE TBPM PROCESS

The initial stage of constructing a time-based process map is to identify the core processes that the product goes through during its creation and transfer to the customer, an example illustrated in

Figure 10.1. A core process is defined as a set of related activities that directly add end user value to a product. These are particularly those processes on or close to the critical path of the supply chain. The non-core or support activities should also be considered in order to understand the effects they have on the use of resources and hence their contribution to situations such as 'project overload'.

Having identified the core processes the ownership of the activities within the process needs to be analysed (see Figure 10.2). This is important for two reasons. First, it acts as a reference point as to who or what controls the process, which proves important in order to obtain accurate information. Second, some clues for generating and implementing a solution may lie within the ownership issue, particularly where process linkages, overlaps and trade-offs may be involved.

Non-core processes relate to value-adding activities that the customer does not directly care about and which can be performed at any time. Examples of the types of core process we often find in the

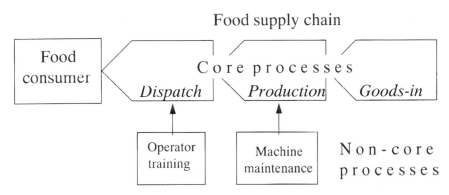

Fig. 10.1 *Identifying core processes*

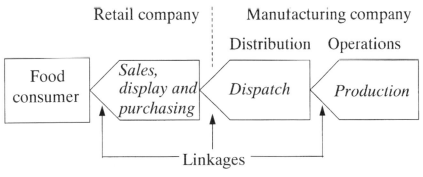

Fig. 10.2 *Relating process ownership*

Time-scale in days

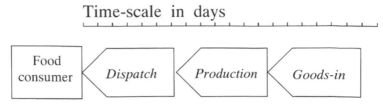

Fig. 10.3   *Aligning core processes to time*

supply chain and new product processes are shown in Figures 2.2 and 2.4 as we described in Chapter 2.

The next stage is to identify the average times for an item of product or information to move through each of the core processes (Figure 10.3). It is important to choose an appropriate unit of time for the scale of the processes being mapped. In the case of H&R Johnson most of the core and non-core processes that people raised at the level of detail mapped fitted into the context of daily units of time. However for more detailed mapping, at say the factory floor level, units of hours or even minutes would be appropriate.

To aid the task of linking the processes together, dependencies are identified that relate to both the physical and information inputs and outputs for each process. This is a form of input/output analysis approach, whereby the interviewee is asked what information and physical material is required at the start of the process and what appears at the end of the process. This simple but rigorous approach ensures that all the relevant linkages are identified without too much preoccupation on how the transformation within the process operates. The latter is usually a favoured subject of most interviewees and can sometimes distract the conversation away from the actual information needed to perform the mapping. If however the process owner wants to get an issue 'off their chest' it is often helpful to the interview process to lend a sympathetic ear and record the facts or the perceived problem. This information is often of use at a later stage in the diagnostic process.

COLLECTING INFORMATION

Time-based information might be found in the form of lead-times quoted by different departments, however this information may require validation to ensure that it reflects what actually happens. Our experience suggests that the best way to find out about a business process in the context of time is to ask the person you are interviewing to walk through exactly what happens to a product whilst in their area of control. The stages that the product goes through are not just those where value is added, but also where the product is waiting for something to be done. Consideration should also be given to whether the paperwork holds up a product and is actually needed. The interviewee should be asked how long, in their experience, each stage takes. It is useful to use a typical product related to a generic customer which avoids the reply 'it depends'. In the new product process it is often appropriate to ask the interviewee to give examples of the best case, worst case, typical case and time when the managing director was beating the door down for a particular type of new product. The latter of these cases gives something approximating to the value-adding time in the absence of carefully recorded data.

DRAWING A TBPM

Having understood and obtained the three critical pieces of information we are ready to proceed with drawing a basic gantt chart which forms the foundation of the TBPM.

The process map should ideally start at the point of end user demand or as close as possible to the point of final consumption for which data are available. This is based on the assumption that all interconnecting processes must stem from here. The importance of this point to a company has led us to position it in the top left-hand corner of the TBPM, unlike the convention for a project plan where it would be at the bottom right-hand corner. This starting position forms a good point of control and focus, even if the industry being described is more of a 'supply push' than 'demand pull' environment. This start point also makes the map diagrammatically easier to construct because the structure of the business process expands from this single reference point by cascading down, backwards in time, along a path of interdependent processes that are required to take place to satisfy the demand. A TBPM can be built following the steps below:

1. Identify and extract the relevant data and information from interview notes and/or questionnaire.
2. Sketch a flow diagram of some of the detail so that the linkages and dependencies can be clarified before constructing the TBPM.

3. Using the above flow diagram and the detailed time informa-
    tion, determine approximately how much lapsed time the total
    business process consumes from beginning to end. At this stage
    ignore the parallel (multi-dependent) and supporting process
    linkages.
4. Plot the scales of the TBPM as shown in Figure 10.4. The total
    lapse time (from point 3) will determine the time unit values, for
    example days or weeks, and the range, for example, 0 to 17 days.
    List the sequence of business processes, starting with the generic
    customer. At this stage it may be helpful to leave gaps for the
    stock that exists between the linkages.
5. Draw in the process bars by representing their duration measured
    against the time-scale. Ideally these should be average times,
    however if maximum and minimum times are potential key
    issues, then this can also be incorporated in the TBPM in two
    ways. Either draw a TBPM for each scenario or incorporate all
    scenarios on one map with a sliding bar feature illustrated in
    Figure 10.5.

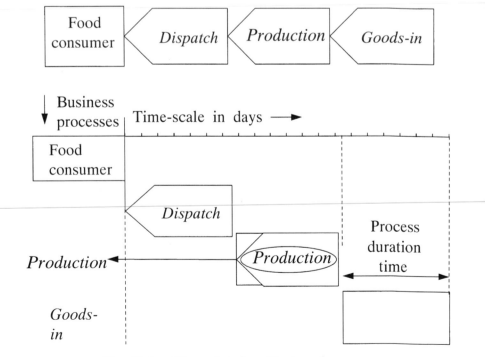

Fig. 10.4   *Time-related positioning of processes*

6. Link the sequential processes together and split off the parallel multiple dependant activities into separate process legs, as shown in Figure 10.6.

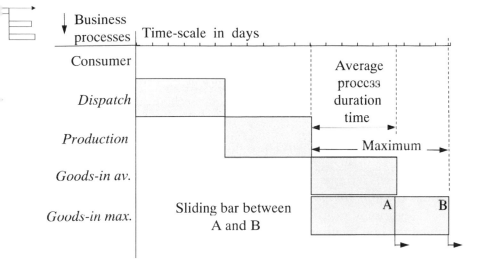

Fig. 10.5 *Adding process bars*

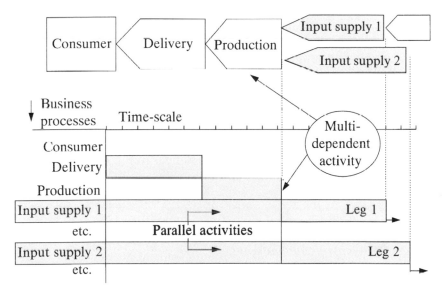

Fig. 10.6 *Sequential processes and dependencies*

Value-Adding and Non-Value-Adding Time

In Chapter 3 we explained the importance of value-adding and non-value-adding time to Time Compression. These can be shown on a TBPM. Value-adding processes are defined by the following criteria:

- The process, or elements of the process, is physically changing the nature of the consumable item (that is, the customer's product)
- The change above produces something that the customer values or cares about and may be willing to pay for
- The process is right first time and will not have to be repeated in order to produce the desired result that is valued by the customer

Going through a list of the core and non-core processes and applying these criteria to them will show which activities add value and which do not and will require further analysis to split them into different categories (Figure 10.7).[3]

The categories of non-value-adding time we discussed in Chapter 3 are queuing time, waiting time, decision making time, and rework time.

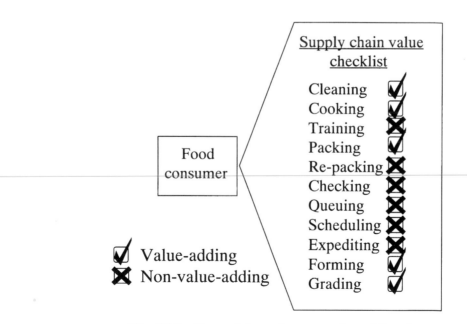

Fig. 10.7 *Determining value–non-value-adding time*

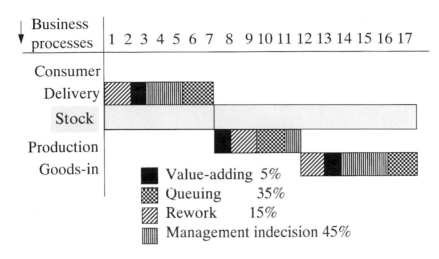

Fig. 10.8 *Defining value–non-value-adding segments*

The accuracy of the time consumed within each category can be difficult to define, however the fact that non-value-adding time usually accounts for around 95 per cent of the total time means that this should not be an overly vital issue. There is usually ample opportunity for change before accuracy at the boundaries of these definitions becomes a problem. Value-adding analysis can be applied to non-core, for example, support activity, processes.

Segment the process bars into the value-adding and non-value-adding categories detailed above. Classify and quantify these categories against the time-scale, as per Figure 10.8.

Value-Adding Time Analysis

The identification of value and non-value-adding time is one of the most powerful features to analyse. To do this you need to first evaluate the total time consumed by all of the core processes. This must include the parallel core processes as well as the critical path (time to customer) process times. This is achieved by totalling the value-adding time of all of the processes and expressing them as a percentage of the total time consumed. The percentage information as shown in Figure 10.8 as a 'label' is supported by a related graphical representation.

Coping with Stock

Having constructed the basic map we have a framework that can be used to position features that are of relevance to understand a specific business process context. In the H&R Johnson situation many of the processes were either supplied, or fed by a stock holding point. Certainly within the supply chain context stock is an important feature that needs to be recognized and understood in the 'as is' business process situation. The type of stock that was being referred to within H&R Johnson was stock held as a result of a deliberate inventory policy as distinct from work-in-progress stock. Stock of this type should theoretically obey rules that are consistent with the stock time curve (see Figure 10.9).[1]

The stock time curve describes the level of stock required for any particular stock keeping unit (SKU). The desired stock level equates to two elements, cycle and buffer stock. The cycle stock is the level of stock that is required to cover the average rate of consumption during the order replenishment time. Therefore cycle or lead-time stock is directly relational to order lead-times and therefore the process times associated with the lead-times.

Buffer stock is the level of inventory required to cope with any variance of demand and supply. For example, if demand is known to occasionally exceed a known average, a desired level of buffer is held to cover this variance. The size of the buffer is determined from historical demand and supply profiles which help to establish the

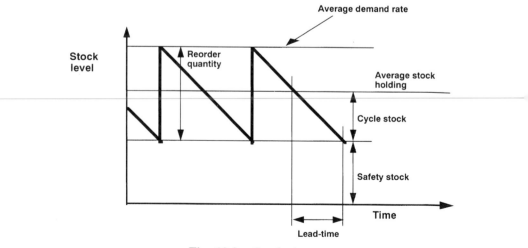

Fig. 10.9 *Stock time curve*

statistical relationship between stock levels and the probability of going out of stock. This probability relates to the well recognised concept of service levels, which can be set by inventory policy if the information is accurate and kept up to date.[2] Service levels are also directly related to time because the longer the lead-time, the greater the amount of stock required to cover for a defined level of service in statistical terms. Consequently the longer the supply lead-times, there is disproportionately a greater amount of stock required at any given point. Therefore, if a 'make to stock' policy is required, the reduction of process times can reduce the level of stock required.

Stocking points that contain buffer and cycle stock under the control of an inventory policy, or at the very least by management intention to hold stock, can be represented as stock bars on a TBPM. These bars are illustrated in Figure 10.10 and are usually positioned between processes that feed the stock in and the processes that remove the stock from the storage location.

The length of the bar represents the number of time units of stock cover found on average at a particular point in the processes. This level of cover is a function of the rate of consumption of the forward processes, for example sales turnover or machining rates.

The positioning of the right-hand edge of the bar is in line with the process order point which initiates and enables the replenishment of the inventory. The left-hand edge of the stock bar may sometimes run over the left-hand edge of the TBPM because of scaling and the length of certain bars. The number of days' stock cover denoted in

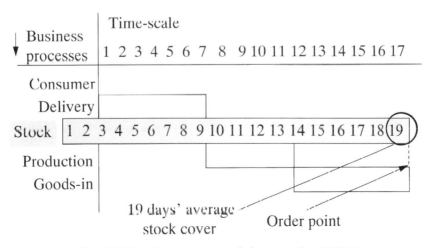

Fig. 10.10 *Positioning stock bars on the TBPM*

the stock bar will illustrate how much stock lies off to the left of the TBPM, for example three days. This is useful because if it is not possible to represent stock to the left of the 'Y' axis then the numbers would denote the existence and magnitude of the stock holding to the left.

Cycle and buffer stock can therefore be examined with respect to the TBPM as demonstrated in Figure 10.11. The length of the stock bar that lies to the right of the critical path lines represents the number of days' stock required to cover the replenishment period. This is commonly known as the cycle stock requirement.

The lead-time that the end user receives can be read off against the TBPM's scale. There are two possible scenarios. One is where 'customer lead-time' is the time a customer has to wait for his product to be delivered from stock. The second scenario is if the item is not stocked in the chain or is a 'make to order' or 'JIT' item. In this case the 'customer lead-time' is the time taken to make the product from raw material, that is, the 'time to customer' of the entire supply chain (Figure 10.12). Therefore the time consumed by the processes and the value of stock can both be challenged.

Best-case and worst-case information can be used to determine the effect of process time variability in relation to the total process lead-time. This may be an important feature to analyse for each respective horizontal channel.

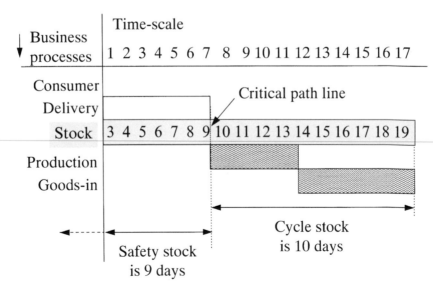

Fig. 10.11 *Examining cycle and buffer stocks*

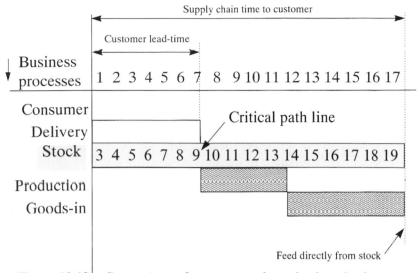

Figure 10.12 *Comparison of customer and supply chain lead-times*

Drawing a TBPM on a PC

We often find that the managers we work with wish to use a PC to draw TBPMs so that they can be updated easily. One way we have found to do this is by using a spreadsheet such as Microsoft Excel or Lotus 123. The value-adding and non-value-adding times can be tabulated against the different activities required on the TBPM. An additional column is inserted between the activities and the first of these values. This is used to calculate the starting point of each bar relative to the axis. It is the sum of the values in the row above, including the value of the starting point. These values can be plotted on a horizontal bar chart graph. The colour of the bar that represents the starting point is altered to 'none' to make that bar invisible, thereby creating a TBPM. In the event of parallel activities the value of the starting point is changed.

TIME-BASED PROCESS MAPPING AT H&R JOHNSON

Having established how a basic TBPM with stock bars can be put together and analysed we can now demonstrate its application.

H&R Johnson Tiles Ltd. has a turnover of around £60 million selling 5200 varieties of floor and wall tiles to 1000 customers in the

UK and abroad. Although the company is still the UK's largest supplier of ceramic tiles, its UK market share has fallen from a peak of 80 per cent to around 20–30 per cent in 1996. This shift is largely due to less expensive foreign imports entering the UK market combined with the introduction of fashion-led designs that H&R Johnson had not been able to compete with. If the company was to retain its status within the UK market and to increase its sales abroad, it needed to address the competitiveness of its operations.

From the end customer perspective, the market is split between four key UK sectors: namely the contract tile fixer, the contract market, the independent retailer, and the multiple do-it-yourself (DIY) retailers. The majority of contract work is made to order, however the multiple DIY retail market was serviced, for historical reasons, through a network of wholesalers fed from a factory warehouse. The lead-time between Johnson's and the actual consumer was 11 days providing that the product was available from stock. Twelve weeks' stock was held between the consumer and the end of the production line, but service levels were running at 85 per cent order fill. To regain customer loyalty and market share Johnson's needed to address the service issues.

A number of other issues lay within the business. Multiple retailers were increasingly requesting 'quick response' daily stock replenishment at a time when the business only scheduled its manufacturing on a weekly basis. This meant that additional stock requirements had to be forecast and held in the warehouse to satisfy the retailer. The system of internal stock replenishment and scheduling was complicated by the fact that kiln firing was done on a 24-hour, seven-day-a-week basis against pre-fired tile production arrangements that only operated on a conventional five-day-week operation. The marshalling of pre-fired tiles was not on a 'first in first out' (FIFO) basis and this added a further complication to phasing and scheduling stock. All of these production constraints added to the stock replenishment complexity.

Batching rules and poor inventory control allowed semi-finished goods stocks to become disproportionately large compared with cycle and buffer stock requirements. Further down the supply chain long supplier lead-times, inappropriate inventory policies and poor reliability meant that substantial raw material stocks had to be held.

In summary, the company was over-stocked in many respects and therefore had high costs and lacked the responsiveness to tackle the customer service issues. The company, prior to the use of the time-based approach, had recognized these issues and had started to address the service issues. This was principally achieved by integrating many of the logistical functions under one director into an open plan room, thereby creating visibility of the customer service issues, aiding communication and enabling changes such as:

- Removing the credit clearance process from the critical path
- Compressing the time to obtain product availability information
- Utilizing express transport arrangements
- Purchasing linked to manufacturing schedules

Time-Based Analysis

The first TBPM undertaken at H&R Johnson was an overview of the entire supply chain. Figure 10.13 illustrates the TBPM for the total supply chain stretching from the commodity in the ground, clay, to the supply of a tile on the shelf of a retailer. The key features evident from this map are the total time to customer (seen as A + B in the diagram), 44 days from the ground to the retail shelf, and the large proportion of stock that exists throughout the chain.

Analysis of the time-based process map led to the realization of the extent of time consumed by the process and the associated volume of stock needed to support the operation. This state of affairs led to the identification of a number of projects based upon the information in the TBPM and the strategic priorities of the company. These included:

- **Time to supply** – looked at the finished goods stock within the supply chain
- **Time to schedule** – addressed the 14-day planning period (C + D on the TBPM) which was shown to be significant
- **Marshalling** – looked at the queuing time around the kiln operation

The 'Time to Supply' Project

This project examined the front end of the supply chain. From a strategic viewpoint, finished goods stock was no longer appropriate for a number of reasons, which became clear when they were

208

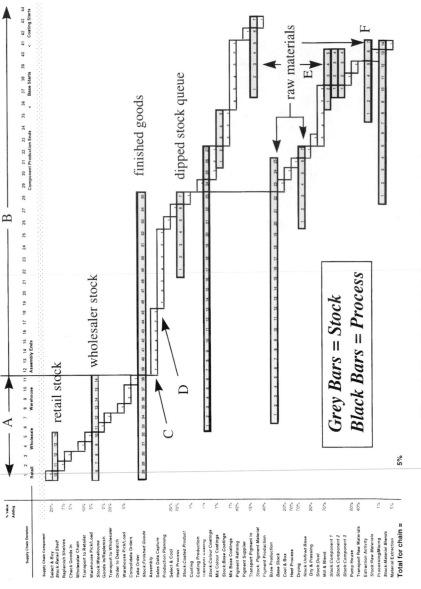

Fig. 10.13 *The H&R Johnson total supply chain*

examined against a framework of supply chain principles. The basis of the principle of the end user customer being served by logistically distinct channels did not favour the correct supply route. It was one of the weakest links in the channel in that it did not serve the interests of H&R Johnson.

It was clear from the TBPM that the wholesaler link in the chain added to the total 'system' process time which was made more critical by the fact that it directly related to customer lead-time, 11 days (see 'A' in Figure 10.13) with an average 28 days' stock held, 14 in retail and 14 in wholesale, at this end of the chain. The retailers were pressing to hold less stock and to be offered greater variety, consequently there was a compelling need to compress the time between the customer and the factory-finished goods stock. TBPM highlighted the implications of these issues and provided a visual focus for initiating change. Simulation had to be used to accurately predict the operational outcome of removing the wholesaler and generally compressing the customer lead-time. This was because the various operational options had to be tested before an implementation plan was agreed with warehouse operations, order management and distribution to enable a smooth transfer to direct customer supply.

The actual Time Compression was achieved by using a national express overnight delivery service between H&R Johnson and the retailer. However to enable this to take place a competence in customer order picking, as opposed to palletized bulk order dispatch, was developed. In the main this transformation required some attitudinal change in the workforce and the use of TBPM helped substantiate the case for the change with simulation demonstrating how multiple order picking and dispatch would operate. The result was the removal of 14 days' wholesaler stock from the end of the supply chain and Time Compression of seven days. From a competitive stand point this enabled the company to retain its most important market sector, the DIY multiples. This is a good example of customer channel focus through the use of restructuring company boundary positions to remove an echelon of the supply chain.

The 'Time to Schedule' Project

Moving further down the TBPM it is evident that two long process bars exist. These represented the sales data capture (C) and production planning process (D) times, each consuming seven days. This management practice, which represented weekly scheduling, operated well and was seen as a rational way of working. The TBPM immediately illustrated the fact that the 14-day planning period was a core process on the critical path consuming a disproportionate amount of time compared with the surrounding process times. For example, actual product assembly only took a matter of hours or even minutes. The other TBPM feature that compelled interest in this part of the process was the fact that the 14 days accounted for the majority of the product supply lead-time from manufacturing (see example in Figure 10.14). Therefore 14 days' cycle stock needed to be held plus any associated buffer required to support any uncertainty that existed in the system. If stocks were to be reduced and manufacturing flexibility enhanced, daily scheduling had to be considered. This would automatically compress the total process time to three days.

The issues surrounding the achievement of this objective were not simple to overcome. A bill of materials had to be comprehensively constructed and adhered to on a daily basis by the supplying processes further down the chain. Similarly, sales information had to be communicated from various segments of the business on a daily rather than a weekly basis. All of these requirements involved the use of new procedures, IT systems and new ways of managing manufacturing. None of the latter was difficult to achieve technically. The key issue was creating the right cultural environment by making the people responsible for downstream processes realise the need for change. The TBPM created the agenda for the change and was the

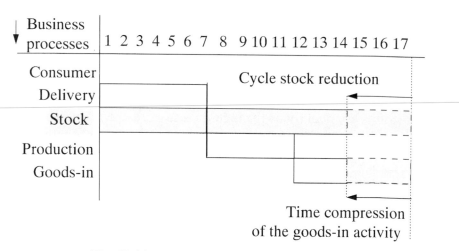

Fig. 10.14 *Equating lead-time to cycle stock*

vehicle for communicating the commercial imperatives using time as the measure. The cycle stock time and its associated inflexibility could be clearly linked with the process that needed Time Compression.

In this example the 'goods-in' process is the process that initiates the feed of stock to the main stock bar. The cycle stock will reduce as the process times within the replenishment period are compressed. Therefore if non-value-adding activity in the replenishment processes (for example goods-in operations) is removed, cycle stock can be reduced. The length of the stock bar that lies to the left of the critical path line is excess stock although it may be required in many situations because it acts as a buffer and a source of customer service. There is a direct statistical relationship between the time-based value of the cycle stock and the amount of safety stock that is required for given levels of service within the business process. Therefore if the replenishment processes are time-compressed less safety stock is also needed.

This project and the use of TBPM demonstrated two of the supply chain principles. The first was that of the need for trust between the internal functions within the company. The map created visibility and the implications of any possible change. The second principle is that of demand dynamics. TBPM is not able to formally deduce that dynamics exist, however the tool did demonstrate all of the conditions that drive dynamics, for example, multiple stock points and a planning and scheduling system that read and compensated for demand in batch and not real time mode. The symptoms of the Forrester Effect (see Chapter 4) were also present, such as large volumes of stock throughout the supply chain and poor customer service levels. The compression of the planning link would reduce any potential demand amplification and thereby enable inventory reductions and improve service levels.

A feature that is associated to the existence and level of dynamics also relates to product variety and associated component complexity. The structure of the supply chain in relation to product component levels relates to how demand for these components might affect different parts of the chain. This can be satisfactorily analysed using a TBPM. Bars can be labelled according to the complexity and variety levels that exist. Figure 10.15 illustrates a decision taken in production to commit the 20 components available into 100 product varieties for stock. A profile can be plotted of each value of variety and complexity, and how it changes with time as progress is made along the supply chain. This may raise a number of issues such as:

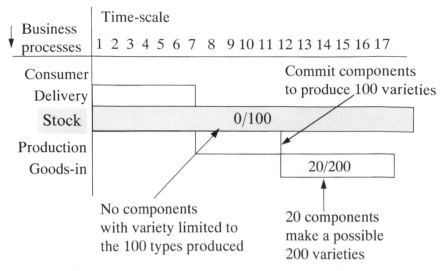

Fig. 10.15　*Product variety and complexity in TBPM*

- The ratio of component complexity to product variety
- The balance between complexity and the available variety for an acceptable customer lead-time
- The potential for outsourcing component sub-systems to reduce complexity

In order to facilitate daily scheduling, changes further down the supply chain were required. A detailed bill of materials had to be identified so that demand could be accurately scheduled along the supply chain on a daily basis using a centralized Materials Requirements planning (MRP) system. Organizational functions guarded material composition and process details as 'secrets' that outside functions would not understand and therefore should not be allowed to influence. The production of glaze was a so-called 'black art' and the exclusive domain of the 'potter' (a person who has a tradition of working in the potteries). The need for change was assisted in part by the time-based approach enabling the release of bill of material information, providing a means of constructively determining the feasibility of daily scheduling. For some of the glazes the production of small (less than a week's demand) batches were uneconomic because the size of the mixers required a certain volume of mix. This was made more critical by the fact that the glaze product had only a short useful lifespan and therefore could not be stored for long periods of time. A compromise was reached whereby a weekly glaze requirement was established and adjusted on a daily basis in line with agreed levels of inherent flexibility within the process and product composition. This was done by considering, where possible, late configuration to minimize wastage.

The Marshalling Project

The TBPM indicated that the volume of stock held in the queue due to the physical constraints of the marshalling layout was a problem. Single-track entry points forced a 'last in first out' (LIFO) stock rotation which made it very difficult to schedule and predict the availability of stock for customer orders. At first this particular problem was tackled using simulation which generated some sequencing planning rules, but later it was overcome by tackling the root cause of the problem as described below.

The dipped stock queue highlighted on the TBPM is due to a bottleneck caused by the ovens/firing process being out of phase with the dipping of tiles. The solution to this problem was implemented recently by the introduction of weekend shifts which have brought dipping capacity and sequencing into phase with firing. This demonstrates a time-based focus in the context of utilizing all of the time available which a TBPM must illustrate. The effects of non-operational time has to be incorporated into cycle times for stock calculations, therefore TBPM's need to map what is happening 24 hours a day, seven days a week irrespective of the actual hours worked.

Other H&R Johnson Projects

Some of the subsequent projects were in direct response to the application of the TBPM. The analysis of value-adding time using the TBPM showed itself to represent just 5 per cent of the total process time. This percentage was judged on the knowledge acquired from the interview process and, without detailed map decomposition, some aspects of this calculation are subjective. The percentage was, however, regarded as being representative by H&R Johnson's management and because the percentage was such a small proportion of total time, its accuracy was not an issue. Note that figure 10.13 is not shaded with the categories of value-adding time because at this level of detail it is difficult to estimate, and would have been visually complex to review. The estimated percentages for value-adding processes are placed down the left-hand side of the map aligned with the processes.

H&R Johnson's main board was presented with the TBPM, shown in Figure 10.13, during a project review meeting and this initiated action. An internal team was established to compress the non-value-adding time from 95 per cent to 70 per cent by analysing the queues, management indecision and rework. This analysis used cause-and-effect forms of diagnosis similar to that described in Chapter 11. One of the most notable outputs from this 'value time' analysis has been a focus on stocks (shown as E in the figure) in the lower levels of the supply chain. This is an example of where other parts of the business process have been organized to a synchronized 'drum beat', referred to by Goldratt,[3] thereby eliminating queues and stocks. This has been most notable in the biscuit area where biscuit production, the baked clay base of a tile, is now being linked to the main glaze dipping and firing production schedule. The production of biscuit and the glazing of tiles were previously controlled by two unrelated scheduling activities.

Further down the supply chain, Time Compression has been achieved together with the elimination of stock duplication through the use of mechanisms such as supplier development and EDI. This has been aided by sharing the TBPM with key suppliers. An obvious example of this was the identification of identical stocks on either side of two company boundaries (F in the figure). The rigorous analysis that TBPM demands during its compilation clearly highlighted where duplicated inventory did not need to exist. This was an important learning point because although the idea of removing identical inventories either side of the company boundaries was not new, the use of TBPM to enable the change was innovative. Many companies are involved with a variety of forms of relationship to enable cooperation and coordination of the supply chain. Some of these activities such as partnership sourcing may involve the use of open book accounting. This form of activity has obvious commercial sensitivities associated with it, and therefore in the early stages of the evolution of any supply chain management initiative it may be easier to share less sensitive time-based information using TBPMs .

A form of product channel focus was also developed with the introduction of jobbing shops. These channels were established to provide a focus for high-variety low-volume product which was

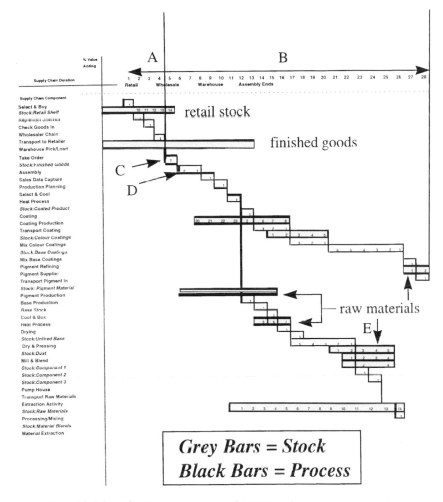

Fig. 10.16 *The time-compressed H&R Johnson supply chain*

originally produced and scheduled down the same channels as the mass volume product. By separating the two distinct logistical as well as physical product requirements, channel stability was created enabling less disruption and time consumption.

In summary the most notable contribution that a time-based approach has delivered to H&R Johnson is the fact that the company has recognized 'time' as the central issue. The TBPM has helped to show the agenda for change and has illustrated the areas for improvement as well as acting as a visual demonstrator of what Time Compression can achieve (see Figure 10.16). Several of the best principles have been demonstrated in action within this case study, however it must be pointed out that the principle of inventory positioning and the idea of 'make to order' or 'make to stock' has only been addressed in relation to the internal supply chain. With further developments in the area of partnership and trust more extensive analysis may be possible in terms of positioning inventory in a more holistic supply chain context. The conditions for demand dynamics certainly appear to exist and the Time Compression initiatives will ensure that the degree of amplification present will be minimized.

From a broad Time Compression perspective the key deliverables of a Time-Based approach do appear to be emerging. Benefits such as productivity increases, risk reduction and market share increases/ retention are all demonstrated. H&R Johnson agree that the Time Compression approach has had a major influence on the following figures although other secondary factors that cannot be isolated will have contributed to these achievements:

- The actual Time Compression for the total supply chain was reduced from 44 to 28 days as illustrated in Figure 10.16. The pipeline time has also been reduced with inventory reductions of 30 days. It must be noted that not all of the potential stock reductions have been implemented.
- From 1993 to 1996 sales per employee rose by 4.8 per cent; during 1996/97 sales per employee were expected to rise by 16.8 per cent.
- Work in Progress was reduced by 9.5 per cent between 1993 and 1996; during 1996/97 WIP was expected to be reduced by 33.7 per cent.
- Market share was estimated to have grown.
- Productivity increased by 23.4 per cent from 1993 to 1996.

- Further reported but unquantified benefits: reduced product obsolescence, reduced material obsolescence and increased return on capital employed.

The only missing factor is that of the ability to increase prices. This was largely inhibited for the foreseeable future due to 'hard' trading conditions in the UK building supply sector.

OTHER FEATURES THAT CAN BE REPRESENTED ON A TBPM

The TBPM framework provides a good platform for annotation of information relating to the features that support analysis of business processes. Information relating to process capacity such as shift-time, up-time and yield can be represented within any of the process bars. The example illustrated in Figure 10.17 shows that the delivery process has a capacity of 504 units per day; this may represent a lower rate of transfer than the preceeding process and is therefore a (local) bottleneck. Flexibility issues and opportunities for the reallocation of resources become highlighted at a macro level. Within complex networks discrete event simulation tools may need to be considered to cope with the dynamics and non-linear relationships between processes.

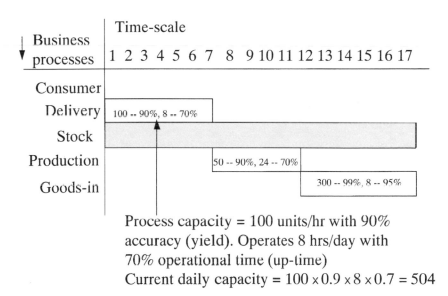

Fig. 10.17 *Additional features in the process map*

Other notes that provide financial or other forms of information complementary to future analysis of the process can be positioned on the map. These may include:

- The identification of process and company boundaries
- The financial value or costs associated with stock bars
- Cost constraints that exist in processes
- Problems, opportunities and solutions associated with the business process

TBPM can be seen to provide a framework to represent a variety of forms of information in relation to process and its positioning in time. One of the key objectives of the TBPM is to provide a set of clear messages about the configuration of the current process structure. It may therefore be appropriate to produce different versions of the TBPM for various purposes in relation to the same business process.

OTHER CONSIDERATIONS

Other general options for analysis and ultimately the achievement of Time Compression are highlighted in Figure 10.18 and for summary purposes are explained as follows:

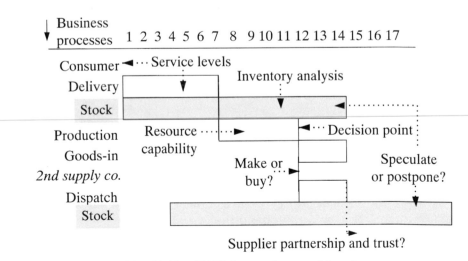

Fig. 10.18 *TBPM emerging considerations*

- Are service levels in balance with inventory?
- Do resource capabilities cause bottlenecks?
- Are there correct decision points such as whether to schedule manufacture of a product?
- Is there a logical 'make to order' or 'make to stock' decision process?
- Can the supply chain benefit from supplier partnerships? For example, is there trust between suppliers and can business information be shared on how to compress lead-times and reduce buffer stocks?
- In the context of supplier cooperation, where total visibility is possible, is there scope to consider the positioning of stock in a supply chain context rather than just a company context? Can companies speculate on where to place stock and think about postponing manufacture or ordering in the supply chain context?

The above are just a few of the avenues for exploration and further investigation. The mapping activity will reveal more detail and new issues will emerge such as: market segmentation, product and service needs, supply channels logistics performance characteristics, manufacturing structure from cells to large-scale continuous processes, contributor motivation and flexibility requirements.

A FINAL NOTE

Time-Based Process Mapping (TBPM) is a technique that aims to provide a quick high level input of knowledge which facilitates diagnostics, action and continual monitoring. It is designed to also act as a catalyst to enable managers to focus on Time Compression opportunities by identifying the time consumed within a business process from the holistic supply chain, though new product development, and down to the micro level of detail such as a machining cell. This chapter has explored how the tool relates to the supply chain and its application. It has been shown that not all of the business process features are directly addressed, however Time-Based Process Mapping does make a significant contribution to fill the deficiency gap identified by the Time Compression project at the outset.

CASE STUDY – BRITISH STEEL

The Company

British Steel is a major producer of steel products for Europe as well as a number of key world markets. It supplies a wide variety of products to a range of industrial sectors. The steel market is still very much commodity based with price fluctuations acting as a source of uncertainty. The company also sells specialist steel and value-added steel products to niche markets. British Steel therefore has to operate as both a commodity and specialist product supplier.

The company is one of the few remaining semi-vertically integrated enterprises. The high level of vertical integration is due to four reasons:

- Inherent structures and management processes traditionally associated with the industry
- Economics has demanded a large scale operation. This argument applies equally as well to the extensive introduction of new technologies and associated automated processes in the business
- A technology dependency due to the processes having to be linked without letting the steel cool
- For market control purposes particularly for control over selling and distribution channels

These characteristics of the business have major consequences on how the company operates from a time-based perspective as well as from the point of view of being able to make changes in such large, complex and well-established industry.

Strategic Drivers

- A large integrated enterprise that may need to face smaller and more flexible competitors
- The degree of competitiveness within the industry as a whole
- Costs are under control but service levels require attention
- Increased product variety is providing competitive differentiation in the market but at the expense of production efficiency and reliability

The Programme of Change

The investigation using TBPM and its rigorous approach to diagnosing lead-time, stock and value-adding time has opened a significant debate within British Steel. This is because the company is one of the lowest-cost producers of strip steel in the world and this has been achieved by a rigorous cost reduction programme throughout the business with inventory being a prime target. The culture of the company is therefore cost-driven with a fierce resistance to producing inventory in any form. This low-cost, low inventory structure has arisen partly due to British Steel's position in the supply chain as a large and powerful company with considerable influence its supply chain partners. The indications are however that this may have been achieved at the expense of the rest of the supply chain. Competitively this may not be a pressing issue because other steel producer's supply chains are in a similar or worse situation. British Steel however has recognized that the way forward strategically is through the supply of service excellence to customers at a competitive price. The introduction of a time-based perspective was therefore the next logical move because the company knew that from a change management perspective, a focus on time was better than the 'fatigued' cost-based approach to change. However further to this is the basic reasoning of British Steel being a commodity producer operating a wholly 'make to order' process in the context of the rest of the supply chain. This has influenced thinking at the top of the organization and some of the ideas from this study are taking root, as described below.

Data collection and project structure

A formalized questionnaire was not used because open questions are proven to be appropriate for acquiring useful general information about the business process. The data collection focuses around getting the interviewee to mentally 'walk' the core process and make comments with respect to the consumption of time. The main problem was obtaining information at the correct level of detail. Attempts to construct a high level TBPM as part of an initial top down approach was difficult because the information that was generally available was detailed in nature. This necessitated a bottom up consolidation and it was often difficult to identify the relevant detail. However, this information proved to be very useful for the bottom up form of more detailed analysis.

A high level TBPM, similar to that in the H&R Johnson case, was constructed and an extract of the core processes with their respective duration times. Average process times were difficult to establish as they depend on a range of constraints and circumstances that related to the unpredictable outcomes of certain processes. Consequently a range of times exist for different processes. The data generated in the maps were next used to determine channels for specific products and customers. The main channels listed take account of process time variability. An example of this is the lead-time variability for the dispatch of steel slabs for general export being very high, plus or minus 20 days compared with only two days' variability and a much shorter overall lead-time to a particular customer in America. This can be explained in part by the fact that the specific orders for this American customer are scheduled for a particular shipping departure date whereas the general exports are produced and dispatched to the docks to accumulate and await a suitable vessel. These variances have significant repercussions on the channels and the ultimate end user served. If lead-times are long, someone somewhere in the chain needs to hold a proportionate amount of cycle stock. TBPMs are a snap shot of the process in time and therefore do not give information related to the historical performance of the chain. This is important information because, although variability is high, there is no indication of predictability. Analysis of the British Steel orders indicate that the average order backlog on promise dates was one week across the total business. Consequently the high variability is linked to poor predictability which drove disproportionately large buffer stocks further down the supply chain channels.

Table 10.1   *Classifying value and non-value-adding stock*

Value-adding stock (*If it is being applied correctly and is reduced the customer would be affected*)	Non-value-adding stock (*If it is being applied correctly and is reduced the customer would not be affected*)
Buffer/Safety Stock	WIP/Batch
Display Stock	Consignment Stock
Maintenance Service Stock	Reserved Stock
Demonstration Stock	Cycle Stock
Distributed Stock	Investment Stock
Kanban Stock	Status Stock

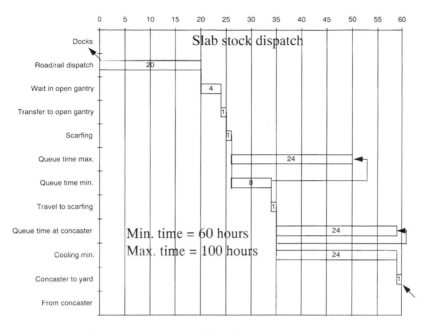

Fig. 10.19 *TBPM for the dispatch of slabs*

Analysis of TBPM value adding time indicated that for core processes listed in Table 10.1 have a high percentage of value-adding time. This was not a surprise because the utilization and productivity demanded from this type of high-value plant is to be expected. The big opportunity however lies in the queues between the core pro cesses. Figure 10.19 illustrates a TBPM for the dispatch of slabs of steel to the export market.

It can be seen that there is a 24-hour queue before the move to the scarfing area and a further delay of between eight and 24 hours immediately before the scarfing process. There is a further delay of 20 hours before road or rail dispatch and the delay at the docks (not shown here) can be as long as three months. These queues present an enormous opportunity for the reduction of non-value adding time. The start point however for value adding analysis will not initially address these queues, as greater benefits were to be found elsewhere as we will explain.

Inventory analysis
Significant difficulties were experienced in analysing and plotting the stock onto the high-level TBPM. The levels of stock held at the British Steel plant are of significant value or tonnage. The company executives

believed that the majority of the inventory in the business offered customer service, however the reality was somewhat different. The available stock information was plotted onto the TBPMs and an investigation ensued to determine the stock drivers. This was a difficult task because inventory data was held in a consolidated form at different points along the supply chain. Without detailed stock analysis and map decomposition, the accuracy of the distribution of stock along the TBPM must be regarded as a representation to facilitate further analysis. At a high level this constraint did not prevent some meaningful interpretation of some key stock issues. The main outcome was that actual stock bars could not be drawn on the maps because free stock, as defined by inventory rules requiring cycle and buffer stock, did not exist. Therefore British Steel do not directly control customer service through the use of stock. The conclusion from this work was that the majority of stock was held in queues with a large proportion held in dispatch bays nominated to specific orders. It was found that stock was held in dispatch by British Steel because customers were refusing to take delivery for a number of reasons. As a result of the lead-time analysis above it was suspected that the majority of this stock was delayed because customers were placing orders well in advance of actual requirements due to poor supply reliability. When the steel became available the customer usually had their own stocks to consume before taking the next consignment. The stock in dispatch was offering service in that it is part of the customer's buffer (although title had not been taken to the goods). From a British Steel perspective this did keep its strategic customers well serviced but this was generally an inefficient way of feeding the overall supply chain. These features are symptoms of demand dynamics which are very likely to exist at this commodity level within the supply chain.

During the investigation of stock several drivers were considered. Listed below are some of the typical drivers for the existence of stock:

- Replenishment time or cycle stock
- Tactical service stock
- Strategic stock for a known shortage
- Seasonal stock
- Merchandizing stock, for example, retail display requirements
- Speculative stock
- Stock held for some form of (usually perceived) financial security
- Uncontrolled stock, for example, the company may not know what it is or why it is there

If the inventory system is out of control it may be difficult to distinguish the actual stock drivers that are listed above. The first task of inventory analysis is to identify the purpose of the stock and therefore understand it in relation to the customer's service needs and the business process. The stock can be segmented into logistically distinct groupings which may follow some form of natural product grouping, for example large and small products. The prime focus in any segmentation must be based upon some rationale relating to the logical segmentation of the end user generic customer. Stock analysis may therefore form the basis for fragmenting and splitting any TBPM into channels feeding specific customer groupings and thereby enabling detailed analysis and process dissection. This form of analysis can help to breakdown the stock bars into manageable units for solution generation.

It must be pointed out that stock bars may not be the sole reason for segmenting the customer groupings but it is a good start point because most businesses usually have more information about their products than their customers and the market structure. The market dimension can be considered in broader terms at strategic level once an understanding of the current stock situation is established. Various forms of stock such as work in progress, bottleneck stock and batch stock can be represented on the TBPM as follows.

Work in progress (WIP) is illustrated in Figure 10.20 as parallel bars concurrent with the duration of physical conversion process

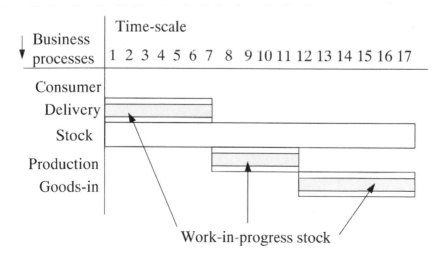

Fig. 10.20 *Aligning work-in-progress in the TBPM*

bars. Therefore the length of the process bar is proportional to the volume of WIP. Bottleneck stock exist as a queue that forms in front of a bottleneck process. The TBPM in Figure 10.21 illustrates four days' average stock accumulated in front of a production bottleneck.

Batch stock is an accumulation of inventory that occurs because the stock feeding process oversupplies stock into the business. Inbound material shown in Figure 10.22 causes an accumulation of three days of stock waiting for take up by production. This may occur because of economic order constraints and/or a minimum delivery quantity.

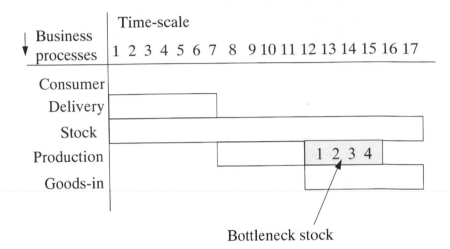

Fig. 10.21   *Incorporating bottleneck processes*

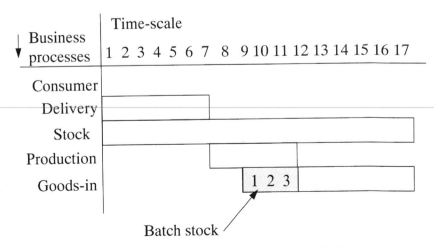

Figure 10.22   *Recognizing stock accumulation*

Figure 10.23 portrays all of the different inventory forms that can be related to process-based explanations or constraints. Note that some attempt to analyse and display value-adding and non-value-adding stock will help with challenging the reasons for the existence of stock.

?/£ Table 10.1 lists some possible criteria for classifying value-adding and non-value-adding stock. The most basic example here is the use of inventory to buffer demand variability with customer service, which is a classic trade-off. In contrast *kanban* systems add value by controlling the flow and demand for inventory and therefore, from a customer viewpoint, it facilitates the timely arrival of what is demanded. If it was removed the operation would collapse and the customer would suffer; however, with a reduction in WIP the customer would not necessarily detect the change and therefore WIP is not adding value. WIP may of course have value-adding implications relating to the continuity of flow in, say, a steel plant situation. The other value-adding activities associated with holding stock, particularly at the retail end of the supply chain, are equally as vital, for example display stock. There is the need to hold inventory at minimum levels within a supply chain in a variety of forms. The fact that there are value- and non-value adding forms of stock endorses the need for establishing the principle detailed below.

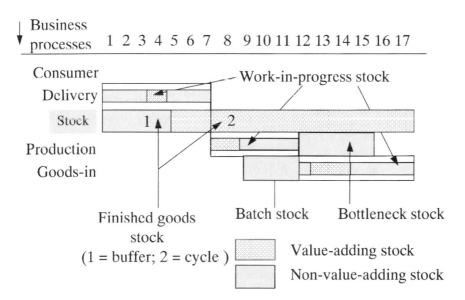

Fig. 10.23 *Appending additional inventory forms*

Analysis beyond challenging the levels of stock held can move to issues of inventory positioning in the total supply chain context. The concept of optimized inventory positioning and the ideas surrounding the use of speculating with stock and postponing the use of stock were addressed next within the British Steel project. The actual cost drivers behind the model of speculation and postponement are hard to determine but the underlying logic has enabled the project participants to use it as a framework to challenge the current supply chain structure. In very basic terms, what had to be understood were the costs associated with using stock (that is speculation), and not using stock (that is postponement), at a particular point within the total supply chain. As with any cost-based considerations all of the holistic cost implications had to be considered across all business units, something that is often difficult to establish.

The first consideration was to identify the point in the supply chain where production could be postponed in favour of holding stock. The start point was the raw materials in stock piles by the plant at British Steel. These materials were mainly imported in bulk, therefore supply flexibility aligned to demand requirements was impractical in terms of cost and time-based service. The next process is the blast furnace which is physically 'hot metal' linked to steel making. The postponement costs associated with not keeping these facilities operational 100 per cent of the time were totally uneconomic. Consequently the next point in the supply chain where stock could be held was in the slab stock areas. Slab could be 'hot connected' to the rolling mills. However, due to demand and scheduling rules less than 10 per cent of the volume flowed directly through to rolling.

Analysis of the existing situation in the slab stock areas showed that substantial stocks were held in queues because some is produced unintentionally, allocated to an order for future processing, or held in a queue waiting to go into the reheat furnace. At this level in the process the number of SKUs (products) that need to be held is 187, however, these relate to 50 parent chemistries. From this low product complexity level in the supply chain an infinite variety (because of all the combinations of length and width) of products can be produced. It would therefore seem logical to postpone upstream production in favour of positioning 'freestock' in a slab form.

In order to determine the costs associated with this scenario, demand analysis is currently being performed by converting product sales data into equivalent slab requirements. This will help establish the variability of demand for slab at this level within the supply chain. The results from this work so far substantiate Pareto, show in Figure 10.24, whereby 20 per cent of the product variety accounts for 80 per cent of the product volume by tonnage.

This is significant because the future of the company could be compromised from a marketing perspective as the product range was being continually expanded. This was not compatible with the existing supply chain operation because increasing product variety is gradually reducing the logistical service capability of the company. Consequently a manufacturing strategy to support the marketing requirements was required. This strategy was considered the logic of producing 80 per cent of the volume (that is, 20 per cent of the product range) on a 'make to order' basis with the residual 80 per cent of the range on a 'make to stock' basis. The reason for this is that the removal of as much product variety as possible from 'live' 'make to order' scheduling enables stability and predictability of the production process as batch sizes are increased. This factor is one of the key variables behind conformance to schedule. Consequently the levels of stock required at this point are substantial, and this required a trade-off analysis with the costs of speculating on holding inventory

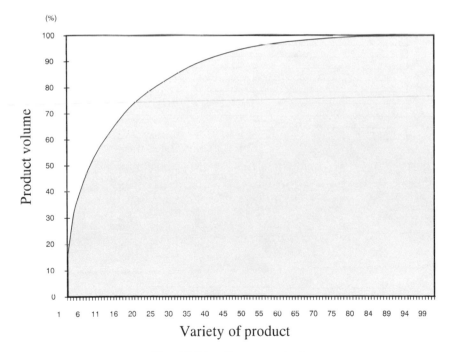

Fig. 10.24 *Pareto analysis*

230

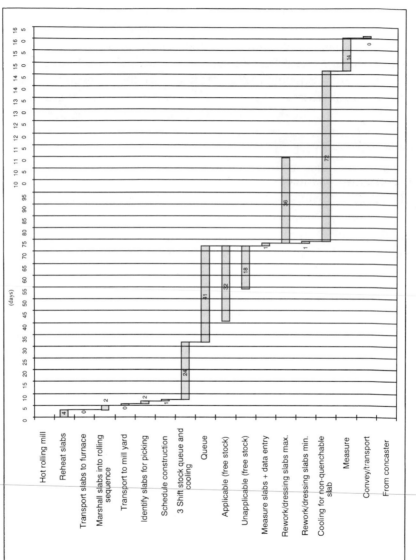

Fig. 10.25 *Decomposition of TBPM*

further down the supply chain. It was known that inventory levels further down the supply were very large because of the size of British Steel Distribution company and the stocks of coil held by their customers.

In summary the time-based focus has motivated British Steel to address a key strategic issue relating to the positioning of stock in the supply chain. There is confidence in the business that this will result in a 25 per cent overall reduction in order backlogs. The business will also be in a stronger position to offer the market an increased range of speciality products.

Results to Date

The company has accepted that it needs to re-evaluate the role of stock within the supply chain. The time based approach has specifically created a focus on using stocks of semi-finished material to improve customer service. This has meant a change in policy from a purely make to order environment to a combined make to stock and make to order system. As a result, inter-production stock has actually increased to provide massive benefits in customer service and possible stock reductions further along the supply chain.

The processes that release the semi-finished materials, that is slab, have been targeted through a Time Compression approach with reductions of up to 50 per cent being implemented.

Learning Points

This project has emphasised the need to take a holistic view of the business process otherwise key issues such as stock positioning would not have been recognised.

- The rigorous approach demanded by TBPM has identified key issues and helped to challenge beliefs held in the business such as 'there is plenty of stock and it is giving customer service'. By taking the financially accepted stock figures and then distributed across the process map demonstrated how inventory should be used for the benefit of the total supply chain.
- Difficulty was encountered with trying to make the data fit the TBPM. This was a problem from two perspectives, firstly some of the data collected related to purely the value adding activity. This

is a common problem encountered with interviewees because they do not view the process initially from the perspective of a TBPM which recognises queues and average historical instances. Secondly a large mass of detail was collected which has to be interpreted and abstracted into a high level map. This was a time consuming process and made validation problematic.

Training, facilitation methods and the computer mechanisation of TBPM are currently addressing these issues, however they are not insurmountable for the current would-be user. This is because time provides a very clear focus and TBPM is in concept relatively simple to apply even in the context of a large integrated supply chain.

11 Tools and Techniques

Every good change agent keeps a selection of useful tools which can be used as and when the need for them arises. The Time Compression Programme has established its own collection of tools and techniques which we have found useful in time-compressing business processes. Although many of these tools are already prevalent within the business arena, many of them have been specifically developed by ourselves to focus on time and the removal of waste. The objective of this chapter is to introduce these tools, explaining how we have used them and in what context. We hope that this will help you to select appropriate tools for diagnosing your business.

Although previous chapters have covered the subject of tool selection, it is worth repeating that the purpose of a diagnostic tool is to promote a particular way of thinking about a familiar process, thereby giving a different perspective. The appropriate tool also provides a structure to hold the information gathered and to help communicate it to others. We have tended to find that simple, visual tools work best in most situations. Hence, many of those we cover fall under this description.

When beginning to use a tool it is important to understand the scope of the process being investigated and level of detail required. Taking an overview and highlighting the key opportunities for further analysis is a good approach. This should help you to avoid 'paralysis by analysis' where a process is analysed to great detail but no one has time to do anything with the results.

The following table, Table 11.1, provides a list of tools which we have found most effective in time-compressing business processes. The table displays a general overview of the tools, together with their strengths, which should assist in tool selection and application. The remainder of the chapter is then dedicated to explaining how to use the various tools and techniques described.

Table 11.1 *Tools and techniques for Time Compression*

Symbol	Tool	Overview	Strengths
	Time-based process mapping	Provides a time-based perspective of business processes in terms of value- and non-value-adding time	Simple, visually attractive, ability to cope with any size business process and a range of time-based features
	Cause and effect analysis	Identifies the root causes of problems, highlighting causes of delay and turbulence	Simple, visual, already well-established as a diagnostic tool
	Causal loop diagrams	The application of systems thinking to complex environments providing a holistic analysis of the business	Explains very complex dynamic systems relatively simply
	Flowcharting	Represents the relationships between system elements in a pictorial form	Logical and very simple. Commonly utilized in systems analysis
	Runner, repeater, stranger analysis	Provides method of classifying business processes into three manageable categories	Simple way to manage diverse operations, provides clarity
	Pareto analysis	Technique of ranking data against frequency or cost to provide visual of process occurrence	Versatile tool to identify volume/variety issues, highlights variances
?/£	Decision/pay-off matrix	Objective means of evaluating worthiness of potential solutions or improvement strategies	Systematically tests solutions rapidly, ease of use, applicability

	Name	Description	Benefits
	Solution effect analysis	Minimizes the likelihood that projected benefits are not impeded by unforeseen events	Simple, visual, quantifies risk potential in simple elements
FMEA	Failure mode and effect analysis	Recognizes potential failure modes and their causes across any business process	Prioritizes actions, can be used where any failure mode can be identified
	Decision node analysis	Provides a perspective of a business process in terms of the decisions taken within it	Maps processes where activities are ambiguous, solves decision delays
	Benchmarking	Quantifies performance gaps with world-class rivals focused upon key processes or product attributes	Provides external perspective for goal setting
	Competitor analysis	Appreciates reality of competitive forces and how a business might respond to certain eventualities	Thorough, summarizes large amounts of market intelligence
SWOT	SWOT analysis	Analyses the general strategy of a business, reviews the effectiveness of operational processes	Basic positioning of company in its market, complements other tools
WIN QUAL	Order winners/qualifiers	Provides an understanding of which criteria a business can gain competitive advantage through	Easy to use, provides a clear and objective evaluation of products
	Simulation	Computerized method of evaluating solutions to complex and expensive business processes	Low-risk testing of solutions graphical and meaningful outcome

TIME-BASED PROCESS MAPPING

Time-Based Process Mapping, as we saw in Chapter 10, was designed by the Time Compression Programme to provide a time-based perspective on a business process. Through representing value-adding time and the different types of non-value-adding time on a time axis, the greatest opportunities for Time Compression can be readily identified. Stock can also be represented on the map, allowing the connection to be made between it and the processes it serves.

TBPM was utilized on most of our projects to identify the best opportunities for Time Compression. It was first used to provide an overview of the whole process, identifying areas where more detailed analysis must be developed. Whilst it is possible to use the tool at all levels, the important criterion is to apply it appropriately. This may mean the top-level mapping of a total supply chain or at a detailed level such as the physical movements of goods on a shop floor. TBPM has been found to be particularly useful with large complex supply chains where clarity in the process is a key requirement. However it proves just as effective with much smaller, less complex business processes.

Strengths

- Simple
- Visually attractive
- Can cope with any size of business process and different details
- Provides a good framework to display time-related features
- Can cope with approximate data

Weaknesses

- Takes a static view of a process
- Difficult to represent out-of-control processes
- Identifies opportunities but does not explain why they exist

Use in conjunction with

- Flow charting should be used to initially identify processes
- Cause and effect diagrams to provide a representation of the causes of the opportunities presented

CAUSE AND EFFECT ANALYSIS

Cause and effect analysis provides a simple means of identifying the ultimate causes of a problem. Recognizing the root cause is essential in order to resolve a problem, not just treat its symptoms. Through removing the cause, its effects are eliminated. This analysis method uses an *Ishikawa*, or 'fishbone', diagram to capture information in a succinct, visual form. The tool has proven useful for highlighting causes of delays and turbulence across business processes. Actions required to time-compress business processes become clear through its deployment.

The diagram can be constructed in the following way:

1. Define a word or phrase that describes the 'problem' or effect being felt.
2. List the general factors that could influence the problem on the ribs of the fishbone. Typical manufacturing starting points are shown above in Figure 11.1. Administration areas can be alternatively summarized under the categories of people, procedures, plant and policies.
3. Decompose these general factors into more specific factors, adding them to new bones coming off the ribs. This stepwise decomposition is continued for each factor and all sub-factors as far as is logically possible.
4. Identify causal relationships that exist between the factors, for example, large batch sizes caused by long machine set-up times. In this way major cause and effect chains are identified.

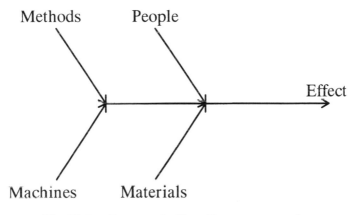

Fig. 11.1 *Cause and effect diagram protocol*

5. Different branches of the diagram are allocated to non-related cause and effect chains. Root causes are displayed on the outermost branches.

The diagram can also be deployed to communicate improvement activities. For example, the diagram can display cause and effect relationships on the shop floor, providing feedback of how a problem's root causes are being tackled.

Strengths

- Simple
- Visual

Weaknesses

- Does not cope well with dynamic systems

Use in conjunction with

- Time-Based Process Mapping to identify causes of non-value-adding time
- Combines well with statistics to prioritize improvement opportunities
- Solution effect analysis to check the robustness of the solution

CAUSAL LOOP DIAGRAMS

This tool provides a perspective for thinking of systems as a whole, originating from the Systems Thinking school of management. A holistic approach to business issues analysis is promoted. As pointed out in earlier chapters, such a view is important to take when investigating a system. This ensures that the causes and not just the symptoms of a problem are understood, including those that are not immediately obvious. Understanding these issues will help to identify which are key to success whilst anticipating possible sources of resistance to change. Points of leverage, where a small change in procedures can result in considerable benefits, are easily identified.

Dynamic interrelationships are capable of being mapped with this tool. Complex cause and effect relationships between different variables can then be identified. Unlike cause and effect diagrams, causal loop diagrams allow multiple feedback loops to be linked. This is important when the effects of delays in a system need to be understood.

1. Select an issue that you wish to understand better.
2. Identify a suitable time horizon for the issue. Variables that change over a longer time horizon may then be assumed to be constant.
3. Identify the key variables as follows:

    - Think of the issue, its anticipated outcome and any unexpected consequences that may occur
    - Identify things that can be measured and which are variable,
    - Draw out the behaviour of key variables over time
    - Determine the boundary of the issue. Ask if a change in a variable is significant in altering the behaviour of the system as a whole
    - Determine the level of detail of the diagram. The variables should be appropriate to the time horizon used and describe patterns of behaviour

4. Describe each variable as a noun, for example 'lead-time' rather than 'increasing lead-time'. The noun should be the positive sense of an action, for example 'grow' rather than 'diminish'. Distinguish between perceived and actual states as the two can be different and affect the behaviour of the system.

5. Link the variables with arrows indicating the direction of the influence. Where there are both long- and short-term consequences of actions, draw the short-term results nearest to the centre of a loop.
6. Identify the polarity of the change. Where an increase in A results in an increase in B use a '+' sign. Where an increase in A results in a decrease in B use a '−' sign.
7. Identify significant delays.
8. Identify reinforcing loops which can become either vicious or virtuous cycles depending upon which direction they move in. Loops that tend to stabilize should be identified as balancing loops.

Strengths

- Explains complex, dynamic systems visually and relatively simply
- Facilitates a good understanding of a system through the process of drawing the diagram

Weaknesses

- Takes practice to do well
- Difficult to segregate major high-level issues from the detail
- Becomes very complex and branches out if boundaries not enforced

Use in conjunction with

- Flowcharting to clarify the level at which the cause and effect relationships operate

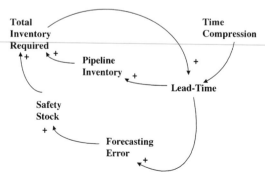

Fig. 11.2 *Causal loop example*

FLOWCHARTING

Flowcharting represents the relationships between system elements in a pictorial form. This may be the physical movement of work, tools, people or paperwork, or the logic in a decision-making process. Its value is to enhance the overall understanding of a system's operation, describing it graphically.

Through sharing understanding, the actual process can be charted. Against this a chart can be constructed showing what steps should happen when the process operates correctly. For example, charting the movement of work across an office or factory can highlight improvements in layout. This is particularly advantageous, when the arrangement is process-based (cell layout), rather than product-based (functional layout).

A number of different standards for symbols exist for the description of process plant and for work study. Depending on the application, an appropriate set of symbols should be chosen.

Remember, when working with flowcharts, the aim is to keep the flow of information as simple as is possible. If the resulting flowchart is still complex, then it will be necessary to simplify the system first and then flowchart it.

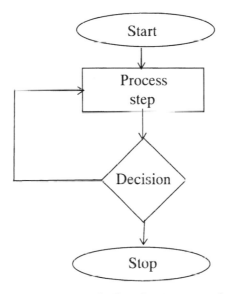

Fig. 11.3 *Simple flowcharting procedure*

Use in conjunction with

- Time-Based Process Mapping to clarify the overall business processes prior to developing the complete map

RUNNER, REPEATER, STRANGER ANALYSIS

Runner, repeater, stranger analysis is useful in a number of ways when carrying out business systems analysis. It provides a way of classifying the type of business; it can help in identifying strategic business units; it can help in identifying autonomous working groups within business units; and it can assist in identifying the most appropriate work control system.

The work is classified into three categories:

- Runners – Work that is being done continuously
- Repeaters – Work that is done regularly, but not continuously (for example, once a week or once a month)
- Strangers – Work that is done infrequently, or may only be done once and never repeated

Note that the major emphasis is on the frequency at which the work is done, rather than the quantity of work. Within different industry types, products classed within the same category will be made at varying frequencies. For example, in the consumer electronics industry a part classified as a runner will be made every day. Within the aerospace industry however, a runner may be a part made only once a week, due to the long lead-times involved.

Few companies will carry out all three classes of work at the same time – indeed, if they do, then this is an indicator of inconsistencies in the business. However, many companies have to manufacture two of these at the same time – runners and repeaters, or repeaters and strangers. In such cases it may be appropriate to create different working units, groups, or cells to handle the two categories of work. It would be difficult to provide a single facility to handle both efficiently, especially where more flexibility is required to manage the low-frequency work.

Work that is running continuously lends itself to simple methods of work planning and control. In the case of manufacturing, a pull or *kanban* system is appropriate, while other types of control are required when many different jobs are being handled (for example, MRP). A runner, repeater, stranger analysis in a company carrying out routine and infrequent work, might result in creating a flexible, quick response unit to deal with the service work, while employing a simpler, less responsive unit to manage the routine, repeater work.

Use in conjunction with

- Pareto analysis to help quantify the emphasis or frequency

PARETO ANALYSIS

Pareto analysis is used in selecting the most important items to receive attention when presented with a problem. It is also known sometimes as ABC analysis and relies on the '80/20' rule. The technique involves ranking data against frequency, cost or time. Pareto charts can be used in a number of ways. However they will typically follow one of two approaches. The first is to prioritize efforts in order to resolve the most important problem. This is used extensively by quality groups. For example, defects may occur for a number of reasons within paint finishing. The causes of these defects may be arranged against their frequency, as shown in Figure 11.4.

Plotting the cost of these problems will reveal a different picture, highlighting that the most important problem may not be the most frequent. Plotting the time delays they cause will reveal the most important opportunities for Time Compression.

The second approach is to group data in different ways, examining each for usefulness in highlighting clear differences. For instance, there are many aspects of factory production that require improvement, for example, scrap, rework or defective product. The procedure of Pareto analysis is to gather data about a specific problem and list all the causes that contribute to the problem over a period of time. This is undertaken using tick sheets. These simple charts are used to tell us how certain events happen. An example is to consider some of the ways the factory can be looked at. The aim is to highlight where differences exist.

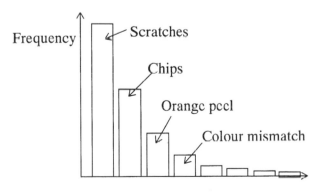

Fig. 11.4 *Pareto analysis*

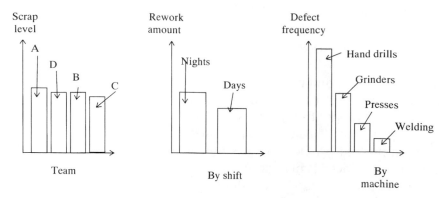

Fig. 11.5   *Pareto analysis for problem diagnosis*

Use in conjunction with

● Cause and effect diagrams to accentuate problems

DECISION/PAY-OFF MATRICES

?/£ The decision or pay-off matrix provides an objective means of evaluating the relative worthiness of particular solutions or potential improvement strategies. It does this by systematically testing each solution against the strengths, weaknesses, opportunities and threats of the system in question. In its simplest form, alternative strategies or solutions are listed on the vertical axis of a matrix. Major strengths and weaknesses, opportunities and threats are written on the horizontal axis. Each strategy is evaluated for its effect over each of the horizontal factors. In a more complex form, weightings can be allocated to the strengths, weaknesses, opportunities and threats, so that a numerical rating of each strategy can be calculated.

For example, suppose that a British company wishes to expand into mainland Europe with a new product and is considering three alternative strategies. It needs to evaluate these against opportunities and threats, identified in the previous analysis. The three strategies are listed on the vertical axis and major opportunities and threats across the top. The consequence of each strategy can now be systematically reviewed (see Table 11.2). It can be seen that each opportunity and threat has been ranked in order of likely positive effect of the strategy. For example for the first threat, 'vigorous response by competitors', strategy B is ranked first, strategy C second and strategy A third.

Many weighting and scoring systems can be devised to obtain a quantitative evaluation. The virtue of this methodology, however, is that it encourages the system designer to consider and explicitly write down the effects of the strategies against the strengths, weaknesses, opportunities and threats of the system being designed.

A variation on this technique, which is used particularly in the analysis of risk, identifies the factors that can affect the decision. It then assigns a factor representing the significance of each and then assigns a likelihood factor to each. The significance and likelihood factors are then multiplied together and the factors are ranked. Those with the highest score are the ones to which most attention should be paid. The procedure is shown in Table 11.3.

Table 11.2 *Decision Matrix*

Alternative strategies	Vigorous response by competitors	Devaluation of pound	Labour unrest in UK factories	Labour unrest in Europe
A Set up factory in southern France and develop market over ten years. Total cost £4m	3 Could result in failure of project but could sell factory for £1m	1 Improve UK profits	1 Not affected	3 Could be serious due to inexperience of European labour
B Joint project with European competitor, making in UK, selling through their outlets. Total cost £2m	1 Should be able to withstand virtually any attack	3 Partner would object to change in transfer price	3 Partner would be irritated by unreliability	1 Probably no direct effect
C Acquire a small European competitor, expand his factory to launch product through his outlets. Total cost £6m	2 Profitability of project not dependent on new products	1 Could improve UK profits	1 Not affected	2 Not as serious as A because of know-how acquired from competitor

Table 11.3 *Risk Decision Matrix*

Factor	Significance	Likelihood	Overall Importance
First factor	0.5	0.5	0.25
Second factor	0.3	0.4	0.12
Third factor	0.6	0.1	0.06
Fourth factor, etc.			

SOLUTION EFFECT ANALYSIS

Having undertaken an improvement exercise, the likely outcome is a solution which will resolve the root cause of the problem. Implementing this should release benefits to the business. The purpose of the Solution effect analysis is to minimize the likelihood that whilst one problem is removed, others are not created. In its simplest incarnation, the analysis inverts the procedure followed in a Cause and Effect Analysis, as shown below:

From a single point solution, the cascade of potential effects are explored to where they could materialize. Essentially, this is a simple, graphical version of a Failure Mode and Effect Analysis. Whilst such a systematic, element-by-element assessment cannot be replaced, this approach is accessible, opening the mind to potential side effects. Defining these enables the solution to be modified and refined before deployment.

Strengths

- Simple
- Visual

Weaknesses

- Not a guarantee of success

Use in conjunction with

- Any solution-generating activity

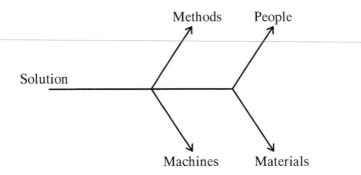

Fig. 11.6 *Solution effect analysis syntax*

FAILURE MODE AND EFFECT ANALYSIS (FMEA)

Failure mode and effect analysis is an assessment of the effects of a failure to meet customer requirements. Typically, its application is perceived as a product design tool. However, identifying potential failure modes and their causes is just as relevant across the manufacturing or commercial system.

The objective of the exercise is to guide the user to where the most serious potential problems exist. This is achieved through assessing the occurrence, severity and detection rate of each failure mode on a scale of one to ten, with ten being the most serious case. Potential causes of that failure and the control systems that are in place to catch it are similarly evaluated. These three scores are multiplied together to give the risk priority number, where high numbers will require immediate attention.

In essence, FMEA signposts the user to where serious potential problems exist. From there, other tools can be deployed to rectify, minimize or manage the failure.

Strengths

- Use where any failure mode can be identified
- Prioritizes actions

Weaknesses

- Where failure ratings appear subjective they lose authority to direct action

Use in conjunction with

- Cause and effect analysis
- Solution effect analysis

DECISION NODE ANALYSIS

Decision-making is a key activity of management. In order to understand a managerial process it is important to understand the series of decisions that are taken. Decision Node Analysis provides a perspective of looking at a business process in terms of the decisions taken with it. Where a process is ambiguous, it can be much easier to determine the order of necessary decisions than the exact order of activities that take place. This is especially true where delays in decision-making are seen to be crucial when time-compressing a business process.

For an effective management process to exist it is important to have effective decision making. For effective decision-making it is necessary to take into account the following factors:

- The quality of the decision
- The level of confidence in the decision
- The time taken to arrive at the decision
- The costs incurred in taking the decision
- The timeliness of the decision

Time Compression improves this decision-making process through the timely delivery of information. In addition, the decision-making process can also be a factor in causing delays in a business process. Thus, understanding the information requirements for a decision and delivering that information at the right time can speed up the decision-making process, and remove some of the administrative burden upon other business processes.

DNA mapping syntax is based on those of IDEF0 and SSADM, which are traditional methods used for mapping information flows. The mapping starts at an overview level and defines the principle decisions and activities. Each of those decisions and activities can then be mapped within the framework set by the high-level map.

At each decision the following are identified:

- The information into and out of the decision
- The events that trigger the taking of the decision
- The constraints placed upon the decision
- The tools available to help in making the decision
- The people who are able to make the decision
- How the taking of the decision is recorded

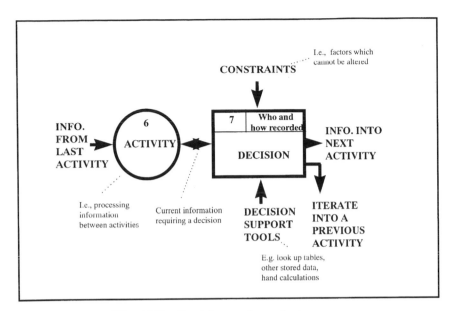

Fig. 11.7 *Decision node analysis syntax*

Tools include information sources such as competitor information, quality data or previous design histories. They may also be quality function deployment charts, computer models, prototypes, or decision support software. Constraints might be legal issues, cost and weight targets or supplier capabilities.

Decision Audit List

The gathered information can be incorporated into a decision audit list which can be used as a checklist against decisions. Understanding those decisions taken in a business process, and how they control the activities within the process, is very powerful. Ensuring that the right information is available in the right place at the right time reduces the time to make that decision. Correspondingly, the time to undertake the process will decrease.

Analysis can also identify unnecessary decisions or inappropriate levels in the organization. Through understanding the decisions, underlying problems can be resolved, thereby improving the performance of the management of a business process.

Strengths

- Can be used for mapping processes where the activities are ambiguous
- Good for solving issues around delays in processes due to decision-making

Weaknesses

- DNA can be quite complex and is sometimes seen as being abstract

Use in conjunction with

- Decision/pay-off matrices

BENCHMARKING

Overview

The signal which spawns the deployment of benchmarking is the realization that someone else is better at something than you are. Typically, this is your toughest competitor but will also be leaders in other industries. Delivering superior performance found there back into your organization is dependent upon being wise enough to learn how to surpass them.

Searching for best practice implies that the organization has become externally focused. Proactive activity such as this enables the firm to understand its industry. This understanding of competitive drivers and their dynamics can then be deployed back into the firm but only where it is receptive to improvement.

Benchmarking is typically used to quantify the performance gap with rivals. This needs to be focused upon key processes or product attributes which define and underpin competitiveness. Identified at the strategic level by senior management, these then need to be translated to a tactical level. Each level of the organization is then aware of how it impacts upon the overall business's objectives. Improvement efforts at each level can then be focused towards these, with appropriate product or process measures deployed to ensure this is the case.

Undertaking a benchmarking exercise requires deploying significant resources although moderating this is possible. Designing the exercise correctly, however, is the wrong area to scrimp upon. Understanding what makes an organization successful, that is, identifying the key processes it undertakes and the factors which lead to the success, is absolutely vital. The firm then needs to define how it undertakes those processes and establish appropriate performance measures for them.

These measures can then be compared against a competitor's process. To start with, objective measures of performance are not vital. 'Ball-park' assessments are sufficient to establish the extent of performance gaps. Where the gaps are significant, an organization can use this as the spur to reviewing their existing process. At this stage, all they know is that improvement is real and entirely possible. Once internal process improvement ideas have been implemented, performance is reassessed. Should it still be inferior and the ideas exhausted, the superior process should be examined more objectively with a focus not upon 'what' they achieve but 'how' they achieve it. This process is repeated systematically with increasingly more sophisticated bench-marking partners.

This activity is more effective if undertaken through a formal process. These are extensively written about, for example by Camp, and align closely to Deming's Quality Cycle: Plan–Do–Check–Adjust. Also, employing the stakeholders in the process with them taking responsibility for the benchmarking and the subsequent improvement activity provides a significant pay-off. Whilst this requires an investment in training and off-line activities, its value is undisputed.

The factors to be considered in carrying out benchmarking are many and varied. Although benchmarking is typically associated with manufacturing operations, its potential goes far beyond this and should cover all aspects of a company's operations. This should include sales and marketing, public relations, customer service, R&D, engineering and design, product and process innovation, human resources and the supply chain.

COMPETITOR ANALYSIS

Typically, the competition companies face is becoming fiercer. The opening of markets and the globalization of competition only serve to increase this. Another perspective on this situation recognizes that rewards from success have never been greater. Responding to the competitive pressures means resolving functional antagonism within the company and aligning efforts against the external competition. Achieving this requires common objectives and a coordinated company-wide plan to be enacted. Supporting these there needs to be a well-formulated and communicated strategy.

To ensure that a company is fully competitive and that the systems that are implemented will be fully effective, it is useful to understand the competitive forces that operate in the industry. To plan adequately for operation within this competitive environment, it is important to consider the different forms that competition can take, the effect of these different forms of competition and how the company may respond to certain eventualities.

Amongst the useful tools devised by Porter is his Five Forces model.[1] This is a means of representing the general competitive environment within which a company operates. The model offers a framework for summarizing the main forces experienced by a firm.

In addition to considering the overall strategy of the company, the relevance of these issues to the firm's functional strategy should be

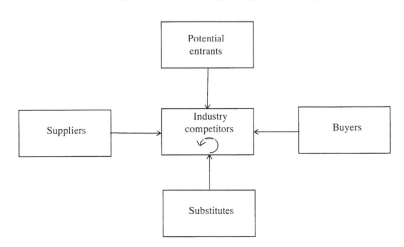

Fig. 11.8 *Porter's Five Forces model*

considered. For example, the 'suppliers' and 'substitutes' categories are particularly relevant to the manufacturing/operating activities.

A careful consideration of all of these factors will quantify the strategic positioning of the company. Cascading this shows how systems at the operational level support the overall strategy and where they need to take into account the forces acting in the market. It should be remembered that the environment is not static, so that the relative importance and effect of the factors will change with time. Review processes should be included in the system, which is designed to monitor these effects.

SWOT ANALYSIS

Strengths, weaknesses, opportunities and threats analysis is used as a basis for examining a situation and categorizing the factors involved into the four key areas. This strategy tool can be employed when determining the overall strategy of an organization and is also used to consider detailed operational aspects. Typically, this type of analysis is very general. Nevertheless, it forms an excellent starting point to provide an insight into the company and its operations.

SWOT is most commonly used in the analysis of a company by its own management, or others who aim to evaluate and develop divisional or corporate strategy. Strengths and weaknesses refer to internal capabilities whilst opportunities and threats focus attention on the market-place. Such analysis is just as applicable when assessing the position of external organizations. This can be the first step in assessing competitor capabilities or the development of supplier and customer relations.

How to use SWOT:

1. List the four headings, brainstorming each in turn.
2. In forming strategy, concentrate on the main issues — no more than ten per heading. It is acceptable to list more factors in the analysis of suppliers or functional departments.
3. Initially, list the weaknesses, without too much discussion or trying to quantify the data. They can be studied in detail later.
4. Strengths and weaknesses should usually refer to internal factors relating to the company and to its existing situation.
5. Opportunities and threats are more concerned with external factors that are envisaged in the future.
6. It is possible for the same factor to appear as a strength and as a weakness.

The analysis will not in itself determine the action to be taken. It does provide a valuable background to the system design and the factors against which the design can be measured. Used at a functional level, it can indicate where action is required in order to make improvements.

Strengths

- Assists in understanding the positioning of a company within its market environment
- Complements other analytical methods

Weaknesses

- Encourages response to specific problems, rather than carrying out a systems approach
- Optimization of subsystems by solving particular problems whilst retaining an inefficient total system

ORDER WINNERS AND QUALIFIERS

The concept of order winners and qualifiers provides an understanding of how a company's products can gain sales in the marketplace. Order-winning criteria are those that provide a competitive edge over competitors; order-qualifying criteria are those necessary to be considered by the market.

The order-winning and qualifying criteria can be many and include:

- Brand image – company reputation
- Technical specification – features and innovation
- Warranty and service
- Availability – delivery speed and reliability
- Product quality and reliability
- Price

The process of evaluating order-winning and qualifying criteria can be made more objective by using the following steps:

- Identify all the factors that could be order winners or order qualifiers.
- Rate each for its **importance**, using the nine-point scale below.
- Rate the **company's performance** against each of these criteria on the nine-point scale below.
- Compare the performances against the chart that shows how the results should be interpreted.

Table 11.4 *Nine-point importance scale*

	Does this performance objective . . .
Order-winning objectives	Provide a crucial advantage with customers?
	Provide an important advantage with most customers?
	Provide a useful advantage with most customers?
Order-qualifying objectives	Need to be up to good industry standard?
	Need to be around median industry standard?
	Need to be within close range of the rest of the industry?
Less important objectives	Not usually important, but could become more so in the future?
	Very rarely rate as being important?
	Never come into consideration?

Table 11.5 *Nine point performance scale*

Is our achieved performance . . .

Consistently and considerably better than our nearest competitor?
Consistently better than our nearest competitor?
Consistently marginally better than our nearest competitor?
Often marginally better than most competitors?
About the same as most competitors?
Often close to the main competitors?
Usually marginally worse than most competitors?
Usually worse than most competitors?
Consistently worse than most competitors?

SIMULATION

Computer simulation provides a way of testing out solutions to a problem without taking the risks of implementing those solutions. It is a good way to optimize solutions where a system is complex and expensive to experiment with. The colourful graphics and visual display which most packages provide help to communicate the results of the simulation to employees.

Simulation requires the development of a systems model of a business operation. The scope can extend from a single manufacturing cell to the complete supply chain. The models provide a logical representation of the relationships between factors in the industrial environment. The activities within these environments may be represented to varying levels of detail according to the requirements of the analysis. The systems model then forms the basis for 'what if' experimentation, during which a range of solutions may be considered. Computer simulation can give a graphical display of the dynamic performance of the system. This can be used to indicate flows of information and material in supply chains. It can identify the causes of process instability and the associated influencing factors. The simulation can also highlight the effect of internal control changes on neighbouring companies within a supply chain.

Strengths

- Can provide an accurate picture of the effects of a given change to a system, particularly with respect to resources and through-put levels
- Provides a low-risk way to test different solutions
- Graphics help sell solutions to others

Weaknesses

- Building a system model can be expensive and time-consuming
- Usually requires an expert, particularly for interpretation

SUGGESTED READING

Camp, R. C., *Benchmarking: The Search for Industry Best Practice That Leads to Superior Performance*, Quality Press 1989.

Kim, D. H., 'A Palette of Systems Thinking Tools', *Systems Thinker*, Vol. 1, No. 3, 1994.

Porter, M. E., *Competitive Strategy: Techniques for Analysing Industries and Competitors* (New York, The Free Press, 1980).

Senge, P. M., *The Fifth Discipline: The Art and Practice of the Learning Organization* (New York, Doubleday, 1990).

Senge, P. M., Kleiner, A., Roberts, C., Ross, R. B. and Smith, B. J., *The Fifth Discipline Fieldbook: Strategies and Tools for Building a Learning Organization*, (Lava, Nicholas Brealey, 1994).

Notes

1 Why Time Compression?

1. H. Ford, *Today and Tomorrow* (Cambridge, Productivity Press, 1988).
2. Ibid.
3. G. Stalk Jr. and T. M. Hout, *Competing Against Time: How Time Based Competition is Reshaping Global Markets* (New York, The Free Press, 1990).
4. H. Hart and A. Berger, 'Using Time to Generate Corporate Renewal', *International Journal of Operations and Production Management*, vol. 14, no. 3 (1994) pp. 24–45.

2 Time Compression and Business Strategy

1. M. E. Porter, *Competitive Advantage* (New York, The Free Press, 1985).
2. G. Hamel and C. K. Prahalad, *Competing for the Future* (Boston, Mass., Harvard Business School Press, 1994).
3. The idea of fit between strategy and business processes and its history is discussed in detail in A. K. Bhattacharya and A. M. Gibbons, 'Strategy Formulation: Focusing on Core Competencies and Processes', *Business Change and Re-engineering*, vol. 3, no. 1 (1996) pp. 47–55.
4. M. E. Porter, *Competitive Advantage*.
5. Ibid.
6. G. Stalk Jr. and T. M. Hout, *Competing Against Time: How Time Based Competition is Reshaping Global Markets* (New York, The Free Press, 1990) p. 77.
7. P. G. Smith and D. G. Reinertsen, *Developing Products in Half the Time* (New York, Van Nostrand Reinhold, 1991).
8. G. Hamel and C. K. Prahalad, *Competing for the Future*.
9. P. M. Senge, *The Fifth Discipline* (New York, Doubleday, 1990).
10. S. C. Wheelwright and K. B. Clark, *Revolutionizing Product Development: Quantum Leaps in Speed, Efficiency and Quality* (New York, The Free Press, 1992).

3 The Fundamentals of Time Compression

1. M. Hammer and J. Champy, *Reengineering the Corporation: a Manifesto for Business Revolution* (London, Brealy, 1994).
2. G. H. Stalk Jr. and T. M. Hout, *Competing Against Time: How Time Based Competition is Reshaping Global Markets* (New York, The Free Press, 1990).

4 Time Compression and the Supply Chain

1. R. C. Lamming, *Beyond Partnership Strategies for Innovation and Lean Supply* (London, Prentice-Hall, 1993).
2. J. W. Forrester, *Industrial Dynamics* (London, Wiley, 1961).
3. J. B. Houlihan, 'International Supply Chain Management', *International Journal of Physical Distribution and Materials Management*, vol. 17, no. 2 (1987) pp. 51–66.
4. Tow, II, D. R., Nain, M. M. and Wilkner, J., 'Industrial Dynamics Simulation Models in the Design of Supply Chains', *IJPDLM*, vol. 22, no. 5, 1992, pp. 3–13.
5. Sterman, J. D. 'Modelling Managerial Behaviour: Misperceptions of Feedback in a Dynamic Decision Making Experiment', *Management Science*, vol. 35, No. 3, March 1989.
6. T. Ohno and S. Mito, *Just in Time for Today and Tomorrow* (Cambridge, Productivity Press, 1988).
7. M. Sako, *Prices, Quality and Trust – Interfirm Relations in Britain and Japan* (Cambridge University Press, 1992).
8. J. C. Jarillo, *Strategic Networks: Creating the Borderless Organisation* (Oxford, Butterworth Heinemann, 1993) pp. 101–22.
9. G. Stalk Jr. and T. M. Hout, *Competing Against Time: How Time Based Competition is Reshaping Global Markets* (New York, The Free Press, 1990).

5 Time and New Product Development

1. See S. C. Wheelwright and K. B. Clark, *Revolutionizing Product Development: Quantum Leaps in Speed, Efficiency and Quality* (New York, The Free Press, 1992) p. 31.
2. Ibid., pp. 88–90.
3. See P. G. Smith and D. G. Reinertsen, *Developing Products in Half the Time* (New York, Van Nostrand Reinhold, 1991) p. 193.
4. R. P. Nayak, 'Forces Driving Rapid Technological Development', *Marketing Intelligence and Planning*, vol. 9, no. 5 (1991) pp. 29–38.
5. See Smith and Reinertsen, *Developing Products in Half the Time*, pp. 193–206, who discuss the concept of 'project overload' in some detail.
6. See Wheelwright and Clark, *Revolutionizing Product Development*, pp. 86–110, for further details.
7. See Smith and Reinertsen, *Developing Products in Half the Time*, pp. 43–60, who describe the 'fuzzy front end' in depth.
8. L. G. Soderberg and J. D. O'Halloran, '"Heroic" Engineering Takes More Than Heroes', *McKinsey Quarterly*, no. 1 (1992) pp. 3–23.
9. Smith and Reinertsen, *Developing Products in Half the Time*, pp. 90–1.
10. J. R. Hauser and D. Clausing, 'The House of Quality', *Harvard Business Review*, May–June (1988) pp. 63–70, provide a good description of quality function deployment.
11. See Smith and Reinertsen, *Developing Products in Half the Time*, pp. 61–79, for information on specification changes and incremental innovation.
12. See Smith and Reinertsen, *Developing Products in Half the Time*, pp. 99–110, for more information on the importance of product architecture.

13. See Smith and Reinertsen, *Developing Products in Half the Time*, pp. 100–10, for detailed information on the concept of modular design.
14. See Smith and Reinertsen, *Developing Products in Half the Time*, pp. 111–31, for further information on selecting teams for new product development. Selection of teams is also covered in Chapter 9 of this volume.
15. S. C. Wheelwright and K. B. Clark, *Revolutionizing Product Development*, pp. 190–6.
16. See Wheelwright and Clark, *Revolutionizing Product Development*, pp. 175–84, for a discussion of the capabilities required for integration between upstream and downstream departments.
17. H. K. Bowen, K. B. Clark, C. A. Holloway and S. C. Wheelwright (ed.), *The Perceptual Enterprise Machine: Seven Keys to Corporate Renewal Through Successful Product and Process Development* (New York, Oxford University Press, 1994), pp. 202–8.
18. See C. Meyer, *Fast Cycle Time* (New York, The Free Press, 1993) and H. K. Bowen *et al.*, *The Perpetual Enterprise Machine*.

6 Time Compression and Change

1. M. Hammer and J. Champy, *Reengineering the Corporation: a Manifesto for Business Revolution* (London, Brealy, 1994).
2. N. Margulies and A. P. Raia, *Organization Development: Values, Process and Technology* (New York, McGraw-Hill, 1972).
3. Examples of the problems of task-oriented change are contained in the following: A. T. Kearney, *The Barriers and Opportunities of Information Technology – A Management Perspective* (London, The Institute of Administrative Management and the Department of Trade and Industry, 1984); G. Symon and C. W. Clegg, 'Technology-Led Change: A Study of the Implementation of CADCAM', *Journal of Occupational Psychology*, no. 64 (1991) pp. 273–90.
4. Examples of the problems of the process-oriented approach are contained in the following: M. Beer, R. A. Eisenstat and B. Spector, *The Critical Path to Corporate Renewal* (Boston, Mass., Harvard Business School Press, 1990); A. M. Pettigrew, *The Awakening Giant: Continuity and Change in Imperial Chemical Industries* (Oxford, Basil Blackwell, 1985).
5. P. C. Nutt, 'Helping Top Management Avoid Failure during Planned Change', *Human Resource Management*, vol. 31, no. 4 (1992) pp. 319–44.
6. P. R. Lawrence and J. W. Lorsch, *Developing Organizations: Diagnosis and Action* (Reading, Mass., Addison-Wesley, 1969).

7 Creating the Environment for Change

1. A. M. Pettigrew, *The Awakening Giant: Continuity and Change in Imperial Chemical Industries* (Oxford, Basil Blackwell, 1985).
2. G. Hamel and C. K. Prahalad, *Competing for the Future* (Boston, Mass., Harvard Business School Press, 1994) pp. 160–5, have also identified the importance of consistency of messages in generating strategic change.
3. A. Coyle and A. Page, 'Consulting with the Flow', *Business Executive* (1995).

8 Wishes to Actions

1. The effect of lack of focus on the top priority organizational objectives on the speed of change is also identified by G. Hamel and C. K. Prahalad, *Competing for the Future* (Boston, Mass., Harvard Business School Press, 1994) pp. 160–5.
2. A good description of this is contained in P. M. Senge, *The Fifth Discipline* (New York, Doubleday, 1990).
3. For example, M. Hammer and J. Champy, *Reengineering the Corporation: a Manifesto for Business Revolution* (London, Brealy, 1994).
4. For example, the idea of continuous improvement.
5. G. Plenert, 'Process Re-engineering: The Latest Fad Toward Failure', *APICS*, June (1994) pp. 22–4.

9 Time to Take Action

1. E. De Bono, *Serious Creativity* (London, HarperCollins, 1992).
2. C. E. Larson and F. M. J. LaFasto, *Teamwork: What Must Go Right – What Can Go Wrong* (Beverly Hills, CA, Sage Publications, 1989).
3. See P. G. Smith and D. G. Reinertsen, *Developing Products in Half the Time* (New York, Van Nostrand Reinhold, 1991) p. 193.

10 How to Get Started

1. A. P. Beesley, 'Time Compression and Procurement' (Proceedings of Ipsera Conference, Cardiff, April, 1993).
2. A. P. Beesley and R. Wilding, 'Time-Based Compression in the Supply Chain', *The Logistician*, Nov. 1995.
3. G. Stalk Jr. and T. M. Hout, *Competing Against Time: How Time Based Competition is Reshaping Global Markets* (New York, The Free Press, 1990).
4. M. Christopher, *Logistics and Supply Chain Management: Strategies for Reducing Costs and Improving Services* (Financial Times/Pitman London, 1992).
5. E. M. Goldratt, *The Goal*, 2nd edn (Aldershot, Gower, 1994).

11 Tools and Techniques

1. M. E. Porter, *Competitive Advantage* (New York, The Free Press, 1985).

Bibliography

Argyris, C., *Overcoming Organisational Defenses* (Needham Heights, Mass., Allyn Bacon, 1990).

Beer, M., Eisenstat R. A. and Spector, B., *The Critical Path to Corporate Renewal* (Boston, Mass., Harvard Business School Press, 1990).

Byham, W. C. and Cox, J., *Zapp!, The Lightning of Empowerment* (London, Century Business, 1991).

Christopher, M., *Logistics and Supply Chain Management: Strategies for Reducing Costs and Improving Services* (London, Pitman, 1992).

Deschamps, P. and Nayak, P. R., *Product Juggernauts: How Companies Mobilize to Generate a Stream of Market Winners* (Boston, Mass., Harvard Business School Press, 1995).

Hamel, G. and Prahalad, C. K., *Competing for the Future* (Boston, Mass., Harvard Business School Press, 1994).

Hammer and J. Champy, *Reengineering the Corporation, a Manifesto for Business Revolution* (London, Brealy, 1994).

Handy, C., *Understanding Organizations* (London, Penguin Books, 1993).

Janov, J. *The Inventive Organization: Hope and Daring at Work* (San Fransciso, Jossey Books, 1994).

Lamming, R. C., *Beyond Partnership, Strategies for Innovation and Lean Supply* (London, Prentice-Hall, 1993).

Porter, M. E., *Competitive Advantage* (New York, The Free Press, 1985).

Sako, M., *Prices, Quality and Trust – Interfirm Relations in Britain and Japan* (Cambridge University Press, 1992).

Saunders, M., *Strategic Purchasing and Supply Chain Management* (London, Pitman Publishing, 1994).

Schaffer, R. H. and Thompson, H. A., 'Successful Change Programmes Begin with Results', *Harvard Business Review*, January–February (1992), pp. 80–9.

Senge, P. M., *The Fifth Discipline* (Doubleday, 1990).

Senge, P. M., *The Fifth Discipline Fieldbook – Strategies and Tools for Building a Learning Organisation* (London, Nicholas Brealy, 1996).

Smith, P. G. and Reinertsen, D. G., *Development Products in Half The Time* (New York, Van Nostrand Reinhold, 1991).

Stalk, G. Jr. and T. M. Hout, *Competing Against Time: How Time Based Competition is Reshaping Global Markets* (New York, The Free Press, 1990).

Wheelwright, S. C. and Clark, K. B., *Revolutionizing Product Development: Quantum Leaps in Speed, Efficiency and Quality* (New York, The Free Press, 1992).

Index